Christina Dodwell was born in Nigeria, West Africa, and educated in England. She worked in London for four years as a secretary for *Queen* magazine (now *Harpers*), and among other jobs she also worked as an interior designer and decorator.

In 1975 she travelled to Africa. Three years later she returned and began working with BBC radio to make four series of travel features for broadcasting. Her work was also published by the *New Scientist*. In 1979 she set out alone on a two-year journey to Papua New Guinea.

Christina Dodwell

IN PAPUA
NEW GUINEA

published by Pan Books

ACKNOWLEDGEMENTS

This book is written with thanks to the people I met along the way; for sharing with me, befriending me and looking after me. Among those I particularly want to thank are:

Paddy Graham, Bangkok

Walter Coleshill, British Consul, Bangkok

Christopher and Caroline Wigan in Singapore

Cathy Hux and Bill Cates in Malaysia

Siswan in Jayapura

Bill and Lorna Bell, who gave me Horse

Joan, Edge and Ray FitzGibbon in Wewak

Jo Harvey-Jones, Ialibu

Heather and Duncan Dean in Mendi

Sue Favetta who lent me a camera

Ursula Saville, Tari

Chris Rose, Tari, for pasture and *kaukau*

Moira Harrington, Tari School

Paul Newell, in Port Moresby

Ben Probert in Tari

Beth and Mike Hayes in Vanimo

Father Hans at Lake Kopiago, and many of the Catholic missionaries throughout Papua New Guinea

Bryan and Barbara Roper in Port Moresby

Mik Plumb in Goroka

Barbara and Owen Slattery in Lae

John Dentist in Madang

Nelson and Esta Tololo, at Tundaka Community School

Korimo and Ginate Rei at Gembogl, Mt Wilhelm

Martin Kiambu, *kiap* at Ama

Councillor Otto

Ex-councillor Gallus

The villagers of the Sepik and Blackwaters rivers, and the people of Kraimbit

April Pisonneault

Earle Lane

First published 1983 by The Oxford Illustrated Press
This Picador edition published 1985 by Pan Books Ltd,
Cavaye Place, London SW10 9PG
9 8 7 6 5 4 3 2 1
© Christina Dodswell 1983
ISBN 0 330 28187 9
Printed and bound in Great Britain by
Cox & Wyman Ltd, Reading

Contents

Introduction

Before setting out on my travels I lived a modern city life, wore fashionable clothes, worried about losing the things I loved, and was literally afraid of the dark.

My initiation into unconventional travel was in 1975, aged 24, when I left England with three other people in a Land-Rover intending to take a holiday overland through Africa. After driving through north Africa and the Sahara Desert, two members of the group stole our jointly-owned Land-Rover and vanished. All my hopes and plans for the holiday were suddenly destroyed.

Abandoned along with me was another young woman, Lesley Jamieson, and although we could have gone to Kano airport and flown back to England, we decided instead to look at the country around us by hitch-hiking and walking. We didn't intend to go far, but as it transpired, some road engineers gave us a couple of horses and so we carried on, right through west Africa on horseback.

The land was semi-desert; we had no map or food supplies, but we soon discovered that endurance and stamina were more important to survival than physical strength. In the year that Lesley and I travelled together we also made an impulsive but successful voyage of 1,000 miles (1,609km) on rivers in equatorial Africa, paddling a dugout canoe.

When Lesley and I split up she flew to the USA and I realised that either my journey around the southern end of Africa would have to wait until a new companion was found, or I could continue alone. I realised at the time that if I could manage being on my own, then the world would be open to me. The matter was quickly resolved when I bought a horse at a slaughter house, and set out alone on a ride of several thousand miles. My travels were not aimless; they were a continual learning-ground that led me to investigate geology, meteorology, anthropology, biology and other subjects just for the fun of learning. Also I learned some important survival skills and discovered that I liked the life of a lone explorer.

Various episodes followed and three years after I had left home I was still travelling in Africa, riding a desert-pony and leading a pack-camel on a journey north up the East African Rift Valley to Ethiopia. The fatigues and hardships of desert travel, such as digging for water in dried-up streambeds and searching for grazing for the animals, were combined with disasters like bandit-attacks and being bitten by a poisonous spider (which paralysed me for a week), until finally, in war-torn Ethiopia, I was arrested by the army as a possible spy. After my release I decided that the expedition had ended and I welcomed the idea of returning to England.

Back in England it was lovely to be reunited with my family, although daily life seemed odd because it felt so easy and normal. My health was in a poor state, as was my bank account which was almost empty. The obvious answer was for me to write a book and fortunately it was simple to find a publisher. But I could not settle down: while writing I toured France and Greece, then went via England to USA and Mexico.

A restless and sometimes reckless nature drove me forward and my confidence grew as I realised that there is little to fear in the world. The life of an explorer was not one I would have chosen for myself, but it had happened, and it felt right. These facts cancelled out any idea of settling down, and while back in England (during the book's publication), I began planning my next trip.

Money was not a problem because the publishers had paid me a good advance, and also I received money for articles in the *New Scientist* magazine, from British television and by broadcasting a regular series of BBC radio features. When travelling my needs were few and inexpensive, so I could afford to be away for several years if I did without luxuries. By looking in a world atlas I considered countries like Brazil, Peru, China, Tibet and Borneo; I didn't make any decisions but I was tempted by their remote and wild aspects.

In the South Pacific, between Indonesia and the north coast of

Australia, I noticed the island of New Guinea which is the second largest island in the world; the eastern half was labelled Papua New Guinea and was shaded green on the map for jungle and white-purple for mountains. Papua New Guinea is also called 'the Last Unknown', being one of the least-explored places in the world, and from an encyclopaedia I learned that among its many primitive tribes are some who still live in the Stone Age. Another book informed me that Papua New Guinea has wilder landscape, and more impenetrable and treacherous jungle than any other tropical region including the Amazon and Africa. The prospect of travelling there excited me.

How to reach Papua New Guinea was a problem I pondered, since to fly there would have meant missing out on many lands below, and yet to travel the whole way by land could take more years and energy than my body could give.

As to why I wanted to visit Papua New Guinea — would it make any difference if I knew why? It wasn't to prove anything or to achieve any pre-set goals; it wasn't that type of expedition. I decided to fly to Thailand, which was on my way to Papua New Guinea, and see some oriental culture. From there I would travel by land through Thailand and Malaysia and then on through south-east Asia, island-hopping by boat to Papua New Guinea.

It was to be a one-person journey. My preparations were scanty but I knew from experience what things I would need: food supplies such as dried beef jerky, nuts and raisins, salt, vitamin pills; and other things like a compass, my hammock, raingear, gifts, photographs of home, and my long skirts which I always wore in third-world countries where a woman is expected to dress with dignity. I didn't take any weapons. It seemed to me that a weapon was likely to get turned on its holder, and I preferred to rely on my wits.

It made me sad to leave my family again but I knew that they accepted my lifestyle, and although my parents worried (as any normal parents do worry), they believed in my ability to survive and gave me encouragement.

Part One

The Approach
to Papua New Guinea

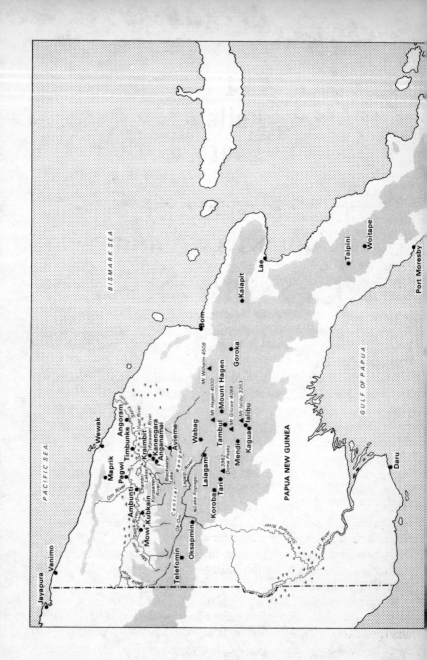

1
Thailand
and the Pearl Traders

Thailand and the Far East were more fascinating than I had anticipated, particularly the hill-tribes with their colourful costumes and customs. I lived with them in the jungle for a while, where I travelled by elephant which belonged to a Burmese man who taught me to control and ride it.

After that journey was over and I had sent the elephant back to Burma I caught a tropical fever which, although it didn't require hospitalisation, reduced my weight from 9st 4lb (60kg) to a mere 7st (45kg) and left me feeling exhausted. This was at the end of December 1979, and so far it had been almost four months since I had left home.

Weak and in low spirits I looked for somewhere to recuperate, and while going south down the Thai peninsula I heard of Pang-yi, a pearl-trading village set in the sea off an isolated part of the coast. Several days later I joined the local Thai passengers boarding a motor-canoe destined for Pang-yi.

The canoe sped through a calm sea which was dotted with humped and cliff-edged islands, and tall limestone pinnacles. Some islands looked black against the sun while the others ranged in shades of blue receding to pale transparency, silhouetted against an open blue sky. There was no sign of habitation and the islands were barren except for sparse mangrove swamps at their base. Finally Pang-yi came into sight. Instead of building on land, the founders of this village had built their homes on stilts above the sea.

When the canoe nosed through the barnacled stilts we scrambled up a wood ladder, with rotted and missing rungs, and we emerged at the level of the huts. It was the hottest part of the day so only few people were around, but as I wandered through the village some young women came to say hello and began to follow

11

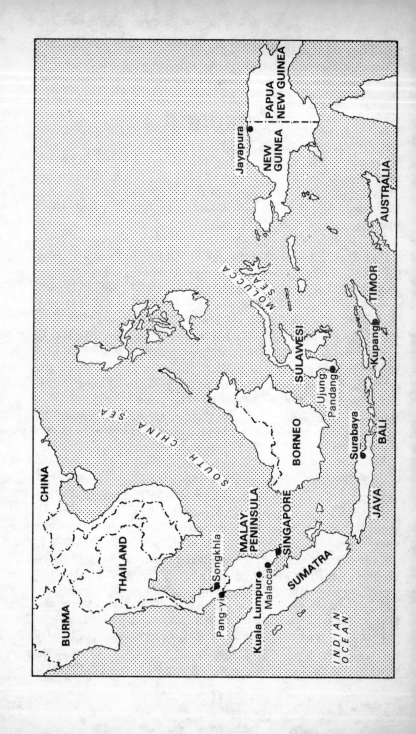

me. They seemed excited and pleased to see me.

Walking was surprisingly hazardous because the walkways were made of uneven and unsecured branches laid parallel between trestles over the sea, and the loose branches often rolled underfoot. Smaller paths, also on stilts, led to some outlying huts. The group of young women had by now overtaken me, and they led me to a hut for a cup of tea. Language was difficult because I didn't understand much Thai, but the women didn't seem to mind and they chattered gaily as they took away my clothes and dressed me as one of them in a sarong and blouse. They smeared my face with white powder, and round my neck and wrists they clasped strings of pearls that came from their local oyster-beds.

Siya, a girl with luxuriant black hair, invited me to stay with her family. The family hut seemed to house about fourteen people, and we all slept on mats on the floor. The floor was merely a series of bamboo slats placed over the platform with gaps where I could see the sea below.

During the days Siya and her friends took me by canoe to various islands that had caves and passages eroded into the rock and which were hung with stalactites. As we swam beneath the caves Siya showed me ancient paintings of faded dark red shapes of fish on the overhangs above us. The paintings had survived the salty air, she said, because the red ochre was mixed with rubber-tree sap. On Pipi island there was an immense cave with scores of bamboo poles leaning against the walls so that people could collect the edible swallow nests at the top. One of the most spectacular caves on more distant islands was the one containing a thirty-foot long (10-m) statue of a reclining Buddha, which was looked after by a yellow-robed monk who sat meditating by candlelight. Other islands had beaches where sea-turtles laid their eggs, or underwater reefs with coloured fish flitting through forests of coral. I marvelled at them all — despite the tiredness which had filled me since my illness — and my senses, which seemed to be closed, now became slowly forced open.

Back in Pang-yi I had been asked to take some English classes at the village school, but I think I learned more Thai than they did English. Thai is a difficult language because it is tonal, so that words can have totally different meanings depending on the tone used: *'Mai mai mai mai'* for example can mean 'New wood burns not'. The villagers appeared to know only three words of English — 'I love you' — which the women called out to me in such a friendly way that I couldn't help but feel welcomed.

They were concerned that my behaviour should conform to their Thai customs, and they taught me that it is an insult to sit with your feet pointing toward anyone, and a rude gesture to put your hands on your hips. Many of the manners I had learnt from childhood were not appropriate here and since I had no wish to offend anyone, I was willing to conform — especially since they weren't treating me as a foreigner, and seemed to have adopted me as one of themselves.

Due to the natural beauty of the whole area there were daily boat-loads of tourists to Pang-yi and the islands (the area had been used as the setting of the James Bond movie, 'Man with the Golden Gun'). The people toured between midday and two o'clock and were an important source of income to the villagers who sold pearls to them at exhorbitant prices.

But although I enjoyed my days in Pang-yi, living in a confined area had its problems and sometimes I felt so crowded and hemmed in by people that I had to look for a quiet place to sit by myself. I wasn't left alone for long though and all too soon some women and their babies (which they tethered to posts to prevent them falling into the sea), would join me while they sat and shelled mussels. On one occasion a large group of women was followed by some goats and their goat-herds until I could count thirty people and ten animals squashed on the little platform around me.

On leaving Pang-yi I said a sad farewell to Siya, and all the women who had drawn me briefly into their lives.

2
Festivals in Malaysia

From Pang-yi I went south by bus and hitch-hiked down the Malay peninsula, detouring to watch a bull-fight at Songkhla where the bulls fought each other instead of a matador.

On my birthday, February 1st, I became twenty-nine. The age itself meant little, and as I thought about it I was aware that growing older was not just an accumulation of years, it was more a process of growing richer inside.

My birthday coincided with Thaipusam, a major Hindu festival dedicated to Shiva, god of destruction. It was celebrated annually at the Batu Cave near Kuala Lumpur and I decided to go there.

On the eve of Thaipusam great numbers of people began to gather near the cave. Dark-skinned Asian women in colourful red, orange, or gold-embroidered saris, their long black hair braided back and garlanded with flowers, were busy making camp, and taking their babies to have their heads shaved and coated with a white muddy paste.

I joined the main flow of people moving towards the cave, which was set high up a 400-ft (120-m) cliff, and reached by a massive flight of 272 steps. The cave-mouth yawned with stalactites and beyond them was an immense cavern that was pitch black and broken only by tiny flickering candles and wide dishes of fire. The smoky air, the smell of incense, and the noise of hundreds of bats being disturbed in their sleep, made my senses reel as I walked in. Niches in the rock held golden images of gods and goddesses that were served by white-robed priests holding trays of flames, which they offered to the people who came to pray. I watched as people dipped their hands in the flame, their fingers moving between the flame and their foreheads. I noticed images of the god Subramaniam, his elephant-headed brother,

15

Ganeesh, and their mother Durga. Durga was portrayed as a fierce ten-armed goddess who rode a tiger; but being a woman she had other aspects. She was also Uma, a gentle goddess of light and beauty; and she was Kali, the most terrible goddess who lusted for blood sacrifices, appearing blood-splattered, seething with snakes, and wearing necklaces of her children's skulls.

At the back of the cave was a deep sunken pothole with a circular patch of sky up above, which threw a beam of smoky daylight to the floor. White stalactites dripped down its sheer limestone walls forming globular curtains, and columns of smooth solid rock. Many passages led off into darkness. On the ground in the centre of the hole sat an old man in yellow robes in the lotus position. His long grey beard was braided and he chanted tunelessly, his whole body jiggling to a beat that I couldn't hear.

He was a fortune-teller. Other fortune-tellers sat on mats and used cowrie shells to forecast the future. On impulse I joined them and practised a bit of palmistry; they were all eager for me to read their hands but I was hindered by not being able to speak their language, so eventually I gave up and walked back down to the river.

It was sunset and some people were bathing in the river, while others on the bank were assembling a shrine-like contraption called a *kavadi*. My legs were tired so I rested there, and found some people who spoke English. They explained that a *kavadi* usually represented a prayer — it being the visible expression of that prayer. The *kavadi* near us was being built on a square frame of poles, and decorated with coloured cloth, plumes, flowers and pictures of various gods. The suffering caused by carrying an overhead *kavadi* (partially supported by spikes and arrows, or by fishhooks into men's flesh) up into the cave, gave power to the prayer. Sometimes they were carried as a penance.

Meanwhile, the evening was bringing more than anticipated. The crowds had thickened and formed tight groups around certain individuals; something was happening but I couldn't tell what. Drums were being pounded in strange powerful rhythms, groups began to chant, long-bearded priests held sceptres of white gladioli; nothing was clear to me.

I turned around and I froze in horror, as I watched a man pierce a four-foot spear through the side of his mouth and out through the other cheek. My eyes couldn't look away. The man showed no pain, and there was no blood. He calmly skewered three tangerines onto each end of the spike, and he started to dance.

A full moon rose slowly above the palm trees on the horizon. The word 'Thaipusam' is a combination of two words: *Thai* which is a Hindu month and *pusam* which is the time of the full moon. In their calendar it was the year 1155. I stayed on the riverbank until late in the night. With every passing moment the crowds swelled, and the drumming and chanting intensified. It was a long time before I could sleep.

The next morning I rose at dawn and made my way back to Batu Cave. A procession was coming up fast behind me and I stopped to let it pass. It was led by a devotee of Hanuman the monkey god, who pranced along with a devilish grin and a long palm-rope tail, snatching some bananas from a food stall and devouring them messily (without peeling off their skins) as he went. He was followed by a woman with bells on her ankles, and skewers through her neck, mouth and tongue.

Next came a *kavadi* carrier, carrying an arched *kavadi* on his shoulders that was a glittering mass of gold paper and tinsel; its front panel displaying Ganeesh, four-armed and elephantile. Another *kavadi* sported an overhead pyramid with plumes of peacock feathers at each corner (there were wild peacocks in the forests nearby; it was dedicated to a god riding a multi-headed peacock, and topped by a bright yellow umbrella.

The man beneath the *kavadi* was in a deep trance, he was jumping and dancing as though the *kavadi* wasn't heavy, oblivious to the chains hanging from it that were attached to him by fish hooks through his skin. Sweat poured off him and his tongue hung out — he couldn't retract it because it was skewered in place by a six-inch spike.

The processions were forced to halt at a single-track railway line by the flashing red lights and ringing bells that heralded the approach of a train. Soon the train came chuffing along looking peculiarly out of context, and when the barrier rose the human traffic-jam began to move.

Back at the riverbank several people were wearing 3-ft (1-m) long spikes through their mouths called *vails*, which served the same mixed purposes as *kavadis*. *Vails* could be any length up to 10ft (3m); those over 10ft were now banned by law because they tended to catch in the crowds and, when they did, they tore the man's flesh and drew blood, causing a scar. A man wearing one usually felt no pain because he was supposed to fast (or take little food) for forty-eight days before Thaipusam which made it easy for him to go into a trance, and so be unaware of the pain.

The last half-mile to the caves was a seething mass of people. Sixty thousand people were present, and over three thousand were wearing *kavadis* or *vails*. Businessmen were usually devotees of the Sarawathi (goddess of money); soldiers preferred Davi, god of fighting (the main god of the Ghurka regiments); while students who were afraid of failing exams carried prayers to Lakshmi, goddess of knowledge. People came from all walks of life; the old and young (children also wore spikes) walking among the beggars and cripples who crawled towards the cave in the hope of a miracle.

A tide of exhilaration helped us all up the 272 steps to the cave. In the dark smokiness I went to Shiva's shrine, who was now shown as the Lord of Creation dancing in a sacred ring of fire. Fire-dishes were everywhere, together with smouldering camphor, incense, joss sticks, piles of broken coconuts and jumbled heaps of *kavadis*, discarded now that they had served their purpose.

Priests rubbed white powder (made from cowdung and ash) on the marks in people's skin when their *kavadi* or *vail* was removed. There was no blood, the flesh simply closed up again, leaving a slight mark for a day. When the priest rubbed powder on people's foreheads, their trance ended.

It seemed appropriate to me that I had spent my birthday at this local celebration among people who had spiritually cleansed themselves and prayed that their needs would be met in the year ahead. My needs were few and I simply hoped that whatever happened to me would turn out happily. The far future lay ahead as an unknown blur as I settled back into the present moment and continued my journey through Malaysia.

Thaipusam is a Hindu festival although the state religion of Malaysia is Islam and most Malays are Moslem. So there is freedom of religion, and the Chinese who comprise almost fifty per cent of Malaysia's population, follow their own mixture of Buddhism and Confuscionism.

The Chinese New Year is celebrated early in March (by our calendar), and during it I visited Malacca, an ancient, predominantly Chinese port whose ties with China have been long-established.

As I walked along its narrow streets lined with vertical signs painted in bold red Chinese characters, I heard the clatter of mah-jong tiles and of ancient printing presses which mixed with the hiss of steam from a laundry. Many buildings were decorated with gold-tasselled red Chinese lanterns, and fluttering banners that proclaimed 'Kong Hee Fat Choy' (Happy New Year). The shop-fronts were open showing tailors using sewing machines, cobblers at work, noodle shops, bicycle repairers, acupuncture clinics, coffin makers, and junk shops where I browsed among birdcages, oil lamps, brass urns, old ship's wheels, Chinese wedding-beds and opium benches. The sensations of history were almost as tangible as the objects themselves. Chinese apothecaries were selling natural cures made from dried octopus and lizard, eyewash from boiled snake-skin, python-heart tonic, and rhino-horn aphrodisiacs. It was as if nothing here had really changed in generations.

Squeezed into the rows of shop-fronts and houses were some small temples. I watched a man painting a mural of dragons and mountains on a temple's outer wall. My favourite temple was Cheng Hoon, built in 1400, and the oldest temple in Malaysia. On the ridge of its pottery roof and upswept gables were porcelain statues of dragons, and along the eaves was a glass-mosaic frieze of mythical reptiles, animals and flowers. The entrance gate was set between two smaller moon gates. I couldn't pass any temple without stopping to go inside, and over the next few days built up impressions of dim light mixed with smoke from countless smouldering joss-sticks and large coils of incense, gold-embossed dragons wrapping themselves round black marble pillars, and gold lions standing guard at the inner doors.

There were main altars and side altars for different gods, and statues or pictures of wise men like Ta Pay Kong (Old White Man), Kwan Kong, shown with a fierce red face and black beard, or Ackwaning, goddess of mercy with sixteen arms. There were also rooms full of long flat wooden pegs, with writing on them in gold characters. They were memorial tags for family ancestors, some with photographs pasted on, and some with tape over their names — the latter meaning that those people hadn't yet died. Ancestor worship was particularly popular and by New Year's Eve the ancestor altars were laden with offerings of roast duck, rice cakes, fruit, flowers and incense. Various people talked to me, and I noticed that they generally believed in a mixture of Taoism, Confuscionism, Buddhism, ancestors and household gods, all combined into one belief framework.

The Chinese New Year was a religious and a family occasion; a time of family re-union. It made me feel homesick for my own family, remembering other New Years with nostalgia, and feeling the emptiness of being alone during a celebration. But my unhappiness was short-lived because I met some students who wanted to practise speaking English and we all spent a light-hearted day together. Also they showed me where the 'lions' would be dancing for the New Year, and they pointed out some poles jutting from first-storey windows, which were baited with Ang Pows containing money that the lions would try to reach in their dance.

On New Year's Day I watched this dramatic traditional dance. The 'lions' were pairs of men wearing a black body cloth with wavy yellow lines and a grotesque headmask. The mask had eyes and ears out on stalks and it had a rhinoceros-type horn on its nose. Its tongue lolled out and its chin waggled as the men performed their dance. To an orchestra of drums, gongs and cymbals, both parts of the lion danced with the co-ordination of one entity. The lion cavorted, thrusting its head from side to side, the back man lifting the front one high off the ground, frequently turning and pirouetting.

The music's unfamiliar jarring sounds reminded me again that I came from another culture, but this time instead of longing for familiar music I felt the excitement of being doubly alive, as a stranger from the West travelling in the East. Some other lions arrived from down the street, to compete for the Ang Pow money. The original lion grew fiercer, prowling angrily and crouching as if ready to spring. Then the man at the back hoisted the man at the front up onto his shoulders to make an attempt to reach to the Ang Pow by the upstairs window. They couldn't reach it but managed to grab the lettuce which also decorated the pole. Suddenly appearing drowsy, the lion lay down to sleep, stretching with catlike grace and wriggling to make itself comfortable. A moment later it spat out the lettuce. Cymbals clashed in a cacophony of sound as the lion leapt into its final dance: jerking, rolling, gambolling, rearing and reaching up again for the Ang Pow. It snapped its jaws and swayed with the effort as it inched higher. With an extra thrust it seized the prize, then bowed down to thank its benefactors.

On the third day of the Chinese New Year I left Malacca and went by bus to Singapore, where apart from the continuing New Year celebrations, my time there was refreshingly ordinary. I stayed with friends in a large house with a swimming-pool and servants, enjoying the contrast and luxury for a brief while. It was reassuring to know that in the midst of this exotic world, western life was going on simultaneously.

To leave Singapore, a chauffeured limousine took me to the docks where I caught a passenger boat to Java, Indonesia. It surprised me to realise that Indonesia is made up of more than 13,500 islands, with over 350 ethnic groups some of which are still primitive while others had civilisation long before Europe. The major islands such as Java, Sumatra, Celebes and Bali differ from each other in culture and creed by having Moslems, Buddhists, Hindus, Taoists, Christians and animists. I crossed Java by train stopping to browse among ancient ruined cities like Prambanan (the most extensive Hindu temple ruins in Indonesia), and Borobudur (erected about 800 AD, the largest monument in the southern hemisphere). Scenes in stone relief ran around every tier, depicting the path from earth level through perfection to Nirvana.

I am an addict for ruins and temples and Java has a wealth of them from many different ages and cultures. I particularly loved the decaying temples and gateways that could only be reached by walking through rice paddies and onto open hills.

One of the many that I visited was a ruined Hindu temple situated on a shoulder of Mt Lawu, overlooking two volcanoes. It was a step-pyramid of dark stones set among pine trees. From the top of the temple the view stretched out over broad valleys to mountains terraced with rice paddies, that made scalloped patterns of emerald green, yellow, mud-brown and the blue of the water reflecting the cloudless sky. Farmers could be seen ploughing, deep in mud with white oxen yoked to their wooden ploughs. As I sat enjoying the view and peaceful atmosphere, the music of a village gamelan-orchestra drifted up in the breeze from the valleys.

For a change of scenery I went to a smoking volcano, Mt Bromo, in eastern Java. At a village near the top I hired a pony and rode across the vast outer crater, now a cold grey plain, to the two younger craters inside. Of the two, Bromo is the more recent. Grey cracked tongues of lava had solidified as they spilt down its slopes, and inside, the crater funnelled down to a black abyss, with clouds of sulphur steam coming from its depths. Walking around the crater's rim was like travelling through lunar landscape for three miles. Such places always give me a sense of awe at the power of nature which makes the power of man seem puny in comparison.

To the south a larger volcano spewed smoke, and to the east I could see the island of Bali.

Bali was a disappointment to me; it seemed that commercial greed and the influence of hippies and package tours had changed Bali's national people, corrupting their values and morals, although I could see that the old ways were still sketchily followed.

On my way out of Denpasar I stopped to watch a cockfight, and stood by a group of men who were betting heavily on the outcome. The fighting was unskilful, and the cockerels each had a three-inch razor blade attached to one leg. Fights were brief (20 seconds) and usually both birds died. It seemed a messy way of slaughtering chickens, and reinforced my unfavourable first impression of Bali.

However, I toured the island, seeing temples, volcanoes and extinct craters holding crater lakes. At Mt Batur the local people were decorating their temple for the festival of the full moon which would last for ten days. The Balinese calendar contains many festivals, though fewer are observed today than in the past. Their calendar also contains 420 days (this was the year 1902).

On the northern coast were long beaches with numerous shrines among the palm trees. Many temples had ticket booths that were not necessarily expensive, just commercial.

A village called Peliatan did much to restore my spirits. I stayed in a *losmen* (lodging house) set in a warren of mud-walled passages, courtyards, houses, temples and traditional split-gates, which were heavily ornamented. Gamelan orchestras practised continually, and neighbouring families let me see their rituals of offering to their deities for a marriage, and also a tooth-filing ceremony! Bapa Togod, who ran the *losmen*, was teaching me to play a bamboo *gengong* (jew's harp). After supper there was often some local entertainment such as a shadow-play (*waywang*), that would take place in the open-air courtyard with fireflies in the grass and a background chorus of croaking bullfrogs.

There were forty temples in the vicinity and some royal tombs at Tampaksiring. The tombs were hollowed in the cliffs of a canyon, set among waterfalls, palm trees and slopes of terraced, vibrantly green rice paddies. Dripping moss covered the honeycomb of tombs and temples also hewn into the rock: royal memorials for a king, queen, son, concubines and son's concubines. Legend said that a giant had carved out all the tombs in one night with his fingernails.

Denpasar, the capital city, was quite a contrast after the relative peace and tranquility of the countryside. I had to go there to collect my mail from the *poste restante* but I found that the continual demands for money, the bribes, rip-offs and stealing were a bore. I expected to have to bargain over every price in the markets, but here it even applied over the bank-rate in the bank. For transportation it was necessary to bargain because prices were often inflated not just twice, but four or five times for those tourists who were gullible or inexperienced enough to pay them. Although I strived to enjoy it all I felt like an outsider to it. Attitudes seemed superficial and commercial, and I decided that it was time to find a way forward to Papua New Guinea.

So I left Bali and went to the Javanese main port of Surabaya to find a boat to take me there.

3
By Cargo Boat
through the South Pacific

As soon as I arrived in Surabaya I wanted to leave it; I disliked the heat, the noise and particularly the exhaust fumes. At the Pelni shipping office I learned that there were no passenger ships operating within the Indonesian archipelago and that I would have to wait for a cargo boat. They were not frequent but I was lucky: a boat called *Tombatu* was due to depart in a few days and although only deck-class space was available and it didn't go all the way to Papua New Guinea (none of the boats did), I could buy a ticket to Jayapura in West Irian, at the furthest end of Indonesia. The ticket-clerk told me that the voyage would take about three weeks and the cost of the ticket (which included three meals a day) was 20,000 rupiah (£28).

When I boarded *Tombatu* a few days later, the decks were already crowded with deck-class passengers and the sun was baking hot, even though the time was only 8 o'clock. To add to my depression, the sailing-time, already delayed by forty-eight hours, was now put back another six hours. I learned that cargo boats didn't run to a schedule (even the proposed ports-of-call had changed), and it seemed that the only certain thing was that *Tombatu* would at some time end up at Jayapura, its destination.

There wasn't any space for me to camp on the deck because it was already piled high with cargo and full of passengers carrying bundles of bedding and baskets containing chickens. People were also camping in the ship's holds, where although there was some space left I found the stifling heat, the dark airlessness and the mosquitoes, unbearable, and I went back out on deck. Eventually I found somewhere to camp on the ship's prow; there was no available ground-space but I staked my claim to a big coil of mooring rope and slung my hammock above it, between two tall ventilation funnels. It was midnight before the *Tombatu* finally left Surabaya.

Even though I know that I am going to have good and bad times while I'm travelling, it still doesn't make the bad times any easier to bear and the next few days continued to be depressing. I was furious at myself for having got on the boat; I had given no thought to the reality of it and now I was discovering what I had let myself in for. Being the only white person on the boat people crowded me continually and never gave me a moment's privacy. I couldn't seem to get away from them anywhere. They even stared at me while I brushed my teeth, and I was constantly pestered by silly young men who said things to me in Indonesian and laughed uproariously at me.

Meals were served three times a day, but they were a monotonous and unappetising combination of boiled rice and fish-heads flavoured with very hot chili. Tepid, colourless tea was provided in big tubs, into which we all dipped our mugs. Sometimes I tried to wander round the ship, but the passageways were blocked with boxes, baskets, and sacks of onions and rice, making any form of exercise impossible. Tied onto every rail and wall was more cargo of red plastic jerrycans and hundreds of plastic buckets. In a better frame of mind I would have described the scene as colourful, but as I couldn't seem to shake off my bad temper, it all just irritated me.

Underfoot the deck was slimy with washing-water, soapsuds, squashed fruit, and rotting leftover food which had been thrown down and trampled. Now chickens were pecking through it. It surprised me that people could create such squalid conditions for themselves. The bathrooms were unusable within two days, even though they were hosed down with sea water every day, and since the only water available for washing was sea water, my skin felt permanently dirty and unpleasantly sticky.

On the second day *Tombatu* broke down. It was sunset and a travelling Muslim priest began chanting the call to prayer. *Tombatu* drifted idly. All the Muslim men laid their prayer-mats facing towards the east for one of their five daily prayer-sessions. I sat in my hammock and contemplated. I felt calmer and there was something magnificent about the flat, circular horizons, the slow convection of air currents which changed the shapes of the clouds, mushrooming upward in anvil shapes, darkening slowly at the base, then letting rain fall as a distant grey smudge against an an empty sea.

At our first port of call, Ujung Pandang in Sulawesi (formerly called Celebes), I took a freshwater shower using buckets from a well, washed my clothes, then bought supplies of coffee, fresh local bread and groceries. I felt much better and re-boarded *Tombatu* in a happier frame of mind.

From Ujung Pandang we set course for Kupang (two days away) on the island of Timor. The evening was stormy, and because the ship's prow was so exposed, my hammock swayed too violently for sleep and I had to move camp down to the back hold. Like the other two holds it was crammed with people, but they were all friendly and we were drawn more closely together when some water came flooding in through the rusty open portholes, and a few people got soaked.

Over the next two days *Tombatu* threaded its way between various small islands and from an upper deck I had a good view over the choppy sea. Suddenly I heard shouts of *'ican paus, ican paus'*, and someone was pointing out to sea. We stared at the water but saw nothing unusual; there was a shoal of flying fish, but they were common here. Moments later the vast dark back of a whale appeared; it played for a while on the surface and spouted a jet of water before diving out of sight again. It was a thrilling moment.

Perhaps my new good humour was because I had begun to accept the way things were, and to adapt myself to them. Until now, I hadn't bothered to learn to speak the language and had even been frustrated when no one spoke English, so now I brought out my dictionary and set about learning to speak Indonesian. It passed the time and I was delighted when everybody helped to teach me. Also I was gradually getting to know the people camping around me in among the baskets of onions and spices, bulging boxes and ship's winches. My closest neighbours were a soldier and his family, who were being posted from Djakarta to Jayapura (and not looking forward to the change); several Javanese college graduates desperately seeking employment (Java was so densely populated that work was very difficult to find); a Sulawesian christian preacher; some aggressive Moslem traders from Sumatra; two prostitutes from Ambon, and a shipbuilder from Ujung Pandang who called to me each time he saw one of the tall-masted schooners with long pointed prows from his home-port.

26

Although I hadn't adapted to bathing in sea water, I had come to terms with the food and occasionally varied the meals by rejecting the fish-heads and adding some of my own groceries to the rice. Occasionally the meals were good, such as when there were chunks of deep-fried fish to eat, and soon I didn't even mind eating the hot chili sauce.

At Kupang the already overcrowded *Tombatu* was scheduled to collect an additional cargo of no less than 800 cattle and 100 goats. Kupang had no actual harbour, only a jetty, so we anchored offshore while some cattle pens were hastily constructed on *Tombatu* from bamboo poles ferried out by small boats. In equal haste many passengers had to clear away their camps from the decks and holds where the cattle were to go. I had already moved and was living on a closed-over lifeboat. My hammock fitted neatly between the lifeboat's davits and from it I had a bird's eye view of the following events.

Loading the cattle provided forty-eight hours of non-stop entertainment. *Tombatu* was tied up alongside the jetty, and herds of wild young 'steaks' (as the kitchenboy called them) arrived, fifty at a time, galloping wildly onto the jetty. Opposite *Tombatu* the cattle were halted and forced to mill in a circle until they quietened and the small aborigine cowmen could group them onto a big rope net spread flat on the dock. As soon as three cows were on the net, the crane hoisted them into the air and slowly aboard *Tombatu*. Cows' legs and heads with incredulous expressions stuck out at the weirdest angles, making a hilarious sight. It was surprising that there weren't more accidents but I saw only one cow fall out and she landed safely in a net that some one had wisely strung between the ship and jetty. To extricate her, a cowman climbed down and tied a rope round her horns, and the crane hoisted her up. While everyone was watching this, no one was tending the main herd and the cattle stampeded back to the shore. Dozens of people rushed to help round them up and in their panic two cows jumped into the sea. They swam to the beach and escaped toward the hills.

The last of the cows to be loaded were the troublesome ones, many now with broken neckropes, which left them almost uncatchable. It took twenty-four hours to get them all on board, and they still had to load the bulls.

When the bulls arrived at the jetty, they wore double neckropes and the wildest ones were blindfolded with sacks. Both they and the bullocks were unwilling to be led and instead charged with heads lowered at their would-be captors. Others skirmished together, their horns locked in battle, and when three spectators moved out of their way they fell backwards into the sea. The cowboys must have been exhausted, but it was very funny to watch.

Loading continued at night by floodlight, and I dozed and watched the show in turns. With the passengers out of the way, conditions for the cattle weren't too cramped (in fact they probably had more room than the passengers) and, since *Tombatu* had also taken on three large haystacks for them to eat on their journey, they would be well fed. The haystacks also provided a useful sleeping place for many passengers.

Finally we left Kupang. *Tombatu* chugged along in the lee of Timor, across gentle turquoise sea and past desolate mountains carved with forested valleys. When the cattle grew restless *Tombatu*'s loudspeaker system broadcast romantic lyrics from the old movie 'South Pacific'. The songs made me feel homesick, but it amused me to be in the south Pacific listening to them.

From Timor we cruised through the Moluccas; it was ten days since we had set out from Surabaya and although *Tombatu* was behind its schedule it went slowly, being hampered by cross-swells which made it roll unpleasantly. Many passengers became seasick but fortunately I wasn't among them. The crew carried out its work despite the rocking motion, and I listened while they hammered off the rust in different parts of the ship. Ten hammers were in use and each one worked to a separate rhythm that blended into one extraordinary metallic harmony.

Coast-hopping along the northern shore of West Irian, we had to put up with rough seas, stormy skies and frequent downpours of rain until we reached Sorong where we were due to pick up a large consignment of oil. We entered Sorong harbour with our loudspeakers blaring 'The Circus Comes To Town' — which I thought was an amusingly appropriate choice.

As soon as we docked, a horde of young men streamed down the gangplank and went running towards town. Their job was to race to the market place and secure good positions for the travelling traders. Other traders had semi-permanent market stalls in *Tombatu*'s front hold, and people from town came aboard to shop for cloth, tape cassettes and T-shirts. While the oil drums were being loaded I went ashore to the immigration office, to try and sort out my visa which was about to expire. The officers were helpful, but said they couldn't extend my visa and that it had to be sorted out in Jayapura; they assured me that there was no cause for worry.

Although the number of passengers was gradually decreasing — the number of people disembarking not being fully replaced — the boat was still crowded and I was curious to see how the crew were going to find room for the quantity of 44-gallon oil drums they were taking on. Their solution was ingenious: they stood the drums upright in the cattlepens so that they formed a series of stepping-stones thereby helping everyone to move around the boat more easily. The only snag was that the cattle's horns were taller than the oil drums, so we had to negotiate every step with care.

We left Sorong and chugged eastwards along the coast, past miles of dense rugged jungle that showed no signs of habitation. I attempted to spend a night sleeping on one of the big haystacks but it was terrible and I had to abandon the idea. Rain had dampened the hay right through and whilst the sun had managed to dry the top layers, the inner core was steaming hot and damp. Being just north of the equator, and in sweltering heat all day, the last thing I needed was a hot wet bed.

The cattle were destined for delivery to various 'transmigration projects'. Sponsored by the Indonesian government, the projects were designed to ease Java's overpopulation (eighty million) by inducing peasant farmers to emigrate to West Irian, which was bigger and had an estimated population of only one million. Several hundred migrant farmers had now moved there and were pioneering their own smallholdings for subsistence farming. Each family was credited with one cow. A transmigration centre called Runsiki was our next port-of-call; though it wasn't a port, didn't have a jetty and was in fact just a village. Somehow *Tombatu* was going to deliver 300 cattle to them.

We anchored off a thin sandy beach backed by dense jungle that reached endlessly up a shaggy mountain range, until it was lost in mist and grey rainclouds. Children in outrigger canoes paddled excitedly out to us. Some bamboo rafts and two ex-

World War II army landing craft came alongside to receive the cattle. They started with the cows from the holds, chasing them in threes into the spread rope-net, then hoisting them by crane into the boats. It began raining heavily as the first cattle were lowered. The whole six-hour operation was carried out in that dark and rainy night.

It was still raining when I woke up next morning. Behind us was a ragged hole in the blanket of dark clouds, through which the sun's rays slanted onto a tall-masted sampan, its billowing white sails shining silver against the thundery seascape. We were heading west, going back on ourselves, towards the army outpost of Manokwari. Five dolphins played around *Tombatu*'s prow, swimming along at exactly the same speed as the boat, but moving in leaps and dives.

In Manokwari we were stuck for four days because *Tombatu*'s main crane broke down, so I spent some of the time exploring the Arfak peninsula, home of the most notorious headhunters of West Irian. When the crane was mended and the ship had taken on its new cargo of several tons of coffee and chocolate (raw in sacks), we left port. By now we had become like a floating village, and I had come to know some of the passengers well. My closest friends were Siswan, a college graduate who was going to join his parents in Jayapura, and Bapa Roos, a knife-maker and metal smith. His best market was West Irian, where he said the people were still using tools of bone and stone. It was Siswan who had explained to me why so many people had looked blank when I told them that I was going to Papua New Guinea. The country was better known as Irian-Irian, and some Indonesians believed that it should belong to their country. They had already claimed West Irian (formerly Dutch New Guinea) back in 1963 when they had gone in to 'pacify the natives'. Nothing was heard in the outside world until heavily-substantiated rumours began circulating about massacres and tribal genocide performed by the Indonesian army against the villagers, and many refugees had fled through the jungles into Papua New Guinea.

The last few days of the journey were enjoyable and companionable. Having delivered most of the cattle and passengers, *Tombatu* was less crowded and it was with mixed feelings that I saw Jayapura was not far away and that we would soon be landing. More dolphins accompanied us for the last few miles and as I looked back on this eventful trip that had started so badly, I knew it was an experience that I did not regret, nor would ever forget.

4
Problems at the Border

Disembarking in Jayapura, I found myself in a small-town capital which seemed more like an army camp. Whistles blew, orders were rapped out, men stamped to attention, and the army practised their military manoeuvres in the streets. The streets were hot and dusty, and littered with a handful of trading booths and endless shanty-type housing. If the housing and hotels looked cheap it was misleading since everything in Jayapura was expensive: a hotel room for instance would have cost 7000 rupiah (£10) a night. I was lucky that Siswan had invited me to stay with his family. They were warm and hospitable people and, after *Tombatu*'s rice and fish-head menu, their Indonesian home cooking was a real treat.

Siswan took me to see the various wrecks from World War II, that were located around Jayapura. On the beaches there were rusted wrecks of army-landing craft, troop-carriers, artillery and tanks. The tanks were parked in a row half-buried in the sand facing the sea, their corroded cog-wheels and segments of caterpillar tracks glowing with rust. War shells poked up through the sand and some women were digging for brass cartridge cases to sell for scrap.

Siswan also inspired me to visit the interior of West Irian; we sat on the sand and he told me stories about the Sibillers or 'worm children', who believed their ancestors were worms. Now they were warrior-farmers (like most mountain tribes in this part of the world), and though similar in appearance to others who wore penis-gourds (long curly bean gourds attached at the top with bush-string) and covered their bodies in red ochre mixed with pig fat, they could still be distinguished by their long waistbands of 'magical' dogs' teeth.

Siswan frowned as he remembered something else, and he

recounted the deaths of four Dutch missionary families in the area I proposed to visit; the families had been killed and eaten by cannibals in 1974. (According to a guide book which he later showed me, the cannibals killed their victims with a bone-knife or spear, then cut a small hole in the skull. The brains were shaken loose then sucked out, and were usually eaten by male children. The body-meat was distributed, and the fat was used for polishing spears or drums.)

However, this didn't deter me from making a brief visit to the Dani tribe who live in that area in the Baliem valley, and protect themselves against neighbouring enemies with a three-mile frontier marked by thirty watchtowers. Each tower is made from bundles of branches roped together with vines to make a tall pillar, and is topped by a small thatched platform. Fighting and the survival of the fittest is their way of life, but during my visit all was calm, and for several days the people went peacefully about their daily lives.

That peace was disturbed, however, when a large party of anthropologists descended on the valley. In a very short time they seemed to be everywhere and their presence made me feel uncomfortable. I didn't want to be associated with them; I was a lone traveller, not one of a group of scientists. I wanted to get away from them, to places beyond their reach and influence. Therefore I cut short my visit, deciding to return to Jayapura and make haste to Papua New Guinea.

On my return to Jayapura, I realised that my Indonesian visa was now several weeks out of date. This was a serious offence. I went to the Immigration Office to apologise, and to my relief the situation didn't become unpleasant: they gave me time to catch the next plane out of the country. There was only one external flight per week, which flew to Wewak in Papua New Guinea, so I went immediately to buy a ticket. Without a map I didn't know where Wewak was situated, but that didn't matter; it was in Papua New Guinea and that was the important thing.

I arrived, as ordered, at the dusty airstrip one hour before departure time, and checked out through immigration and customs control. There were three other passengers. We were all about to board when an official approached me and asked to see my vaccination certificate. He flicked through the pages until he reached the cholera vaccination record and stopped. Mine I knew was out of date, but it had never been required at a border before and I didn't expect any trouble. But my luck was out — here I was told, it was compulsory.

Suddenly the affair blew up. The pilot refused to allow me on the plane (since the airline would be legally responsible for keeping me in quarantine), and the airport officials wouldn't let me remain in Indonesia (because my visa was already extended over the maximum allowance). The Indonesians demanded that I go on that flight, but the pilot refused, so they grounded the plane. Tempers rose and soon everyone was shouting angrily. Everyone that is, except me. I sat quietly in a corner, cursing the ticket agency for not warning me and praying that I would be allowed on the plane. An hour later the pilot won the argument and the plane moved off without me. As it taxied down the airstrip a customs officer asked to see my passport and noticed that my entry-permit to Papua New Guinea would expire the very next day.

I had twenty-four hours to get into Papua New Guinea, or my visa would be invalid. And my last hope had just roared into the sky.

It felt as though the bottom had just dropped out of my world; it had taken me eight arduous months of travel to reach Papua New Guinea and now it seemed that the door was to be slammed in my face. I couldn't bear to think that I could be sent home when I was so close to the border.

Tears welled up and began pouring down my face. I felt crushed, helpless and alone. I no longer knew what to do. People tried to help, but there seemed to be no way out. An official drove me to the Missionary Society but they had no flights lined up, and the air charter company offered me a plane for 600,000 rupiah (£800); again tears blinded my eyes and I couldn't speak. The airport manager kindly took me for a cup of tea and a hot meal, then to a Sumatran doctor who gave me the cholera jab, and finally deposited me with the Chief of Immigration.

The chief smiled to see me again. In our previous meeting we had established that I wouldn't pay bribes, or let him play power games, so this time he didn't try. Perhaps he could see that I was distraught, and sensed that the slightest upset would reduce me to tears again. I struggled to stay composed, though four hours of crying and misery had left me weak. It was almost reassuring to know that *something* had to happen next.

5
Arrival
in Papua New Guinea

The immigration chief took charge of the situation. After a harrowing interval he issued me with orders, and wrote out some instructions for me to take to the coastguard's canoe-keeper. At dusk I located the canoe-keeper and gave him the instructions. I slept on a floormat in the boatman's hut and at six o'clock next morning the boatman loaded me and my backpack into his canoe. At last we were setting off along the coast towards Papua New Guinea.

It was an outrigger canoe with a motor, and as it sped through the choppy sea, waves sprayed over us. The boatman was wearing a windbreaker and an old-fashioned flying helmet. I nestled behind my plastic rainsheet, but my face and arms were soon crusted with salt from the spray.

The boatman announced that we were now in Papua New Guinea waters. I felt a sense of elation which was similar to fear. Far to our right the inhospitable coast stretched into malaria-infested marshes and mangrove swamps. Behind the swamps was thick jungle, smothering the land as it rose toward mountains. There were neither people, nor signs of habitation. So this was the country that I had travelled half way round the world to visit.

According to history, the first European to report sighting the coast of Papua New Guinea was a Portuguese ship's captain in 1526. The first landing (on the island's south side) was made by another Portuguese captain who named it 'Ilhas dos Papuas'. Papuas was a Malay word meaning fuzzy-haired. The natives were seen to be unfriendly and none of the European powers expressed any interest in the island except the Dutch who laid claim to the western half in order to protect the wealthy Dutch East Indies empire in Indonesia. The name New Guinea was given to the whole island by the Dutch, and later during its colonial period the island was divided into Dutch New-Guinea (the western half before it was claimed by the Indonesians), German New-Guinea (the northern quarter) and British New-Guinea (the southern part). After World War I Australia became administrator of the German portion, and later when the British also handed their southern territory (re-named Papua) into Australia's care, the two quarters were eventually joined into one country.

At mid-morning, in the sea ahead of the canoe, we saw a dugong. These creatures are said to have caused the mermaid legends; they belong to the Order Sirenia, named after the mermaids of Greek mythology who lured sailors to their deaths on the rocks. (Actually, dugongs are a distant relative of elephants, having shared an ancestor about 70 million years ago.) This dugong was sunbathing, floating lazily on the water; it was about the length of a human adult, with mammalian body and fishy tail, but it didn't fit my image of a mermaid. As soon as the boatman saw the dugong he seized his spear — a 9-ft (3-m) pole with ten sharp harpoon-prongs — and hurled it at the unfortunate beast. The spear hissed through the air, trailing its rope, and splashed into an empty sea: the dugong had already dived to safety. The boatman cursed it as he pulled in the rope and retrieved his harpoon, and I tried not to look glad that he had missed. Dugong meat was a delicacy.

My first sights of Vanimo were of a fishing boat tied to an old jetty, a collection of bungalows and local administrative headquarters. Although there was no official immigration post, I located a man who said that he could stamp my passport. He had not previously had the opportunity of checking a tourist into the country, and he couldn't resist the desire to find out what tourists had in their luggage. He unpacked the lot. He looked a bit amazed by the innumerable plastic bags, my catapult, tobacco pouch, and strips of dried meat (jerky). He confiscated my jar of salt in case it was heroin.

His signature on my visa told me that at last I had entered Papua New Guinea. I felt exhausted by trauma and drained of all reactions. Nothing really mattered, except that I had arrived. I had no idea where to go from Vanimo. There was nowhere to buy a map.

An American missionary family in Vanimo invited me to stay at their house while I decided my next step. They were Protestant bible-teachers. Formerly they had been drug abusers, but their new-found beliefs and pure Christian goodness made me feel ashamed of my lack of faith.

The next morning was Sunday. In the bamboo chapel beside their home they held a church service, conducted in Neo-Melanesian (known as pidgin, the national language of Papua New Guinea).

I sat on a roughly-hewn pew among the local womenfolk, listening to the flow of the preacher's intonations. Frequent English words jolted my meditation, but I couldn't understand much of what was being said. Pidgin is based on Melanesian grammar and the words are a mixture of English, German, Chinese, Malay, Portuguese and other languages, with many regional dialects added. Pidgin is no one's mother tongue, it is a second language which is taught in schools in order to unite the country's innumerable tribes who speak different languages (45 per cent of the world's total languages).

Certain phrases did catch my attention, and intrigued me. A stranger was *man bilong long-wei ples* (man belong long-way place), a language was *tok-ples* (talk-place), and home was *arse-ples* (base-place).

Slowly I became aware that it must be Easter, for the lesson was about the crucifixion. It went something like this: *Ol i nail-im Jesus long kros, im i die, na ol i plantim bodi daunbilo long groun. I die, tasol im i no die finis. Bye i kumup wantaim moa, long lukim long yu-mi.* (They nailed Jesus on the cross, he died, and they buried his body underground. He didn't die completely. He will come up one more time, to look at you and me).

Over the next few days I learnt more pidgin, and I relaxed in the feeling of security that comes from being with a family. The missionaries, Mike and Beth Hayes, couldn't have been kinder, and their young children were flawlessly well behaved. Beth was schooling them and while I stayed I helped teach them, to give Beth a break and repay her kindness.

For myself, the most immediate task was to decide where to go next. I borrowed a map and settled down to study it and find a route out of Vanimo. Here I got my first surprise: the map showed Vanimo as a small coastal outpost at the emptiest end of a sparsely-populated land, so wild that no roads led to or from it; it was completely cut off. I looked at the other towns and counted just seven, and they included the capital city. Only very few of them were interconnected by roads and I could see why — a massive chain of mountains ran the length of the country, reaching 15,000ft (4,575m) in parts — that formed a natural barrier.

My first option was to continue the journey by sea, but that would have entailed an uncomfortable three-day ride by cargo boat to Wewak, and it seemed pointless to go around the outside of a country that I had come to see. Neither was I too keen to make my first stop a town — I really wanted to explore the interior and to meet the tribes-people.

My second option was to continue on foot, but no one knew of any paths from Vanimo going inland long-distance. My third was to get a lift in one of the light aircraft used for local government and mission work, that often landed in some of the more remote places. The country was dotted with grass airstrips, and included some of the most perilous ones in the world. That probably sounds exaggerated, but it is said that for a pilot to have a year's experience of flying in Papua New Guinea and using those airstrips, is worth ten years' experience elsewhere. The flying itself was also hazardous because various mountain ranges were too high for the light aircraft to fly over, while thick clouds often obscured the lower altitudes around the mountains. Accidents were frequent.

These hazards aside, flying seemed to be the best idea. That completed the choice of *how* to continue. But where should I go? The decision could be made by random choice. Spreading out the map, I took hold of a pencil then reaching out I let the pencil drop to touch the map. It landed on the highlands at the remotest end of the mountain cordillera, the least-explored end of Papua New Guinea. I felt some stirrings of excitement as my journey began to take shape; I would fly to the back of that area, then walk through, heading west until I reached the tail end of a jeep-track (shown on the map by a dotted red line), at Lake Kopiago. I had no idea how long the walk would take.

At Vanimo airfield I found a twin-engined plane destined for the patrol posts of Telefomin and Oksapmin. At seven o'clock the next morning I sat on board the plane as it bumped its way along the runway and accelerated into the sky.

I was in the co-pilot's seat and enjoyed a superb view as we flew over the jungle, slowly gained height and rose over some hills to a vast plain. Beneath me lay an expanse of jungled flatness that I could see was dissected by streams which flowed into a larger, muddy brown, sluggish river. These were tributaries of the Sepik river.

Soon we were above the river and I could see its meandering course looping back on itself in sweeping curves, eroding banks and changing its course continually, as it cast-off its horseshoe-shaped lakes. These lakes were stagnant and overhung with lush vegetation. The pilot, an Australian, called them ox-bow lakes and said that they were infested with crocodiles. Then he snorted with laughter and began telling me about his experiences flying with cargoes of live crocodiles. Baby crocodiles were gathered by local tribes-people who took them to Green River airfield when a skin-trader or crocodile-farmer made a buying expedition there.

Cargo for the crocodile farmers had to be air-freighted alive and to ensure safety in transit their jaws were tied shut with twists of grass-string. It was not uncommon however, for boxes to break or spill open depositing panic-stricken crocodiles all over the floor, and he chuckled as he recalled that on one occasion, when a loose crocodile bit his foot, he grabbed it by its tail and threw it out of the open window beside him. It hit the propellor and was instantly splattered to pulp, much of which splashed back through the window into the plane. He also recalled a flight carrying a twelve-foot (four-metre) crocodile, which was heavily sedated and bound with ropes. In its sleep it flexed its muscles and one by one the ropes snapped, but fortunately for the pilot it didn't wake up.

The pilot brought me back to the present by gesturing down and pointing to the sources of three rivers below: the Sepik, the Strickland and the Fly rivers. We were now in the mountains approaching Telefomin and the plane climbed steadily as it cleared ridge after ridge, between which I could see vegetation clinging precariously to the plunging slopes.

When Telefomin came into sight, it seemed to consist of just a couple of buildings and an airfield. A few people had gathered to watch the plane land, waiting with curiosity to see what it was bringing. As we taxied, the pilot told me that many people still regarded flying as magic; planes to them were metal birds (living things), with pilots apparently using magic to control them. Some years ago, when a helicopter had landed, the local villagers had swarmed all over it, patting it and trying to feed it with *kaukau* (sweet potato, the staple food).

We stayed for a short while in Telefomin and, while the pilot went about his duties, I wandered around smiling at people and trying to practise my pidgin. The women were bare-breasted and they wore grass skirts. The men were small-statured, dark-skinned and bearded, with heavy hook noses, either pierced open through the nasal septum or tipped with strange small spikes. They didn't speak any pidgin and their own language was sharp and rapid, making them sound ferocious. I remembered being told in Vanimo about some killings by cannibals in Telefomin not very many years ago.

Oksapmin was only ten minutes flight from Telefomin. We flew past 12,000-ft (3,650-m) high peaks, before banking round and up a breathtaking escarpment, to the lip of the dish-shaped valley of Oksapmin. People beneath us hurriedly cleared the runway and gathered to meet the plane. Included in the welcoming party was Nicky Cape, a young Englishman who had been sent to Oksapmin for two years by the VSA (Voluntary Services Association) to teach people how to cultivate vegetables.

During lunch he gave me much valuable advice about my proposed walk, but said he doubted that I would reach my destination of Lake Kopiago. The problem was that to get there, I had to cross the Strickland river and because it was the rainy season it would be swollen and in flood. Fifty-foot floodwaters had swept away the suspended footbridge that used to span the river several years ago and it hadn't been replaced. Nicky was horrified at my suggestion that I would swim across and warned me that many people had already drowned attempting it. But seeing that I wasn't going to be put off, he suggested that I should walk to the north and loop round so that I could swim across as far upstream as possible, where it would be narrow and not quite so fast-flowing. He added that to his knowledge no white woman had ever walked that route before.

The only thing to arrange now was a guide, so Nicky organised for a message to be spread telling any prospective guides to meet me on the following day. Actually, I didn't really want a guide — the idea of being lost didn't bother me — but since I had a specific destination (albeit randomly selected), I was realistic enough to know that I would need a guide if I was to have any hope of finding it. Another major consideration was the weight of my backpack. It weighed about fifty pounds, and included two weeks' emergency food supplies that I had collected at Vanimo. Because of the jungle's sparse population I couldn't rely upon always being given local hospitality, and the poor local diet of *kaukau* I knew wouldn't be sufficient to sustain me. Among these people I discovered that it was not possible to have just one guide, there had to be at least two, because one man would be afraid to return alone. They feared possible harm from other tribes since by custom they were not friendly to each other, and at best, they regarded one another with suspicion and mistrust. My walk seemed to be turning into an expedition.

Shortly after lunch, when the pilot and Nicky boarded the plane (Nicky was ill with hepatitis and had to go to Wewak for medical attention) and they left Oksapmin, I felt terribly alone. But not unhappy. Nicky had kindly suggested that I stay in his hut and had left me with a large heap of firewood for warmth.

The coldness of the mountain altitude surprised me, I had forgotten what it felt like to be cold — particularly after the month of hot sun and sea on *Tombatu,* and the sweaty coastal climate of Vanimo. Now I felt refreshed and chilly. Late that afternoon I strolled down the broad valley to a grove of hoop-pines, which grew up to 250ft (75m) without a bend in their trunks and whose branches seemed to be ringed by hoops of pine needles. It felt good to be among giants. Standing among those trees, I watched clouds drift up over the escarpment, floating forward and engulfing everything in foggy wetness as they went. When the trees blurred and disappeared I retired indoors, lit a fire, and settled down contentedly for the evening.

The following day I sat outside and waited to see if any prospective guides would turn up in reply to the message that Nicky had sent out. Various people came over to look at me. Some of them were Neolithic-type bowmen, with spikes on the tips of their noses made of beetles' antennae. Nearly all the men carried bows and arrows, which I noticed had points of carved cassowary-bone instead of metal, just as Bapa Roos had told me

41

on *Tombatu*. Several men wore penis-gourds, while others instead wore a narrow piece of woven bush-fibre as a loin cloth. Women wore double-layered grass skirts and were bare-breasted. They carried *bilums* (big net bags slung from a long loop across the forehead) that were full of firewood and *kaukau* and looked heavy. The children hid behind their mothers' legs and seemed terrified of me.

A group of adults began discussing me and since I couldn't understand a word of what they were saying, I had to hope that they weren't being too critical. I smiled and listened to the way they spoke. Their voices had a harsh, staccato quality, their sentences beginning with a sharp gabble and slowing to a low end. It made them sound fierce, though I knew it was just their manner of speech (as in Telefomin), and I didn't feel afraid.

After some considerable time, two men with wild pigs' tusks through their noses stepped forward and informed me that they would be my guides: '*Yu-mi go long wokabaut*'. Their knowledge of pidgin was as scanty as mine, but we managed to communicate and agreed that they should collect me at dawn the next day. They would accompany me for the first stage of my walk, then pass me safely on to new guides. Their pay would be at government-porter rates, approximately two *kina* (£1.50) per day.

I passed the rest of the day quietly and went to bed at eight o'clock, to prepare for an early start in the morning.

Part Two

The Long Walk

6
A Perilous River Crossing

Dawn was foggy, cold and damp. I lay for an extra moment in my sleeping bag dreading the coldness outside, until I remembered why I had to get up, and hurriedly did so. There was no time to waste. Quickly rekindling the fire to warm myself, I made some coffee and breakfast and began to pack.

When my guides, Kom and Arak, arrived I was ready for them. They were impatient to start out saying that we had far to go in the day 'Yu-mi go nau. *Wokabaut bilong yu-mi stap long-wei tru'*. Kom heaved my backpack onto his shoulders, and when both men had picked up their bows and arrows, we set off down the valley at a fast pace.

We went in single file with me in the middle. The damp fog lay thickly in the valley so that nothing was visible except for Kom, who was in front of me, and the muddy path underfoot. When the mud became a marsh I had difficulty keeping up with Kom, for despite his wearing the backpack, he jumped nimbly from one grassy tuft to the next. Sometimes he missed his footing and sank to his knees in mud, but I slipped continually. I had completely forgotten about bringing boots or any other suitable footwear, and was wearing thong sandals which were worse than useless. They went slimy with the wet clay and my feet slid sideways off them with almost every step. In the end I gave up and took them off, realising that I would probably have to do the whole walk barefoot.

Now there was a risk in every unseen step and I could feel the mud oozing between my toes. On the plus side though, I was free to use my feet in a more animal way, to balance myself and to grip the tussocks. As we hopped and floundered forwards, the fog began to clear and the sun shone weakly, but it was still cold.

At a cluster of huts in the lower valley we stopped briefly to collect three women. They were going to visit a relative who lived a day's walk to the north-west and our paths coincided for a couple of hours. The women weren't quite ready, and were still filling their *bilums* with *kaukau* and oddments. While I watched them I observed the patterns of dots and lines tattooed on their faces. The lines on their foreheads followed the curve of their eyebrows; they had stars on their temples and a rising sun in the centre of their foreheads. Several of the men wore pigs' tusks and one had the head of a rhinoceros beetle, complete with antennae, sticking out from the tip of his nose.

When they had finished the women put the straps of their *bilums* across their foreheads and swung them onto their backs. At the top of one *bilum* I could see a baby, sleeping peacefully, blissfully unaware of all the noise and commotion.

The size of my expedition had grown again. Chattering gaily in harsh gutteral tones the party moved off. We had left the swamp and were now walking through *pitpit* grass (like elephant grass), which grew thickly across the narrow path and entwined above our heads. We had to push our way through it, and respect its ability to cut skin; this was no main thoroughfare.

The path was heading north, leading to the base of a mountain which rose steeply into the clouds and had to be climbed. My band stopped gossiping and concentrated on the climb. Forest closed over us, water dripped from dank green foliage, tree trunks were coated in luxuriant moss and lichen, and filmy moss hung in trailing beards from the branches. All was misty and silent. Occasionally one of the men would whistle a long shrill note which I guessed was to give the stragglers an idea of how far ahead the leaders had gone. Naturally I was among the stragglers — partly because I was too busy looking around — but mainly because my lungs were straining with lack of oxygen and I was unfit. Strung out in lengthy single file, we wove our way along the forest floor, between and beneath its huge tangled roots.

To get to the other side of the innumerable ravines we followed the paths to wherever a tree had fallen to bridge the gap. The first few tree 'bridges' were fairly level and although there was little to grasp for balance, it was not difficult to walk across. But at a steeply-angled bridge where we had to jump from one tree trunk to another and proceed up its network of branches high above a swamp, I baulked and my courage failed. I stood there, unable to go forwards, momentarily paralysed. It was unthinkable to sit down and cross on my behind, since I would have felt undignified and the women would have laughed and said that I was afraid. The one ahead of me noticed that I was no longer following her and she came back across the bridge to show me the way again. She didn't even bother to put down her baby, she was so sure of her steps; she walked towards me, erect, and zigzagging the time-worn course.

She shot a question at me, probably about my stillness. I wondered how to react and knew that I couldn't refuse to walk across, so indicated to her that I would try again. Following her dark silhouette and keeping my eyes on the sloping log beneath my feet, I began making my way across. Where the bark had worn off the wood was still wet from recent rain and therefore extremely slippery, but I told myself sternly 'Do it, don't think about it. And don't look down.' After the first faltering steps I began to use the walking stick Kom had picked for me as a balancing pole, and after a few terrifying moments we were across.

Climbing up the mountain we found that the roots across the path made good handholds and helped us to clamber and scramble up over the wet mud. Then with great relief I heard Kom say *'Taim bilong kisim wind' (kisim wind* means to catch your breath). We sat down on some flat rocks to rest and Kom showed me his bow and arrows. Each arrow was differently made for a different use: a four-pronged bamboo arrow was for shooting birds, a knife-shaped bamboo blade was for pigs, another was tipped with cassowary bone, and one had barbed hooks running twelve inches down the shaft, skilfully carved and coloured with ochres. The bow was of sturdy blackpalm, with a bowstring of scraped bamboo.

Kom kindled a small fire and heated some *kaukau,* which must have been pre-roasted before setting out because they were ready to eat in ten minutes. This was my first taste of *kaukau* and it was delicious, just like a sweet potato. The resting-place marked the parting of ways between us and the extra women who went off to the west. We could hear them chattering long after they had vanished from sight — making a shrill and strident noise rather like the raucous birdsong and screeches that echoed through the forest.

As we climbed, so it got hotter and the forest sweated. Trees blossomed with orange and yellow bell-flowers, and were prolific with red berries, nuts, or giant acorns; other fruits were hairy, spiky, shiny and brightly coloured. The fruits that lay rotting on the ground were fermenting. Toadstools were growing profusely on many centuries of accumulated leafmould, while purple fungi sprouted like coral from dead tree stumps, and thick bark was being shed by other trees in the annual cycle of decay and renewal.

My feet were doing well, though it was impossible to keep up with Kom's fast pace and the climb seemed endlessly steep and rough. By mid-afternoon we were on top and, while we rested and roasted a few more *kaukau*, a hunting party came along. We all exchanged greetings and they sat down. They were thin, undecorated and naked except for their long curly penis-gourds. The two groups talked with the rapidity of machine gun fire. The hunters had just caught a reddish-gold animal, a strange furry marsupial with wide goggle eyes and a long bald prehensile tail. Its hands had five claw-tipped fingers and it had in its pouch a miniscule hairless baby. The animal was probably a type of possom, but I had never seen one before. Despite the many years I had spent travelling, there was never a feeling of sameness.

I wondered what caused the animal life of Papua New Guinea to be different from the type I had seen all over the rest of the world and, in trying to figure it out, I recalled (from former brief studies of Plate-tectonics) that Papua New Guinea was once part of a land bridge which attached Australia to the Asian continent and that when the land bridge had sunk, it had left the island of New Guinea isolated before the evolution of many types of animal. So that, although there are few of the world's common wild animals, Papua New Guinea is rich in reptiles, rodents, marsupials and birds. It has giant monitor lizards; crocodiles and tree-climbing crocodiles; pythons, taipans and death-adders; flying foxes, spiny ant eaters, tree-kangaroos, cassowaries and over 600 other species of birds.

I divided out some tobacco between the hunters, my guides and myself, which we smoked before moving on. When we had been walking for eight hours my leg muscles ached and I was exhausted. Twice I asked Kom how much further we had to go. His first reply was *'long-wei liklik'*, meaning a fairly long way, but the second time, when we stood on top of a ridge looking down on the Ok-Om river, he at last said *'klos-tu. Haus i stap klos-tu'*. In the valley below, on the opposite side of the river, I could see two huts.

As we slithered down the muddy mountainside Kom and Arak suddenly began yelping and yodel-chanting. Their combined harmony reminded me of the sound of baying hounds after a fox. It was an exciting noise; it re-energised me, and it also told the huts' occupants that they were about to have visitors. Ok-Om wasn't a big river and was easy to cross on a suspended foot-bridge. Away downstream, beyond our sight, the Ok-Om and Lagaip rivers met in a T-junction and became the Strickland river; it was the Lagaip river, the major force of the Strickland, that I had decided to swim.

It was a relief to arrive at the huts. I was aching with fatigue. The family came out to welcome us and stood in a line to look at me, their faces crinkled with curiosity and amazement.

They stared for a long moment before one of them turned to Kom and asked a question. His reply made them even more curious and they came forward to look more closely at me. Kom told me that they had asked if I was a woman. It seemed that a lone woman traveller was beyond their comprehension, and they were confused at seeing me there. To ease their nervousness I kept smiling and began shaking hands with each person there. I doubted they had ever shaken hands with anyone before, but it was a useful gesture of contact and goodwill, and their wrinkled brown faces smiled back at me. Mothers brought out their babies to shake hands too.

The women were wearing grass skirts, and their earlobes were distended around bamboo hoops. Most of the men wore pigs' tusks through their noses and one wore a chunky tusk-and-cowrie-shell necklet, and about thirty bamboo hoops round his waist which were joined at the front into an up-pointing prong.

Their evening meal was *kaukau* which was roasted in the fire and peeled by hand before eating. As well as tasting like a sweet potato it also looked rather like a potato. The *kaukau* gardens where they were cultivated lay nearby on the riverbank. The people shared their *kaukau* with the three of us and I contributed some canned meat stew, which we heated in my saucepan over the fire. They didn't possess a saucepan or any other utensils, plates, cups or cutlery. They ate with their hands, and without bowls so I had no means of dishing up the stew and, instead had to take some and pass the saucepan round for the others to share. I noticed that there seemed to be a systematic order for taking food: the first to eat were the two men from the huts who also took some for the male children before passing the pan to Kom and Arak. Once they had helped themselves they handed it on to some older men, until it finally reached the womenfolk.

We didn't drink anything with the meal, and after I had taken the saucepan to the riverside and scoured it clean with wiry grasses, I re-filled it with water to make tea. At first the people didn't like the tea and passed it back to me, but when I added several spoonsful of sugar and offered it again they drank every drop.

Later the menfolk sat around the fire and played their long-waisted drums which were hollowed from a single piece of wood. I listened to them talking and drumming until I was too tired to stay awake. For sleeping, I was shown to a small smoke-cooking cubicle where the fire had been allowed to die down and swept away, leaving a clear space. The bamboo walls and floor were black with soot.

I laid out my plastic rainsheet and sleeping bag on the floor, and fell asleep to the sound of drumming.

We looped round to the north of the gorges leaving the huts behind. There was no need to hurry because it was only a short day's walk to our next stop which was to be at some huts called Sisimin. We followed a path along the riverbank and made a short-cut across some crumpled hills, which I was told were the foothills of the Central Mountain range where some very primitive Hewa people lived. Much of their territory had never been explored or mapped, because it had been an official 'restricted' area (closed to outsiders, unless accompanied by an armed government escort) until about 1971.

We met a Hewa as we approached Sisimin. He stood aside to let us pass; he looked frightened of me and seemed unsure whether he should run away. His own appearance was made startling by his hairy headgear: a tall tapering topknot of hair clippings and grasses, held tight with bush-string. His earlobes were pierced and stretched around bamboo hoops and his nostrils were pierced at the sides, with crossed feathers inserted as nose-quills. He hurried on his way and we strolled on ours. I couldn't go any faster because my leg muscles were aching, and my mind was heavy with the worry of swimming the river.

Kom had told me that there was a place near Sisimin where I could swim the river. It was about three miles up from the Strickland Gorge and we went to look at the place before going into Sisimin.

As I stood there on the bank watching the roaring torrent of water foaming over submerged rocks, my blood ran cold. The river was alarmingly wide and although this was the safest place, the river was still in flood and it looked a terrifying prospect.

When we reached Sisimin, our arrival was heralded by a trumpeter with a long gourd-trumpet; this was the local way of conveying information to outlying huts. The gourd-trumpet made a braying noise and someone explained in pidgin '*im sing-aut*'.

My hosts in Sisimin were Yagol-T, who was an evangelist preacher from the Sepik river region, and his wife Tocas. Their hut was clean and spacious; more so after the chickens had been chased outside. Among their chickens I noticed some long-legged cassowary chicks, with their distinctive black and tan stripes and their small wings, which are characteristic of flightless birds. Yagol-T said that the chicks' mother had been killed in a hunt and that the chicks were highly valuable as status symbols, or as meat, or payment of bride-price. One small adult cassowary could be worth 500 *kina*, roughly £375, while the larger lowland species could fetch 1,000 *kina*. The highland cassowaries were smaller, growing only 4 feet (1½m) tall, and were vicious. When a cassowary was slaughtered nothing was wasted. The meat was eaten, the feathers used for human decorations, the wing-spines became nose-quills and the thigh-bones were made into daggers. Not having developed an iron age, tools were usually made of bone, hardwoods and stone.

That night, as we sat around the fire discussing the river, Yagol-T urged me not to attempt swimming while it was in full flood but to wait a day or two for the level to drop. However, he acknowledged that it was equally possible that the rain upriver would continue and the water level would rise.

The first thing I did the next day was to go down to the river and check the water level, but it was still too high to attempt a crossing and I went back to the village feeling despondent and a little edgy — the waiting was almost worse than the prospect of the crossing.

Fortunately, I had some distraction in the form of a steady stream of visitors who came to exchange greetings and news, or just to look at me. Their attention didn't worry me for unlike the Indonesians, they didn't crowd me and they appeared honest. I felt confident that none of these people would try to steal from me. It seemed that the deeper I travelled into the wilds the greater was the people's honesty and integrity, and it was less likely I would be threatened in any way by people. Also it occurred to me that perhaps their 'primitive' moral values were more civilised than in 'civilisation'.

My visitors appeared to come from mixed stock, some had dark brown skin, some light brown, and others had ginger-coloured skin and ginger frizzy hair. The ginger colour didn't look like pigment deficiency so may have been genetic, which seemed reasonable since Papua New Guinea contains at least 700 different tribes, who come from Melanesian stock mixed with some Micronesians, Polynesians, Negritos, Malays and Aboriginals. The tribes, or clans as they are called throughout the highlands, are each made up of 50-100 men (who share their territory and a common male ancestor), but in the more populated eastern highlands the numbers in a clan could swell to several thousand.

Around me the children were pot-bellied with malnutrition and worms, and many people had a skin disease called *grilli*, which is actually a ringworm infestation that causes the skin to peel over most of the body. It is itchy, contagious and almost incurable. Malnutrition was common because of their poor and unbalanced diet of *kaukau*, and the lack of regular meat or fish to eat.

Everyone had something to say about why I shouldn't try to swim the river. I went down to its banks several times more to check the water level, but each time it was too high, though it was difficult to tell with all the surging and splashing. Meanwhile, I learned that the normal method of swimming across was to use a float of logs, which was held with both hands while swimming with your legs. Without a log float, I was told, I would be swept away by the current into the gorges. To help pass the time, I made a miniature model of a float and mentally prepared myself to cross the river. The idea terrified me, and I could see that I would be lucky to get safely across. But I didn't believe in going back or in giving up before trying. It wasn't a question of refusing a challenge — the concept of challenge didn't mean much to me — it was just that here, travelling in this remote country, certain things had to be done just as part of daily life. They may seem extraordinary now, but in their context they weren't.

As the day progressed, the weather worsened and storm clouds built up overhead. I hoped that the rain wouldn't fall upriver and put off my crossing for yet one more day.

Yagol-T noticed my impatience to cross the river, and during the evening he called his flock to a church service to invoke God's aid for my crossing. The church was a bamboo lattice-work hut built on a hilltop overlooking the vast jungle. I stood among a congregation of people wearing necklaces of teeth, and hairy head-dresses decorated with leaves and feathers. They sang a lovely hymn in pidgin, the chorus of which was *laik im yu, laik im mi, o god yu bigfela,* and into the offertory bowl they put maize cobs, bananas and sticks of sugar cane. Yagol-T led them in prayers, asking for dry weather in the headwaters and for strength in my swimming, calling for help also from the spirits of three men who had previously drowned there.

Then he asked me to say a prayer in English. There was no need to be inhibited so I spoke to their God, asking him to bless them for their kindness.

Early the next morning I ran down to check the river, but it was no less violent than the day before and my spirits began to sink. While I was waiting to see if its level was rising or falling, four Hewa men appeared who, it transpired, also wanted to swim the river. They agreed that it was too swollen to attempt for the time being, and they began to make their one-man floats. Chopping down a few smallish trees and cutting them into metre-length logs, they bound three of them together with vines to make each float. They made an extra one for me and said that I could cross with them.

I was just turning to go back to Yagol-T's hut when the Hewas changed their minds and announced that they weren't going to wait after all and that they would cross now. I replied that I was ready.

The Hewas had also offered to guide me for a couple of days after the river, so I paid Kom and Arak off and thanked them for their help. We collected my backpack, wrapped it in my plastic rain-sheet and roped it onto a big float. The only thought in my mind was that if the Hewas were willing to let me attempt the swim then it must be possible.

The first to try crossing were three of the men with my backpack. I watched nervously as they dragged their floats down the sand into the waves, slipped their wrists through loops of vines tied to each float, took firm hold of the logs and launched themselves forward into the churning current. Swimming hard, they shrieked their traditional yelping battlecry, which grew fainter as the roaring water carried them down the river. The water surged over rocks in huge angry waves, and as they met the rapids one float broke apart. We watched horrified as the man was swept away, catching glimpses of him on distant wavecrests as he struggled to gain hold of one log. Finally we saw he had caught the log and was floating safely back to shore.

Then it was my turn. Kom and Arak positioned my float alongside that of the strongest man and they held it steady, pointing it at a slight angle upstream. I slipped my wrists through the loops of vine and called my last goodbye to Yagol-T, Tocas and friends at Sisimin. Cold, calm terror gripped my stomach, far colder than the icy mountain water around my legs. We pushed the floats forward and set off. Yelpings of encouragement were ringing in my ears as I began to swim for my life. The far bank was a blur of green beyond a tossing muddy brown river. I kicked my way along with desperate determination. Water was roaring in my ears, and my knuckles were white with the effort of gripping the float.

Despite my kicking, I was being swept mercilessly downstream and knew myself to be powerless against the river's force. My muscles ached, but I couldn't slacken. The man with the float beside me was still yelping encouragement. When we were nearing the centre of the river, my terror began to turn into a different feeling: a wild sense of exhilaration. Waves were washing over us and we were dragged into heaving rapids; I saw the water meet the sky at every angle, yet it never closed over me.

The opposite bank loomed slowly larger, but when I fixed my eyes on a point it vanished upriver and again I realised how fast I was being swept downriver. Briefly it flashed through my mind that the gorges must be close, and I swam with every last ounce of strength.

Closing in on the bank the current was less turbulent, and I dragged myself to the shore. I sat and trembled with fatigue, too tired to feel elated by success.

The Hewa who had failed to get across made a second attempt which was successful, and he joined us on the bank. Meanwhile the other two emerged safely from upstream carrying my backpack. It was fairly dry and I was pleased to find that my camera inside it was also dry. All too soon the men indicated that we should move on. My legs felt too weak to walk, but somehow I managed to pull myself up from the ground and stumble forward, although I would have liked to have rested longer.

There wasn't any path from the river, so we had to scramble bent double through the forest undergrowth until we reached some rocky land sloping steeply uphill and we could stand upright again. I was so tired that my feet didn't feel the sharpness of the ground. The Hewas were sure-footed and moved at almost a jog-trot, occasionally stopping to examine animal tracks for signs of freshness.

The forest became lower and spikier again, interspersed with patches of open grassland before rising steeply to a series of muddy ravines which had to be crossed on thin fallen tree trunks. My companions were surprised when they saw that I could walk along the trunks — they obviously hadn't expected me to manage them and didn't know I had already been initiated.

At one mud patch someone spotted the fresh prints of a cassowary, so we all stopped and started searching for its trail. Our path seemed forgotten as the men fanned out through the forest, pausing only to check the undergrowth for signs of newly-broken twigs, or fluff and feathers caught on the spiky shrubs. We crept along stealthily; the forest was dim and silent, its thick leafy canopy muffling all sound from outside and making even the snapping of a twig seem loud. When I stepped on a thorn and had to stop to dig it out, I asked the Hewa who stayed with me why cassowaries were considered dangerous, when they were only birds. He explained in pantomime that cassowaries, being flightless birds, had very strong legs and their feet were tipped by a powerful fighting claw. When a cassowary attacked, he struck with the full force of his claw and leg; it was enough to rip open a man's belly.

Suddenly he motioned silence and gestured to a biggish black bird he had spotted in a nearby tree. He selected an arrow and taking steady aim, he fired. The arrow flashed out and a second later I heard the bird fall to the ground and my companion lunging towards it. When he found the bird he quickly finished it off and brought it back to me. It was a black hornbill with long jet-black feathers and a crest on its head. We were still examining it when there was another crashing in the undergrowth, followed by shouts and expressions of dismay: the other men had lost their prey. We re-grouped, and discussed the black hornbill. In their opinion, where there was one of these birds, another would soon be found. So they began to hunt for its mate; their eyes darting through the branches, their hands gripping bows and arrows, their whole bodies alert. I felt slightly sorry for the mate, but for these people it wasn't a matter of sport, meat was scarce and an important addition to their diet.

The hissing of an arrow and an excited shout marked the end of the second bird, and my troupe returned triumphant to their original southerly route.

Twilight came early, which is usually 6 p.m. in places that lie near the equator, and the twilight turned quickly to darkness. Our pace was still fast and I was finding it more and more difficult to keep up; I was exhausted. Without light I couldn't see where in the rocks and mud to put my feet, let alone see where the leaders had gone, and I relied on my Hewa friend to guide and urge me forward. Twice I slipped and fell, but fortunately without hurting myself. Now lagging far behind the leaders, my body aching with tiredness, I could hardly find the strength to keep walking. The effort of just putting one foot in front of the other took all my willpower. But I knew that we would arrive somewhere if I kept going.

Beyond the pitch blackness I noticed a glow of light, it was a man carrying a smouldering bush-lamp. He had come to greet us and take us to his family hut nearby.

7
Feasting and Folklore
at Kaugona

For defence against raiders his family's hut was built on stilts on a mountain slope, in traditional style with twenty-foot (6-m) tall stilts at the back (at the lookout's corner) and a plank in the shallowest corner which was used for access.

Many dark faces looked up through the smoky firelight when I entered. The fire lay in a long hearth of dirt which explained how it was possible to have fire in a timber hut. Gradually, as my eyes grew accustomed to the light I counted twelve members of the family, from grandparents to third generation children, and I shook hands with them all. An uncle wearing strings of beads across his forehead, a rope-grass topknot and a necklet of marsupial teeth, moved up to make space for me. It felt good to sit down.

Men were cutting up the birds they had shot, having plucked them and carefully collected the feathers to make into items of self-adornment. The meat was added to some *kaukau* and green leaves, and put in a big clay pot of water to simmer on the fire.

We 'chatted' (communicated without understanding the words) as we waited, and I showed them some photographs of the country I came from, my parents and of snow. They reacted with delight, pouring over the photographs while I tried to explain where snow came from and what it was. And I watched their animated faces in the firelight.

Hewas are different from their neighbouring tribes mainly because they have developed an artistic culture; also because they are semi-nomadic and related to the Sepik hill-people. Their paintings are made using coloured ochres on slabs of bark, which are created to gain power over the animals or ideas that are symbolised on them. The paintings are never abandoned, but are kept in piles under small thatched shelters. I understood that

57

they were chiefly used before hunting, but didn't understand if the stack of paintings was like a battery charged with power, or if that power only lasted for one hunt.

After eating the tasty meal and when I could no longer stay awake, I unpacked my sleeping bag and looked for a space to sleep. The men indicated that I should stay by the fire for warmth, so I curled up and slept deeply.

Next morning I opened my backpack and discovered a nest of small cockroaches, which scattered in every direction. Most of my gear was packed inside plastic bags, but the cockroaches had got into it all, even my diary. It didn't upset me because there was nothing I could do about it, and I didn't say anything because I didn't want them to think that I was displeased. I had enjoyed my stay, and I was sorry to leave.

My next pair of guides was a one-eyed man called Napat and his brother who took me for a gentle two-day hike along the Strickland escarpment. On the first day we were joined by another Hewa man with hairy top-knot and leafy loincloth, a woman in a grass skirt who carried a big *bilum* with her sleeping child, and a youth who walked in front of us all with a stick to beat the dew off the long grass. Despite his good work, I was soon soaked and had to pause frequently to wring out the hem of my skirt.

As we rounded the curve of a mountain we emerged onto a magnificent escarpment. Towering cliffs rose above tumbling open grassy slopes, their tops lost in the clouds. The lower slopes dropped down into the pit of the gorge. It was wonderful to see such enormous, craggy and uplifting landscape after spending days walking in muddy forests.

By noon we had reached our stopping-point, an isolated hut on a spur of land halfway between gorge and cliffs. The hut was simply constructed with walls made of bark, laced together with thin bamboo strips, and a roof made from thatched *kunai* grass. Nearby some children, wearing leaves, beads and seeds, were shepherding a bunch of semi-wild piglets. In the afternoon I followed the brook a short way to where it expanded into deep rockpools, and there I took a glorious bath. It was refreshingly icy, and after I dried off in the sun, I dived back into the water for more.

When my body felt clean I attended to my wounds with antiseptic and pulled all remaining splinters out of my feet. Later at the hut, I attended to the sores and cuts on the people there. Their skin was leathery to touch, and I could understand why — they needed it to survive that chilly climate and tangled vegetation.

Late in the afternoon Napat's brother said we had run out of *kaukau* (I usually bought it daily for the three of us), and he offered to go and buy some from a hut far above us on the escarpment. I had not spotted the hut before, and it looked to be about an hour's walk. On asking him how much it would cost to buy enough to last us for two days, he said that it would cost ten *toea* (7p). So I gave him the money and watched the speed with which he climbed the steep grassy slopes. The price of ten *toea* reflected the low cost of living, which is how I managed to make my money go further; even the guides' rate of pay was absurdly low, but it was the government rate and if I had paid more they would have thought that I was rich. In their normal lives they didn't use money and, although most of them had seen it, few of them had owned any. They had no real need of it because their huts, clothes and decorations came from the forest (though some wore ragged clothes donated by missionary societies), and they had their own systems of trade. For food they all grew *kaukau* and they looked after each other in a way that helped me to understand the strength of the clan unit.

Napat had collected some firewood and since he had no matches he asked to use mine. But before I could get them he motioned me to stop and said that he would show me how to create fire. He took a branch from his firewood and after splitting the end he wedged a small stone in the split, then looping a flexible strip of bamboo around the wood he sawed it until a spark caught in the tinder beneath. When it smouldered he blew on it gently until it flared into flame. Usually it was not necessary to make fire because in most huts a fire was kept almost permanently burning or smouldering, but this hut was more like a travellers' lodge. Napat said that he seldom had to make a fire because he carried pre-cooked *kaukau* when out hunting and would take home any game that he killed for cooking and sharing. I wondered why I had not seen fire-lighting done during our daily treks and realised that all the men had asked for matches.

59

We dined on baked *kaukau* (each person baking his or her own in the fire), and corned beef that I provided. As I drifted into sleep I could hear the sound of pigs snorting and squealing under the hut, and the patter of rain on the roof. Later when I woke everything was silent and I couldn't remember where I was. Slowly, by tracing the events of the past up to the present moment I realised that I was in Papua New Guinea. In my half-sleeping, half-awake state it seemed an odd place to be.

In the early morning sun I strolled around, looking at the misty cragginess of the escarpment and watching the dampness rising off our hut's thatch. As the sun grew hotter the dampness turned to steam and mingled with smoke seeping through the thatch from the cooking-fire being kindled indoors. Breakfast was sugar-cane (chewed with loud slurping noises and then spat out) and *kaukau* with canned mackerel from my supplies.

Then it was time to hit the path. There was still a heavy mist and the tall grass was so heavily drenched in dew that my back-pack looked wetter than after the river-crossing. Hiking below the escarpment wall, the sun began to shine through the mist and I could see the faint outline of mountain peaks behind the rising cloud. In the distance I could hear the roaring of water in the gorge. The path hugged the contours, rounding the grassy spurs and clinging to the forested ravines. Sometimes distant landmarks came closer quite quickly, sometimes painfully slowly. Napat said that they would cut a proper path some year soon.

One-eyed Napat was good company; he pointed out the plants that man ate and the plants which he said ate men. The latter group included those that stung, scratched, burned and were poisonous. There were plenty of them in the forest thickets, the worst for me being the spiny, thorny ones lying invisible in the muddy path and that were so painful to tread on. Mud came up to our knees, slowing our progress considerably, while overhead the forest dripped and steamed creating a high humidity. It was a relief to emerge from that into patches of open land, across which I could see mountains on every horizon. Butterflies danced in front of us as we made our way along the rocky cliff-hanging trails to some caves where we stopped to roast *kaukau*. I had adopted the mens' habit of eating *kaukau* at least four times daily; continually rough terrain demands energy, and *kaukau* is not strong fuel for a body.

Yet, now that I was getting accustomed to the daily routine of walking, I was growing fitter and acclimatising to the cold, high altitude. It was six days since I had set out from Oksapmin, but somehow the time had been so full of new impressions that it seemed longer; and the lifestyle which at first had seemed so strange I now accepted as more normal. The friendliness of the people and their willingness to respect me as a woman were good points; my only worries were the cockroaches in my backpack and the absurd worry about what would happen if one of my feet went lame. There was also the loneliness of not having anyone to share it all with, or even someone to talk with in English. My understanding of pidgin was progressing slowly because few people here had been to school or learned to speak more than a smattering of it. However we also communicated in tones, gestures and non-verbal expressions. It is possible to understand a fair amount without knowing the words, because when someone speaks, it is immediately clear to me if they are greeting me, warning me, threatening me or passing a comment, and once I know the context I examine the content. I have found that after long periods without hearing my own language I learn to 'tune in', becoming greatly more sensitive to reading facial expressions, gestures of hands and the tonal inflections of the voice. Frequently I had to ask the meanings of certain key words, which were usually explained by showing the object, or drawing it in the mud with a stick, or improvising it in mime.

As we walked on through the jungle, swarms of black flies circled round my head and kept trying to crawl into my ears, up my nose and into my eyes. They didn't bite but they were infuriating and persistent. I tried swatting them and clapping my hands so I could kill several at once, but they were always replaced by more. It made me glad that my eyelashes were very long; I flapped them continually, and although I felt foolish, it did keep the flies out.

After six hours' walking we saw a cluster of huts ahead, so we stopped at a stream to wash the mud off ourselves, and for the men to pick fresh leaves to wear on the string around their waists. The huts belonged to an influential man who had two wives. He offered us some sugar cane — a wonderful tonic after

61

the hike — and he installed me in a spare hut which was empty except for a pile of dry grass in one corner which I made into a soft bed. One wife brought me some firewood while the other gave me some *kaukau*, and we sat down to talk about family life. Families, they told me, were usually small, having an average of just two or three children and infant mortality was high. This seemed to me like a natural and effective method of birth control in an area where despite the profusion of the forest, the soil is too poor to support a large population.

Children, especially the males, were the most valuable thing in life. I couldn't understand all that they said to me but later I read an article by an Enga missionary that helped to explain their attitudes: 'In some New Guinea languages the verbs of existence (to be) vary for men, women and children. Children 'exist' in the same form as clouds, rainbows and vine bridges; they are suspended phenomena, and as such they can relay messages between humans and the environment.

'Babies are born in a partitioned section of the women's hut, but they are given no great welcome because they may not live very long. The top if their skull is considered highly important; potions and magic spells are put on that spot. Babies often wear their umbilical cord round their wrist. Naming doesn't take place until six months to one year because naming would give the babe an identity, and a spirit, and if the infant died then the spirit would need attention. If it died without a name there would be no spirit.'

The fact that the man had two wives told us he was wealthy, because only a wealthy man could afford more than one wife. These two wives obviously didn't get along well together, since their husband had been obliged to build separate huts for them. (Sometimes co-wives are good friends and share a hut.) Husbands in general seemed to value their wives only as beasts of burden and bearers of children, and men were laughed at if they spent time talking with their wives. Wives lived separately from their husbands, usually in collective women's huts, and were forbidden to go in or even to look into the men's hut.

To have a hut to myself was quite a luxury and it gave me the chance to de-bug my luggage, which I couldn't do with people watching. It wasn't that they would have thought it rude, but it would have been unwise to unpack and display all my worldly possessions in front of people who had little. From experience I had learnt that their curiosity would be aroused, leading to questions about what each thing was for, and demands of 'I want' and 'give me that'. So I emptied my backpack in private and let some chickens peck up the cockroaches that fell out. There were more cockroaches than the chickens could gobble at once, and to stop them running up my legs I had to dance around and try to keep my feet off the ground.

The next morning however, I discovered that one evil had been replaced by another. I woke up covered in bites from fleas that had been hidden in the dry grass bedding.

Napat, his brother and I turned east away from the escarpment and entered a region of turbulently upthrust mountains covered in spiky tangled forest. More black flies hovered around my head, and my legs were cut to shreds by thorny creepers. Soft-looking ferns were studded with prickles and innocuous-looking leaves were fringed underneath with stinging hairs. Along with cuts, stings and bruises, my body still itched with the flea bites. But life wasn't all bad. The forest rang with the harsh cries of birds and I saw my first bird of paradise — a small bird with superb long feathery plumage of orange and pink, which came from beneath his wings.

Out of forty eight species of birds of paradise, thirty eight of them live in Papua New Guinea. The Papuans called them 'Birds of the Gods'. Stories of these spectacular birds were first heard in the sixteenth century when the Dutch explorer Linschoten called them 'Paradice-birdes, for ye beauty of their feathers which passe all other birdes; these birdes are never seen alive, but being dead they fall on the Island; they have neither feet nor wings, but only head and body and the most part tayle.'

The idea that birds of paradise had no feet or wings came from the hunters' custom of cutting them off and trading only the head, body and tail. Some were traded as far as Europe, where their feathers were worn as fashionable decorations by women, in much the same way as the tribesmen used them for self-beautification in Papua New Guinea.

Birds of paradise were a common sight until shotguns and rifles were introduced to Papua New Guinea, but now they are rare and hunting them is forbidden by all except traditional means.

The path led up through caves and trees and along, over and under the massive tree roots. I was less nervous crossing the networks of fallen trees having had some practice, but still I used my walking stick as a balance pole. That stick also came in useful for testing depths of mud, and for thrusting in the ground to make footholds in slippery downhill slopes. It saved me from falling over many times, since it was no longer wise to grab branches for support as they were too thorny and spiky.

Napat's brother slowed his pace when he stepped on a thorn and the tip went in too deeply for him to dig it out. It was late in the day when we reached a small garden-hamlet, deserted except for an elderly woman who had to be coaxed out of her hut to speak to us. She spoke shrilly to Napat, explaining that her sons were away hunting, then gestured to a hut where we could sleep and disappeared back into the dark smokiness of her own hut. We ate *kaukau* and had a quiet evening. There was little I could do about the splinter, though I used antiseptic in the hope that it would draw it out.

My feet were doing well, and though they were lacerated and had a couple of small thorn-splinters, they were not too painful. The fleas were more of a nuisance having found their way into my backpack to infest my sleeping bag and clothes. The only way to kill them was to catch them one by one and crush them between my fingernails. So far I had killed about twenty.

The next morning didn't begin very well — Napat's brother said he was too lame to walk and it was raining — which was a little depressing for my happy mood. But we enjoyed a leisurely breakfast and shortly afterwards the rain stopped and two men arrived who were on route to Kaugona, which was the next hamlet in the direction of Lake Kopiago. Napat arranged for these men to be my new guides (the pidgin translation of guide was *soim rot* — show him road).

When I asked them how far it was to Lake Kopiago, Napat replied *'Longwei moa, tasol i no longwei tumus'* (Longway more but not too much further). So I asked how many days it would take to get there, and he said that it depended on how fast I walked, which made me smile for the simple logic. *'Na spose mi wok olsem befor?'* I queried and he said, *'Tupela o tripela dei tasol'* (two or three days only).

Because of the rain the paths were soggy and slippery and the streams were swollen and roaring. We climbed up to the top of a ridge and went along it. The ground underfoot was now soft and cushioned with moss; red flowers and maroon bracken formed a sharp contrast to the greens surrounding me. Sun slanted through the trees and mist, as pigeons cooed and water dripped from the leaves. There was little undergrowth but many fallen trees and thorny bushes. From a slight clearing on the ridge-top we could see out across a jagged complex of massive mountain ridges and deep valleys. It didn't surprise me to hear that 'hidden valleys' had been found in various parts of this whole highland region tucked in between seemingly impassable mountains. The most recent 'hidden valley' was discovered in 1977 and, looking at this tightly-folded, rocky and jungle-covered landscape, there were obviously others still to be found.

The region where we stood had been 'restricted' and closed to outsiders until 1965, because of its inaccessibility and the hostile reactions of the tribes. In such country it is difficult to exercise law and order as the government has discovered. The tribes had abided in the ways of their ancestors for centuries, and naturally they had no wish to accept interference from men representing something called *guvmen* (government), particularly when the *guvmen* tried to impose its laws on them. For the Hewas a good case in point was about cannibalism: according to the government it was illegal, but for the Hewas it was part of their tradition so how could it suddenly be made 'illegal' by outsiders? As I understood it cannibalism wasn't to do with murder but was more commonly a case of the tribes eating their own people who may have died through disease or natural causes, and they did it because they believed that it gave them immunity from sickness. Their traditions were their heritage, and despite having travelled through cannibal-country several times in my past journeys, I had never felt threatened. Partly I think that my safety lay in the fact that I am a woman and a woman is more of a novelty, while a man can be seen as a threat.

As we walked on, my guides explained that we were in the borderlands between three tribal groups: the Hewa, Min and Duna, and that we were heading into Duna territory. I wondered how they would be different. According to one of the men the Dunas didn't bury their dead and instead they left them on a tall

65

bamboo platform until only the bones remained and they could transfer them along with the dead man's bow and some *kaukau* into a nook in a tree.

Before we turned to descend the ridge my other guide pointed out the direction which we would take, and I saw that ahead lay at least three steep, parallel ridges of mountains with deep valleys between them that we would have to cross. Rain hampered our descent; the rain was heavy but of short duration and I was already so muddy and wet that it wasn't worth unpacking my rain-sheet. It seemed that since this was the rainy season I was lucky not to have been caught by rain more often, especially as Papua New Guinea is famous for its two seasons which are generally known as wet and very wet.

Two hours later we reached the base of the first valley and stopped to *kisim wind*, sitting on grey boulders in the swollen grey-muddy river, beneath a stormy grey sky. I had been wondering why I had not seen anyone fishing or eating fish and my new guides explained that although an attempt had been made to put fish in the rivers, they had soon disappeared. Looking at the roaring floodwaters I could understand how the fish had been simply swept downriver. Flash floods were not uncommon and when it rained heavily in the headwaters a small brook could suddenly become a furious torrent.

Mid-afternoon when we arrived at the hamlet we were just in time to join in a feast. The people welcomed us, lent us a hut and showed us the washing-pool in their stream. After washing, my guides joined the throng of men and I sat down slightly apart from them all — I wasn't sure if I had been invited to eat with them and I didn't want to make assumptions. The other women were not invited to the feast because it was not customary for women to eat with men — so they stayed by their own hut and carried on with their work of making bush-string *bilums* and chopping some greens to cook with their *kaukau* which they would eat later.

The willing hands of many men helped to uncover the clay *mumu* (ground oven), roll back the hot stones, and haul open the banana-leaf layer which sealed the smoke inside. Eagerly they pulled out pieces of pig meat and long tendrils of juicy bracken which they stuffed hungrily into their mouths. A choice morsel of pork was passed to me, so I moved closer to the party and several other men also gave me bits of meat. It seemed that they didn't really consider me to be a woman since it was unheard of for a woman to pack her belongings and go travelling, and therefore they treated me as an honorary man. In general, both men and women treated me with courtesy and I still had had no cause to feel threatened. I hadn't been approached for sex, and in fact had met only one man who had looked at me lustfully, so I had simply taken care that we were never alone together.

Underneath the bracken in the ground oven was a layer of *kaukau* and scarlet-red knobbly fruit (*pandanus*). The men lifted the red *pandanus* out onto smoked banana leaves and started mashing them into a seedy pulp; then, taking large handfuls, they squeezed it through clenched hands until thick scarlet juice poured out between their fingers. The remains they pushed into their mouths, eating the pulp and spitting out the seeds. Their faces were smeared with scarlet juice which would stain their skin red for several days.

The headman gave me a banana leaf as a plate and heaped it with plenty of everything. It was the first time I had tasted *pandanus* pulp and it was thick, warm and surprisingly good; it was rather like bland tomato ketchup in flavour. We were sitting in the sunshine outside the mens' hut, on the bald shoulder of a mountain. The forest had been cleared back to make space for *kaukau* gardens, which overlooked grim, narrow valleys that were surprisingly deep. The view stretched above the lush profusion of forest. In the foreground, red-stained men sat on their haunches and pulled more food out of the ground oven.

Two men wore tusks through their noses, others had pearly *kina* shells (flat crescent-shaped shells) on a string round their neck. *Kina* shells had been a unit of currency before money was introduced and their money was named after them. The shells used to be traded up from the coast, so that by the time they reached the highlands they were valuable. In the past, shells had individual names, and a knotted string threaded between two holes in the shell showed how many people had owned it. Cassowary-bone daggers were tucked into their woven grass armbands. Round their hips two men wore multi-stranded ropes of twisted fibre with hoops of cane, or *arse-grass* (bunches of cordyline leaves) over their bottoms and a front flap of woven fibre.

When they finished their meal they rubbed their bellies with contentment, the urgency of their hunger satisfied. Now they picked at scraps in a leisurely way, and sat back to light their bamboo pipes of tobacco.

I sat on a sunny bank beside a man called Krka who pointed to the different trees and plants and told me about their powers or uses. Among the edible plants cultivated in close proximity to the huts, we could see four varieties of *kaukau*, maize, cassava, chili bushes, tomato-fruit (not the same as tomatoes), plantain bananas (for cooking), *pandanus* palms (whose red fruit we had just been eating) and breadfruit trees (the breadfruit needed to be cooked). Other plants had herbal uses, or magic powers. One of the magical ones was used to attract *kina* shells; unmarried girls rubbed the leaves onto their skin to make it glow with a deep sheen like the shell itself.

Magic was generally made from the combination of certain plants and ritual spells. Some magic had everyday application, such as the rituals that were performed during each stage of preparing, planting and harvesting a vegetable garden. Other types of magic, like root spells, involved getting goods for oneself.

Rain began falling late in the afternoon. Several of us sheltered in an open-sided hut, and listened to an old man telling folk stories to while away the time. The old man didn't speak pidgin, so Krka translated some of what he said in pantomime. The story seemed to concern a cannibal giant with the magical power to fly from place to place. He terrorised the local people who ran away into the forest leaving one old woman behind. For years she lived by herself and then mated with an animal to produce a half-animal child. The child grew up and killed the giant so that the villagers could return.

Legends and myths provided the explanations for things being as they were; for natural phenomena, for the existence of night and day, or good and evil. Myths of origin were something which interested me, and those of Papua New Guinea were rich and varied. Among them were legends of a life force which drew people on the sand, and poured blood on the drawings to make them come alive; another was of two men who emerged from the blood of an old woman and another was of men created by union between the spirit of a volcano and a half-snake half-woman. One myth which reminded me of the myth of Adam and Eve went like this: first there was nothing — no trees, no birds, no animals and no people — and the world was flooded except for a small patch of land. Nearby was a volcanic island, and inside the volcano lived Pekoia, father of all. One day he flew out of the volcano, bringing pigs, nuts, and the breath of life. He fashioned two men and one woman out of mud and breathed life onto them. Man's fall from grace happened in jealousy over the woman.

It was a dark rainy night. Firelight flickered in the men's hut lighting up their faces as they talked; one of them began to sing. He sounded lost to the world, existing only in the melody of his song. He was singing as I fell asleep and still singing whenever I woke in the night.

When I woke at dawn it was still raining. Since my guides had reached their destination I needed to find replacements. Krka offered to be my sole guide, and after reassuring me that he wouldn't be afraid to return alone, I agreed to hire him. It rained on us several times that day. Wet clothes were colder than bare skin and I suspected that I was less appropriately-clad than Krka with his bunch of leaves and multi-stranded girdle. He had stuck feathers in his hair and as he puffed uphill, his breath whistled out through the pig's tusk in his nose. Sometimes he got answering whistles from birds and inspired piercing bursts of birdsong, and he taught me to recognise three different kinds of birds of paradise. His sharp eyes picked out things long before I saw them: the movement of a snake or some black forest crabs.

As we crossed the arduous steep ridges, plunging slopes and spurs of mountains, sometimes Krka walked and sometimes he ran. Where the rain-forest thinned out into moss-forest we walked on carpets of rich moss and feeling its texture made me glad to be barefoot. The moss-forests were places of mist and cloud, and vague shapes of trees. Some grew over 200ft (60m) without a bend of their trunks while others were gnarled and crooked, festooned with orchids, lichen and silvery trailing ferns. Their roots were immense, forming flank-buttresses, while their branches were tangled together and knotted with ropes of vines. Heavy orange mosses like sponges of water overflowed from damp wood and filmy moss beards hung from branches. We walked through the opaque gloom of mist which echoed with strident birdsong.

As the mountains gradually dropped in altitude and we descended slowly towards Lake Kopiago (which was not yet visible to us), the path became more defined and the land grew more populated. People who saw us shrieked with astonishment and when Krka told them that I had walked from Oksapmin they shouted the news to others. Their noisy reaction surprised me because I felt sure that they must have seen other white women before, such as nuns and mission-women who would have used the road to reach Lake Kopiago (now only about five miles away). But apparently it wasn't the fact that I was white that surprised them but the fact that I had walked from Oksapmin.

Their noisiness was a contrast to the startled grunts that people usually uttered on catching sight of me, and to which I had become accustomed, but perhaps the mountain-clans were more instinctive and silent than townsfolk. These people were all Dunas, which is a fairly large and colourful clan. The men who came out of their huts to greet me made a fine sight with their opossum fur headbands and cane-stalks through their noses. One wore the outspread wings of a bird of paradise on his head.

The last few miles seemed interminable; Krka pointed out a mountain beside Lake Kopiago, but we had to go up and down so many other ranges that it never seemed to get any closer. My feet suddenly began to feel very sore, and I kept having to stop and rest. I was exhausted.

When the path became a track (presumably the track I had seen on the map at Beth's house) I knew we had finally arrived at Lake Kopiago. The lake lay in a broad basin, its swampy edges were overgrown with lush grasses and reeds and its water rippled with the wind heralding another dark storm. I felt joyful but stupefied with fatigue. Krka and I went to a group of buildings which happened to be the Catholic mission and Father Hans gave us a wonderful reception. Krka stayed for a short while then said he wanted to visit one of his relatives living in the village by the lake, so I thanked him, paid him and shook hands in farewell.

Father Hans called me into his small mission-house and, after a spare bedroom had been prepared for me, I took a hot shower and changed into fresh clothes. It felt good to be clean again, it restored my spirits and I enjoyed a comfortable evening talking in English with Father Hans, and eating real food with delicious home-made bread. Rain poured torrentially all night, but it didn't matter any more: I had arrived. I had succeeded in safely reaching my first destination in Papua New Guinea and I was sleeping in a bed with crisp white sheets.

8
A *Gumi* Expedition

For me, Lake Kopiago was the beginning of a new road, but for Papua New Guinea it was the end of a road: I had reached the furthest penetrating road into the remotest end of the country. Even the word road was misleading unless you pictured a rough dirt road in rocky, forested and mountainous terrain.

Lake Kopiago itself was a small township with a sprinkling of government buildings, a trade-store and three different church missions. On Sunday I went to the Catholic mass which was a subdued affair, without much singing and just a small congregation of Dunas. Since it is their custom to grease their bodies with pig fat (they believe it is good for the skin) that begins to smell rancid after a few days, the smell in the confines of the enclosed chapel was very strong indeed.

I stayed for two days in Lake Kopiago, relaxing now that I had reached my first destination, and thinking about where to go next. It seemed a good idea to broaden my perspective of the country by following the road; I didn't know exactly where to go yet, but since there was only the one road without any crossroads for over 100 miles (160km), there was no need for me to plan a route. From Lake Kopiago the next 'place' on the road was Koroba Catholic Mission which at about 30 miles (45km), was a long day's journey away.

Not long after I set out a government Land-Rover stopped to give me a lift, which was a pleasant change, but it jolted me to pieces as it bounced along the road hitting rocks and potholes, and forcing me to hold on with both hands most of the time to stop my head bumping against the roof. We had to cross several bridges which were in a poor state of repair, and at two of them, the driver advised me to get out and walk across. The tree trunks spanning the ravines had rotted, and frequently the cross-timbers were unattached and broken. The Land-Rover was equipped with hammer and nails (essential for such a journey), and we mended the bridges enough for our crossing. One bridge collapsed just as the Land-Rover's back wheels left it.

The Catholic sisters at Koroba were warm and kindly. Their work was to teach local women about hygiene and nutrition. Teaching nutrition was done by introducing chicken, cattle and more varieties of vegetable to the people to show them what they could do to vary and improve their diet. But people in general were reluctant to accept these 'foreign' ways and preferred to continue their traditional diet of *kaukau* and an occasional soup of greens. Once every few weeks, sister told me, the whole village would feast on pig, and then every so often a man would over-gorge himself and suffer a gut blockage called *pig-bel*, which is usually fatal.

In general, undernourishment makes them a lethargic, depressed people and suicide, often considered a western 'disease' is prevalent, especially among women. One of the sisters said that it is done out of jealousy and spite. She also said that it is common to see women with stumped fingers that have been chopped off at the knuckle. This is a custom and is done to demonstrate either anger (maybe at a husband who takes a second wife), or sorrow over a *Big-man's* death. Even little girls are sometimes subjected to finger-chopping when a clan elder dies.

Another of the sisters showed me around the vegetable garden. She had introduced organic fertilising and had some pairs of treated and untreated plants as examples to show the local people how they could improve their yield if they used fertiliser: beside an untreated, stubby passionfruit vine was an organically fertilised one over 150ft (45m) long. While we strolled around, we saw some school children fleeing in terror from the mission's pet cows; in fact the cows were only being playful, but the children were afraid of them because they were larger than any animal they had seen before.

I admired the work of the Catholics and the way that they integrated with their local community; they didn't seem to try to force their will or their ways onto the villagers, but were content instead just to show them that better ways were available. People's resistance to change made it a slow process, but the Catholics' devotion to their work often held them in one mission for up to twenty years. They did not secure their missions behind tall wire fences, they just shook their heads sadly when anything was stolen; they seemed not to delude themselves about reality, knowing that good and evil went together. But their work was not all disappointments. Among their successes over the years were many families with improved health, children who had reached higher education and gained better employment through their teaching, and men who had started local businesses or small cattle farms.

After leaving the Catholic mission in Koroba, I went east on foot along the road. Although this was my first walk in Papua New Guinea on my own and without a guide, I didn't feel nervous.

I met some women in grass skirts with heavy bulging *bilums* strung from their foreheads, and a widow whose forehead was painted black with a bright yellow stripe across it and one down her nose too. Her shoulders were buried beneath hundreds of necklaces made from *pitpit* seeds known as Job's Tears.

At a small village market I paused to rest, and sat watching people who sat watching me. Most men had white-ochred faces, nose-tusks, headbands of beads and shells, and one had a sliver of pearl-shell hanging from his headband to the tip of his nose. Several men wore headgear decorated with feathers from lorikeet, cockatoo, parrot, cassowary and birds of paradise. I must have made an equally odd picture to them: a white woman, on foot, carrying a backpack and wearing a shirt and long skirt. Their conversation about me was forceful and gutteral, but was accompanied by respectful nods every time our glances met.

The track wound onwards, bordered with yellow-flowering bushes and pine trees. I passed an old man sorting coffee beans, four cows grazing in a fenced area, and a woman leading her pig by a string tied to its foreleg. A man with a toy ukelele stopped to strum a tune. There were occasional timber arches over the road which had spiked outlines for decoration and defence. But there was no traffic. The day was hot and rumblings of thunder came from the valleys as I walked without hurry. I felt carefree and untroubled. My future lay ahead, empty, waiting to be filled.

When it rained I took shelter in a village, entering it through a small fighting-gate. This was triangular, made of spiked stakes

74

fringed with kunai thatch, and like the arches was there for defence. Aged, stooping Duna men, with their women and children kept me company. I thought that there might have been a slight disadvantage in not having a local guide who could introduce me to them and allay any fears about me, but soon it was clear that they didn't regard me as a threat and they listened eagerly when I told them the names of the places I had come from. Actually they made noises of sympathy and I think they felt sorry for me because I had no vehicle and I didn't have a man to look after me.

While waiting for the rain to stop, I looked for some fresh writing paper in a side pocket of my backpack and I found a scrap of paper with a map scrawled on it. It had been drawn by an Englishman called Jo Harvey-Jones whom I had met in Malaysia. It was only a pencil sketch map and apart from showing Papua New Guinea's coastal outline it had only three places marked: one cross marked the Strickland river (he had been telling me about a recent British expedition there), another was Mt Hagen, a town in the middle of the highlands, while the third cross lay to the south and was marked Ialibu, the place where he lived and where he said I would always be welcome. I felt sure that I could get to Ialibu by dirt-road, and so it became my new destination. I mentioned Ialibu to the Dunas, who didn't recognise the name but they could see that I was pleased about something and their dark faces smiled happily back at me.

After a while a jeep came along, and they flagged it down. I couldn't understand where the driver said he was going but since he was driving east it had to be the right direction. It took us three hours to drive to an outpost called Tari, and the road was abysmal. On one occasion the jeep's front suspension jumped right out of its fittings and it took a hefty whack with a crowbar to put it back in place. We stopped briefly in Tari then continued eastwards along the road.

Black outlines of mountains drew closer as we rose up into high-altitude forest and passed fern trees, clumps of bamboo plumes and tall, thin trees hung with dark reddish mosses. The road improved for a long way, but then deteriorated into impassable mud where it took us two hours to cover one mile. I didn't mind, it was exciting in the jeep, getting stuck, backing out and racing again at the mud, even though we were making overall progress in inches. We managed like this for a while until when we were trying to get round a corner, we went too near the outside and the jeep slid right off the road. As the jeep tilted on the edge of the hillside and slid again, I sat still and held my breath, not daring to move. It slid for another few feet until it came to rest against a stunted tree. I couldn't get out as I was on the tree side and wedged at a 70° angle, but the driver got out and a group of men from some huts near the road came over to help. While some of them cut a couple of big saplings for levering the jeep out, others attached a towrope, and with their combined brute force they got the jeep back onto the road. But within a few lengths it was bogged down to the axles in mud. We tried reversing and charging forward, but only succeeded in ploughing deeper and deeper each time. I suggested that I got out to lighten the load, but the driver wouldn't hear of it. It was getting dark and starting to drizzle. Mud was flying from all four wheels and over the men helping to push us. When they pushed against the bonnet to get us out from each failed run, I saw an alarming-looking row of straining, bearded faces through the windscreen: one had a red-painted nose and thick red circles round his eyes, and another had hair roll-braided in mud and a wreath of ferns.

The rain, now falling heavily, reflected in our headlamps like prismic daggers of light. More men materialised and I could hear shouts of 'Oya' and 'Agh' as our wheels spun desperately, and harsh-gabbled speech as they began using spades or their hands or feet as shovels to clear away the sloppiest mud. Others gathered armfuls of branches and *pitpit* grass to throw into the worst patches. The rain eased and fireflies came out. The jeep hurtled forward in another attempt to get through, but it slid over the bank again and the men had to hold a rope to prevent it from sliding right over.

It was ten o'clock before we successfully rounded that corner, and when we became bogged down again, we decided to give up for the night. We made our way to the men's hut but the men wouldn't allow me into the hut because I was female. Sleeping in the jeep was fine with me, but when the jeep's driver decided that he would sleep in the vehicle with me, I said that I would sleep out in the bush. This was my first hassle and it made me feel angry with him. Finally, the men offered me some space in their hut. It stood low to the ground for warmth, and to get inside, we crawled on our hands and knees through a small hole into a warm smoky room. There were no beds, so we just lay around the fire and kept it well stoked all night.

Early the next morning all the men turned out to help again, and we progressed forward at an agonisingly slow rate, with the engine roaring as our wheels spun almost uselessly, unable to grip the soggy clay despite four-wheel drive.

It surprised me to hear that this road was part of the Highlands Highway, the most important road in Papua New Guinea. It was the only road from the coast into the country's highland interior and the building of it in 1970 was responsible for the economic development of the highlands which had previously been isolated and too remote. By 1974 the highway had reached Mendi, and in 1977 it was extended to Tari. We were now stuck on the latter part, six miles before a village called Nipa.

When the weather was dry the driver said it was possible to reach Mendi, but this time he had to abandon the attempt at a broken culvert and begin the difficult task of turning the vehicle round to face back the way it had come, so that he could return home.

I decided to go on towards Nipa, so I thanked him for everything and set off walking. Slippery clay clogged round my feet, making them heavy and clumsy. Each foot had to be pulled free, and each step sank me knee-deep again. My backpack hindered me and I fell twice. Mud, glorious mud. A young man helped me by carrying my backpack for a couple of miles but when I offered to pay him the government porters' rate, he replied that some friends of his had once been paid 100 *kina* by some tourists and that he wanted more. He thought all foreigners were rich. I felt threatened by his attitude and his company, and he was surly when I settled up at the agreed government rate and went on my way alone.

Over the next few hours I passed a gang of workmen trying to remake the road, and walked past rugged mountains, tall grass and low forest, until wearily, I descended down to the village of Nipa.

The first collection of buildings I saw comprised the High School and inside I met a delightful New Zealand couple who seeing my state, immediately offered me a hot shower and afterwards gave me coffee and home-made cookies. An hour or so later an acquaintance of theirs called in and offered me a lift to Mount Hagen.

He was a VSA boss who was on a field trip to visit his flock of volunteers. He had a tight time schedule to keep, and a fast car to keep it in. The highway had now emerged from the wet clay and forest into some open stony mountains where it was surfaced with crushed rock gravel. Time equals money, my companion quoted, as the car raced along the road sending stones flying out behind it. My first instinct was to be afraid of the speed, but he drove well and I began to enjoy it.

In the car he had a map which I looked at eagerly; it was nice to see where I was — to place myself as a dot on a piece of paper. It wasn't through choice that I didn't carry a map, it was simply that I had not seen one for sale in my travels so far. The crumpled sketch map in my pocket had been enough to bring me here and I began to look forward to meeting Jo in Ialibu. Ialibu is located about thirty miles down a side-turning off the highway before Mt Hagen, so I got out at the turning and walked until a pickup truck came along which gave me a lift all the way there. When I arrived I found a thriving outpost built at high altitude on a slope of Mt Ialibu.

Jo Harvey-Jones ran a coffee growing project. He was an energetic person with great zest for life, and to celebrate my arrival, he invited a houseful of guests and took us all on a *gumi*-expedition. A *gumi* is an inflated inner tyre off a truck or tractor. You sit in the tube and use it to race down white-water rapids. It was reputed to be excellent sport. Along the Yorlo river, Jo had found an untried stretch of white-water about six miles long. Eight of us set off, driving for several miles then walking for several more until we reached the Yorlo river. Two of the party gave up as soon as they saw the narrow, rocky river with rapids as far as the eye could see. I was a bit concerned myself, but decided to have a go. The experts of the party thought it looked good, so I put my *gumi* in the water with theirs and hoped for the best. The water was icy cold but that was soon forgotten as we pushed off into the tumbling foaming torrent and were whirled away by it.

The first section contained some large rapids. There was no time to be terrified; it was more important to pay attention, to try to keep myself facing forward and not spin out of control. Down through limestone gorges we rushed along the roaring white water with treacherous rocks above and below the surface. To avoid the submerged ones, I quickly learnt to raise my feet and bottom and to hold on tight. Waves heaved around us, hiding rocks until we were nearly upon them, and if we were too late to avoid them we were sent whirling crazily down the rapids. At one stage three of our group were thrown from their *gumies*. Mine was sucked into the fastest channel and I took the lead. I started to worry that a waterfall could lie ahead and I wouldn't see it until too late. Suddenly I wondered what I was doing racing down unknown white-waters like this. The freezing cold water was spraying in my face and icy waves washed over me. In this altitude it was cold despite blue sky and sun.

The rapids were broken on occasion by cliff-sided pools where I could rest. At one beach, I pulled into the shore and made a fire of driftwood to warm my freezing body. The others arrived, less two who had decided to try and walk back through the bush rather than complete the course.

By river it took us four hours to reach a bridge where a road crossed the water, and we climbed out. It was bliss to get home and drink coffee laced with brandy beside the fire.

Jo took me to see his coffee projects and Mount Hagen, which was the town I had named as my poste restante. It was lovely to get mail for even though some of the letters were three months old, they were news to me. My mother was concerned that a third world war could start over Afghanistan and I wouldn't hear about it.

The Saturday market in Mount Hagen was a colourful affair, selling fruit and vegetables, *kaukau*, live pigs, tobacco and betel-nut. I went for a coffee in the town's hotel and was shocked to discover that a hotel room cost 40 *kina* (£30) a night. No wonder people thought that the tourists were rich. After coffee I did some shopping and found a pair of jungle boots in a Chinese trade store. I had had enough of barefoot travel and my feet were sore and they needed protection. Unfortunately the smallest size of boots available anywhere was a size nine, but I bought them anyway.

My shopping expedition was complete when I found a map of Papua New Guinea for sale in the chemists. I knew at a glance that it was not very accurate because it had solid red lines marking roads between Oksapmin and Lake Kopiago where I had walked on footpaths. Nonetheless, it was a map.

Back in Ialibu, I relaxed for the evening, happy to be among friends and contented with having completed the second step of my journey.

Part Three

The Horse Journey

9
Taim Bilong Eleksen

Ialibu had been a destination, which became a place of rest, enjoyment and good company before turning into a launching pad for the next stage of my travels. I had decided that I wanted to continue my journey by horse. Travelling on foot was tiring, particularly with a heavy backpack, and since I had already ridden about 6,000 miles by horse through Africa I wasn't apprehensive about it. The lack of roads in the highlands also made riding seem a good idea: a horse could go where a vehicle couldn't, it could carry my gear in saddlebags and it was the best form of cross-country transport.

Yet I hadn't seen a single horse in Papua New Guinea so far and when I asked, I discovered that most of the highlanders didn't even know what one looked like. My best bet seemed to be to try some of the remote cattle ranches in the hope that I might be able to buy a ranch horse. Jo entered into the spirit of things and while on a coffee errand he mentioned my intention to an Australian ranching couple.

As it happened, the ranchers (Bill and Lorna Bell) were being forced to move from their house quickly, because the ranching company had just sold out. Moving house included moving their fifteen dogs and cats, eight horses and a stallion. A friend of the Bells had invited them all to stay, but couldn't take the stallion as they already had one. Two stallions together would have fought, so the Bells suggested that I go out and look at him.

The stallion was out on the range with his band of mares when I got there; he had not been ridden much lately but when I tried riding him he behaved very well. He was a pure-bred Arab, but not a showy one. His was the hardy, tough type of Arab; he stood about fifteen hands high and was white with a few brown flecks. The Bells wouldn't take any money for him and gave him to me on the condition that I never sold him and that when I no longer wanted him, I gave him to Father Albert, a Catholic farmer-missionary who lived at Kagua mission and who I had already met and liked. This arrangement was fine by me, especially as it solved the problem of finding a good home for him at such time as our travels together finished.

The stallion's hooves were unshod, and Bill who had blacksmith's tools, offered to shoe him for me. I hesitated over the idea because it might prove impossible to find another blacksmith in my travels and his hooves would need attention each month, whereas if he stayed unshod like most ranch horses, his feet would become tougher and the wear of daily travel would keep them properly shaped without maintenance. Another consideration was that white-coloured hooves are weaker than black hooves, and because of the hard, rocky terrain I finally decided that he should be shod. In emergency I hoped that I could manage re-shoeing somehow, and I watched Bill closely as he worked. The horse stood fairly patiently, without snapping or kicking while he was being shod and I was glad that he seemed to have a gentle nature.

But he was difficult for much of the way back to Ialibu: for twenty miles he shied and swerved, jibbed and stopped, and kept trying to turn home. It was dark by the time we reached Jo's place and I was looking for somewhere to put him for the night when to my great relief I saw that Jo had already solved the problem — he had used all his firewood to build a makeshift corral. We put the horse into it and he grazed contentedly. Jo had also done another great favour by finding an ancient saddle and bridle that had belonged to a *kiap* (government officer). We collected the tack and were delighted to see that it was still usable although the leather was stiff and rotting with age. Later that evening I cleaned and saddle-soaped the tack until it became supple.

I stayed for a couple more days with Jo to give myself time to get used to the horse and to make a pair of saddlebags for my belongings. A nylon flysheet from a tent provided the material which I sewed to make two large satchels with pockets on the front and back end-pieces to hold things which I continually needed like water-canteen, camera, map and compass. The satchels were joined together by straps which would fit over the saddle and also I made an extra cinch to prevent the saddlebags from flapping around when cantering along. It was fortunate that I knew what I was doing, having made my other saddlebags in the past. My last task was to pack all my belongings into the saddlebags, ready to set out in the morning.

And so it was that I set out from Ialibu on horseback. I had no idea how many months our journey might take, or where it would go, except that at some stage I wanted to visit a highland clan called the Huli Wigmen who lived in the Tari Basin about 150 miles (240km) to the north-west of us.

The stallion was good to ride and he didn't object to wearing the saddlebags. We cantered along the airstrip and headed west into Ialibu Basin, a vast basin crumpled by hills, with Mt Giluwe in the north (the second tallest mountain in Papua New Guinea) and Mt Ialibu brooding behind us. It occurred to me that my horse didn't have a name, and although I was sure that the Bells had told me it, I couldn't remember what it was. But it didn't matter and I felt sure that a new name would not be hard to find, and until then I would simply think of him as Horse. It was fun to have started our journey together; I felt happy about life.

After several miles the sandy track grew rougher and narrower until it was merely a footpath across rolling scrubland of silvery-feathered *pitpit* grass. A path was usually a safe bet to follow because it had to be going somewhere, since here there was no reason to have a path unless it linked one place to another; and where there were no roads the villagers had a network of paths. However, I did not expect to see big villages because highland clans generally built small garden settlements (although if I saw more than twenty huts together I called it a village).

Mid-morning we stopped at a cluster of ten thatched huts where some women were tending *kaukau* gardens, their babies asleep in net *bilums* suspended from nearby branches, while the men sat either doing nothing, or gambling, or discussing local politics (the provincial government elections were due soon). They all studied Horse in amazement.

When we left, several of the men accompanied us for a few miles along the path. I would have preferred to be alone, but was grateful for their help when the path became more difficult and we had to cut detours to avoid fallen trees and slash our way through the tangled bushy vegetation. After climbing up into a range of hills, we rested at the top before attempting the steep descent into the valley.

Going down proved hazardous: the path was inside a rocky gulley so narrow that we had to unload Horse to squeeze him through. Once inside the gulley he had no choice but to go forward. I led him on a long rope and left him to use his wits. At the bottom of the valley was a fast-flowing river which he refused to cross with me on his back but crossed willingly enough when I led him. Because the men were still with us I couldn't take off my clothes, so my jeans and boots got soaked, leaving me uncomfortably cold and wet. Going up the other side was hell, the paths had been made for people who could clamber up the banks using the handholds and footholds of tree roots and could climb up the sides of the rock using crevices. Horse couldn't do this, but despite the obstacles we still managed to progress in a forward direction, climbing other slopes, wading other streams.

But if uphill was difficult, downhill was frankly terrifying. The ground was rocky, steep and slippery with mud. On one occasion when I was leading Horse down a slope, he slipped and came down so fast that I had to leap out of the way to avoid being trampled by him. After that I learned to brace myself against his shoulder in order to slow and guide him down mudslides, and it was a good position because I could easily side-step out of the way if he lost his footing.

I had not expected the terrain to be so difficult. Soon I had blisters from wielding a bush-knife and both Horse and I were covered in mud. What I didn't know was that there was worse to follow. As it got more and more difficult, all I could do was go forward and make Horse follow me. Where the path led up a rocky landslide he picked his footings gingerly for a short way, but it was an impossible task and we had to cut a new detour through the wet forest with its tangled roots. Halfway up a bank Horse knocked into me making us both lose our balance and go hurtling back down to the bottom, and at that point I despaired. I wanted to give up, but I didn't know how. Helpers continued to clear the way by cutting out the roots which looked likely to trap or break Horse's legs. Despite many bad moments Horse never actually fell, which was fortunate since he would probably have been damaged and I had no medical supplies that would have helped him. I think that he was as surprised by his abilities as I was.

It started to rain and dusk fell early. The one man still accompanying us said that a village was not far, and we stumbled on in the dark and rain. It was a nightmare, my flashlight shone a thin beam which picked out the dangers of the path until finally, at the crest of a ridge, I couldn't face another descent and I stopped to make camp.

We were 7,000 feet (2,100m) up and it was cold and still raining. My clothes were soaked from the river; the firewood was wet; my water canteen was empty, and I was hungry. It was unwise to camp overnight with a man whom I didn't know, so I tried to make him go away but he was concerned about my welfare and didn't want to leave me on my own. He told me that I had no need to fear him and he began to help me make camp. Between us we found some wood for a fire. It had been an incredible first day: I had been in a constant state of terror throughout most of the afternoon and had gone through places that I would never normally have attempted or thought possible with a horse. If any good had come out of it, it was that Horse and I had learned to trust each other. After a hot meal, my spirits lifted a little and the man and I slept peacefully, each rolled in a sheet of plastic. The plastic was a thoughtful last-minute present from Jo. Horse grazed freely; being a ranch horse he was trained not to stray off and occasionally he woke me when he wandered too close.

We woke to a red dawn stippled across the sky and a blanket of cloud below us that obscured a view of the valleys. My ally revived the fire to make tea, and we set off down the escarpment that I hadn't been able to face the night before. The clay was wet and the footpath was steep; the day promised to be as bad as the one before.

But these bad times were not without their rewards. When the saddle girth broke and we stopped at my companion's home hamlet to repair it, the people there gave me a hero's welcome. The old ones didn't just shake hands, they hugged me — by the waist, legs or arms — hugging in total delight. The old people were small, wizened and bent, and the men wore bamboo waistbands. The women's breasts hung long and empty, their faces were tattooed with lines and dots, and their teeth stained red with betel-nut; they had enormous smiles. My companion introduced me to a man who was obviously important, since his *omak* (a tally of bamboo sticks worn round his neck) reached down to his waist. During our conversation he told me that each stick represented ten pigs given away by him. Pigs represented wealth and giving pigs away represented more wealth. Wealth and prestige in the highlands were based on what you gave away, not on what you owned.

The men had been discussing the forthcoming election and showed me a tattered poster entitled *Taim bilong Eleksen* (time belong election). It bore pictures of the candidates, which someone had captioned with comments such as *Laik dring bia tumus* (like drink beer too much) and *i no gudfela* (he no goodfella).

While I was looking at the poster the women began mending the saddle-girth for me. They used bark string and stitched it so securely that I knew it wouldn't break there again. Some of the women put a pile of *kaukau* leaves for Horse to eat; they were fascinated but wary of him, and when he blew down his nostrils in pleasure at the food, they leapt backwards with shrieks of alarm.

When Horse and I left we said goodbye to our friend and set off with a new gang of helpers. The hamlet was surrounded by *barats* (wide ditches about six feet deep) that were dug to prevent pigs from straying, and for defence in tribal warfare. We had entered the hamlet by crossing a *barat* on a wide bridge, but on leaving I found that the *barat* was spanned by a log-bridge too slender for Horse and we had to get down into it and out at the other side. Several other wide *barats* lay across our path that morning and at one of the narrower ones I decided to try jumping over with Horse. He spaced it well, springing easily over the gap and we landed safely, causing much excitement among our followers.

The afternoon sun shone on the *pitpit* grass, clumps of bamboo, casuarina trees, and stilt-legged *pandanus* palms. When we reached a jeep track, it was a great relief. We turned west along it. The ground was stony but level, and the stream-gulleys were spanned by timber bridges. Partway across one bridge some rotten crossplanks collapsed under Horse. He scrabbled for support, plunging forwards and kicking his hooves. Wood splintered beneath him, the rotten wood tearing like paper and as

Horse clawed his way forward, a hoof caught my leg and I went flying off the bridge. I landed deep below in the water. Shivering with fright I clambered up the riverbank back to the road. Horse stood nearby, and a man who had seen what happened shouted *'Hoss brok-im leg. Skru bilong leg im i brok. Im bugarap tru'* (Horse broke leg. Knee belong leg broken. Him buggered-up true). My heart plummeted as I ran to check him, but actually Horse was alright; the cuts oozed blood but they were superficial. So I shouted back *'Im nogat bugarap'* (pidgin for ruined/broken/out-of-order) *'im lusim skin tasol'* (him lose skin that's all).

We spent the night at some huts on a hilltop among casuarina trees. Instead of *barats* they had fences of spiked wooden stakes around them, and since the gateway was too narrow for Horse, the huts' occupants helped me pull a few stakes out of the ground to get him through. Even so it was a tight squeeze and one saddlebag got slightly torn on a spike. Again the people came to shake hands or hug me, bringing roast *kaukau* for me and *kaukau* leaves for Horse. Horse-pasture was plentiful because there were no big grass-eating animals around, so I put a halter on him and let him eat his fill. After such a physically and emotionally tiring day I slept soundly.

Shortly after setting out the next morning we came to a river where the bridge had been swept away and there was no obvious way to get Horse across. I was considering the risks of swimming it when a passerby told me that other bridges ahead were down and that to cross the Erave river beyond (which was set in a deep gorge), you had to use the 'flying fox', a kind of pulley system with suspended ropes. Obviously this was no good for Horse, so I decided to admit defeat and to turn east on the track and loop around the outside of Ialibu Basin.

We passed the path from which we had emerged the previous day and continued along the rocky, sandy road between banks of tall *kunai* grass, that led us through gently undulating hills. At a small locally-run coffee plantation (part of Jo's project) we called in to say hello but were told that the manager was hiding with relatives because of a payback death threat. Payback was the traditional system of revenge and counter-revenge. An electoral candidate had been killed in a road accident caused by a drunken bus driver so it was now the duty of a person from the candidate's clan to kill one from the bus-driver's clan as revenge. The manager was one of that clan and would remain in hiding until the matter was settled — hopefully by compensation.

Further along the road we passed a local community school where all the children ran out of the classrooms to look at Horse going past. They asked me questions like 'Why are you on patrol?' and 'What for?'. Good question; the past two days had been so depressing that I couldn't think of any reason at all why I should want to be travelling.

But my disappointment was gradually erased by new impressions as the morning progressed: there were yellow and purple flowers in the wayside and sun and dark clouds above. A woman came along taking her pig out foraging for roots; the pig was leashed by one of its feet which the woman explained was the only way to control a pig out walking. Next we met a political candidate carrying a loud-hailer and campaigning for votes; we stopped to exchange greetings and news, but the man didn't put down the loud-hailer, and at close range his voice was deafening. The local interest in the election was great because this was the first time that provincial governments had been elected in Papua New Guinea. The last major election was before Independence in 1975.

The track ended at a junction with a dirt road where we turned north to skirt around Ialibu Basin. Mid-afternoon we reached Muli village just as rain began to fall, so we stopped for the rest of the day. I didn't really trust Horse not to stray so I tethered him on a long rope in lush grazing, while I washed my mud-encrusted clothes. I had been given a hut to myself, but it was full of people sitting cross-legged on the floor and watching everything I did. When more people demanded entry to the hut, one of the women barricaded the door against them, only allowing certain friends to come in. I felt crowded but tried not to show it. They were only curious about me and in their culture the idea of privacy didn't exist so I didn't express my need for it.

Women were clutching babies, and children were clutching more babies. Men wore wigs shaped like footballs on top of their heads. These wigs were made of dry burrs and hair, held in place by head-nets trimmed with leaves and grasses or marsupial fur, and topped with sprays of cassowary feathers. For the many people who were not allowed into the hut every word that I said got passed out of the windows. Later by the light of a kerosene lamp I mended the rips and tears in my saddlebags. The people, still in the hut, were now talking about the election. They spoke in pidgin, and I listened while sewing and remembered an article I had read about the pre-Independence election. During that election on one of Papua New Guinea's islands, New Hanover, hundreds of people had refused to vote for anyone except President Johnson of America. Efforts to convince the islanders that they could not vote for Johnson failed; they had admired the Americans ever since the Second World War when U.S. troops and cargo had landed by aeroplane on their island. Alarmed by the islanders' stubborn refusals, the District Commissioner had called a meeting with them to explain that the American President was already fully occupied. The islanders' response was to collect 450 *kina* (£325) to 'buy President Johnson'. They handed the money to the Commissioner and asked him to make the transaction for them.

Meanwhile, the cult was spreading to other islands, no-one could make the people understand, and a cult-prophet announced that on 10 April a ship would arrive from President Johnson bringing cargo to the islands. On 9 April the District Commissioner was startled to get a radio message from a U.S. ship on survey duty, which proposed to stopover on New Hanover. Urgent messages and explanations followed, and the ship steered clear.

But still the cult grew and 1000 *kina* (£750) more was collected in donations. The affair exploded when some people were seen fitting an outboard motor to a boat, manufactured by a company called Johnson. The locals accused the men of stealing Johnson's gift to the islanders and violence erupted. Police were sent in and many were injured in the heavy rioting which followed.

Horse and I continued from Muli around the eastern side of Ialibu Basin, and after passing again through Ialibu village we went north toward Mt Giluwe. My map showed me that in about fifteen miles we would reach the Highlands Highway. Although this dirt highway ran through Mt Hagen to Mendi and eventually to Tari I didn't really want to take Horse along it, especially since I remembered that during my journey on it by car, the wheels had sprayed stones out behind us, which would certainly be unpleasant for a horse and rider. My map also showed *kiap*-roads which Jo had told me were the original roads of the highlands. They had been made when the colonial *kiaps* and local men had cut trails for their jeeps; many of their roads no longer existed, and those that remained were in various states of neglect. On my map I saw a *kiap*-road going around the back of Mt Giluwe to Mendi, about seventy miles long, which looked like a good route to choose. I put away the map and Horse moved into a canter; the road beneath us was dusty and he cantered easily, his hooves raising the pink dust behind us. We slowed to a walk to pass a procession of women out foraging with their pigs, and a group of men wearing rounded wigs of cassowary plumage. At noon we stopped at a hamlet, where I watched a woman tattooing a girl's face, using a needle and charcoal. The other women who clustered around had lines of dots tattooed on their foreheads and noses in the shapes of suns and stars, parallel lines drawn under their cheekbones, and arrows that led away from their eyes. Round their necks they wore many bead chokers, while their bodies were clothed in brightly-coloured shawls and wraps over grass skirts.

Leaving the Ialibu Basin grasslands and rolling hills, I rode towards mountains that seemed to recede the closer we went towards them. Up and around the side of a small mountain, we passed a lake by the road. A man we met said that if a stick was poked into a specific place in the lake, the depth that it reached would indicate how long the person would live. He also told me a muddled legend about half a pig which was left on a rock by a man returning from a *sing-sing* (celebration), and which somehow managed to run away. Its footprints were still visible in the rock, and it could still be seen on the mountain occasionally, but with foliage covering its raw side!

We crossed the Highlands Highway and went north on the old and neglected *kiap*-road which I had seen on the map. Low clouds gathered and the sky turned grey but I didn't pay any attention. When the rainstorm came we both got soaked. Within minutes my clothes were wet enough to wring out; a stupid thing to allow to happen in this cold high altitude. Local women scurried along using large banana leaves as umbrellas. We stopped at a hut beside the local *haus-sik* (first aid post) and I put Horse in a field of cows for company before going to relax in the family hut.

A roaring fire was built to dry me out, and we all shared supper of *pitpit* shoots (like crunchy asparagus), *kaukau,* greens and canned fish. A woman sat making a grass skirt for her baby girl, with bark-string tassels. Her husband was the local *dokta-boi* (for the *haus-sik),* and was trained in first aid and hygiene; he told me about his work with the regional problems of leprosy, pneumonia, malaria, colds, and tropical ulcers. We also discussed a disease called *kuru* (laughing death). It affects the human nervous system causing death within about six months, and is called laughing death because of the hysterical facial contortions of its victims. The deaths of an estimated fifty per cent of Fore clan-women and ten per cent of Fore men are due to *kuru.* The Fores said that *kuru* was caused by sorcery.

A church mission however, has investigated and discovered that *kuru* can only be caught by eating contaminated meat and that the disease didn't seem to be carried by animals. The Fores are traditionally a cannibal group. They eat the decomposing flesh of the dead in order to free the spirit from the corpse. Without that ritual they thought the spirit would be doomed to eternal limbo. The people knew that cannibalism was now illegal, but couldn't be convinced that their traditions were harmful. Thus *kuru*'s existence seems to show that the old ways are still in use.

It was a cold night. I slept in the *haus-sik* and had no fire. My space-blanket (a modern invention for keeping warm) didn't work. It developed condensation on the inside, and got wetter and more icy through the night. Early in the morning I was woken by a man with an axe wound in his head (from a drunken fight) who wanted first aid. The *dokta-boi* attended him while I had breakfast and afterwards I went to fetch Horse. He was grazing but when I called him he looked up and whinnied softly. Someone tried to charge ten *kina* (£7) for putting him in the field overnight, but it was obvious that he was overcharging me because I was a white foreigner, so I offered him one *kina* (75p) and he accepted it with a smile.

The *kiap*-road followed the base of Mt Giluwe and took us among pine trees, fern trees, and stilt-legged *pandanus* palms, each leg of which divided into many legs, and made interesting patterns. After a couple of hours' riding we stopped for a short break and I unloaded the saddlebags, because they must have weighed about 40lbs (20kg) and it was important to let Horse relax his back-muscles several times a day. Without care his back could become sore, especially since he had not been ridden much before we set out. While he rested I went down to a stream to wash myself. The icy water refreshed my skin.

On my return I found a man staring at Horse. The man was interestingly dressed wearing a large *bailer* shell (a large convex sea shell) that covered his chest like a breast-plate, so I asked him if he minded me taking his photograph. He was pleased by the idea and puffed out his chest, but as I took the photograph my camera made an odd click and I discovered that the shutter was stuck open. On examining it I realised that the shutter-spring was broken and that there was nothing I could do to fix it. This was a terrible disappointment. For once I regretted that I hadn't sought out sponsors to provide cameras.

Further along the road I saw a bush of wild raspberries and since it was past midday I decided to stop there for a picnic. I had some pre-cooked *kaukau* which the *dokta-boi*'s wife had given me for the day's journey, and in my food supplies was some milk-powder and some sugar which I mixed into a sweet cream to eat with the fruit. I had picked quite a nice pile of them when I caught Horse snatching a mouthful. But obviously he didn't like the taste and I laughed as he screwed up his nose in disgust. Fortunately there were plenty more and I was able to enjoy my simple pleasure.

Later that day as we continued slowly along the road, walking because of its uneven rocky surface, I met someone who asked me if I was carrying *'bokis long pepa i go insait'* in my saddlebags. It transpired that he was talking about a ballot box for the election and that a patrolling voting station was expected to arrive at a village a short way further along the road; the voting was due to take place on the following day. We stopped for the night at some huts before the village so that we could arrive with the voters in the morning.

Early morning mist shrouded the peaks of Mt Giluwe and mist-clouds rising up from the valleys engulfed the track. Everything was blurred, and the outlines of landmarks loomed large and then vanished as the mist thickened. In the gloom ahead I could hear the chanting and music of ukeleles before I could see the group of men, their faces streaked with white paint, dancing along the road. As they came closer I could see that their chests and shoulders gleamed with oil, and their heads were crowned with ferns and foliage and tall feathers or outspread birds' wings. They wore wide waistbands of bark with a front apron and freshly-picked cordyline leaves as *arse-grass*. Their legs were painted in white dots, and their feet stamped in enthusiastic dance rhythms. They were making ready to vote, dancing themselves into the right mood. Several men were waving political banners with lifesize photographs of their favoured candidate's face framed with green ferns, and chanting songs about his greatness.

Horse nearly panicked with fright. Head held high and ears twitching, his eyes were goggling with surprise. Equal astonishment was mirrored by the men at the sight of us.

We spent most of the morning at the polling booth, a roped area on a hilltop beside some abandoned huts. Around us crowds of brightly-decorated people thronged, their costumes veiled by the opaque mist.

Festive music sounded, while serious-looking officials, explaining voting procedures, tried to make themselves heard above the noise. All the while more chanting bands of villagers kept arriving, their head-dresses adorned with feathers from birds of paradise.

Voting began. One by one and ceremonially the leading villagemen cast their votes, and the line grew longer behind them until scores of people were stamping their eagerness to vote. Ballots were posted into portable red boxes set in the roped-off area, and indelible green ink was put on a finger of each voter to prevent anyone from voting twice. Afterwards many people were so wound-up that they re-grouped and continued their chanting. Horse and I went along our way.

10
Stolen!

Soft fine rain began falling from clouds which hid the massive slopes of Mt Giluwe above the track. Horse and I called in to say hello at a prospector's camp where men were searching for sites along Kagul river to generate hydro-electricity. There were two Australians and a team of local men; a rough and ready bunch but all friendly.

The road climbed to 7,500 feet (2,300m) altitude, through boggy forest edged with white heather and waterfalls. We passed daisy flowers, trumpet bushes, and moonflowers whose highly poisonous leaves I read would send you mad for a week. As we climbed so the vegetation changed and the thick vines, root-buttresses, and palms were replaced by fern trees, beech trees, some broad-leaf trees, and *klinki* (spider-like) pines. At the outer side of the road the land fell away almost vertically into a valley below.

In Kiripia village we found a Catholic mission. The sister, and her mother who was staying, were welcoming. We put Horse in the cow paddock, and I took a hot shower, changed into dry clothes, and drank a glass of sherry before sitting down at the table for supper. I had to remember not to start eating before the sister had said the grace. During the meal, which was delicious, the sister talked about her work over many years with the mission, and how sadly she felt about the outcome. The mission had started by running a primary (community) school in Kiripia, which after Independence had been taken over by the Papua New Guinea government. The new rule required that all teachers had to be nationals, but since the nationals weren't dedicated, standards had dropped, and now few pupils could speak fluent English. The mission had also started a health aid-post, but this was closed and waiting for the government to send a nurse to staff it. The mission's cattle scheme had also failed, and now the only remaining sister was farming a few cattle and vegetables. She was bitter about the way that things had turned out, but it didn't spoil her love of the people nor her spirit of Christian goodness.

Her knowledge of the people and their customs was extensive, so I listened while she spoke about local types of celebration called *sing-sings* and one type in particular which she called a *pig-kill*. Two hundred pigs were slaughtered at the last big *pig-kill*, and it was not unknown to slaughter 300, 400, or 500 pigs. Because by tradition they had had no metal weapons it was still customary to beat the pigs to death using strong wooden sticks. The dead pigs' bristles were singed off in the fire, and the meat was carved into sections which were distributed among many people. The entrails were usually given to the wives as thanks for tending the pigs.

The mission also had a bookshelf filled with books and magazines concerning Papua New Guinea; I picked out several reports on the highland clans and their ways which I read avidly before falling asleep.

After leaving Kiripia mission in the morning we came to a flat section of road but it was still too stony for speed. The stoniness of the road was aggravating because it was tedious to have to walk all the time and it made Horse sleepy and sluggish. He needed to change his pace to stretch his leg muscles, and it was with relief that I saw a flat grassy verge ahead.

One consolation for the rough road was that few vehicles used it, and those that did went very slowly. At the end of the straight stretch I heard a vehicle approach so I steered Horse off the road to let it pass, but the driver stopped anyway and got out to say hello. He was an Australian *kiap* returning from a patrol of magistrate's duty, and we got into such a long conversation that I unsaddled Horse and gave him a rest. The *kiap* had been visiting some of the remoter villages to hear any grievances that the headman had not the authority to handle. The grievances were aired as court-cases, with the magistrate presiding. Sometimes the charges were of sorcery and these charges were usually made against women, since women were believed to control the evil spirits or *sanguma*, as they are called. *Sanguma* came out at night, and for this reason most men feared to be out after dark.

In one *sanguma* court-case a woman pleaded guilty to the charge of murder by sorcery. It must be difficult to judge such cases, since the evidence is often invisible and the information in the testimonies is based on superstition rather than fact. I had already met men who claimed to have seen *sanguma* or been attacked by them. One man told me that he had been attacked by a shapeless black shadow that had entered his hut and engulfed him, thereby constricting his breathing. The pain in his chest was terrible. In the morning the hut had smelt weird and outside it were footprints neither human nor animal. He had sent for a *kiap* and missionary to witness the evidence.

Other murders were allegedly committed by the insertion of a sliver of bamboo in the victim, either while he slept or by pushing it into him as he walked. The splinter causes a bruise which fades as it works inwards, and is usually gone when the person dies about two weeks later, leaving no visible cause of death.

It was a misty afternoon, the road was stony and we made little progress. I dismounted and walked beside Horse, since long hours in the saddle made me stiff and sore and I often liked to walk to stretch my legs. We were both getting used to each other and to the new routine of a journey. It was a full week since Horse and I had set out together, but we had a very long way to go. As we wandered along I remembered a childish folk rhyme which says 'Thursday's child has far to go', and being a Thursday's child I never doubted that it referred to me.

If distance was travelled quickly it meant little to me; I didn't like to hurry, preferring to move in time with the land and to let our speed be governed by the roughness of the terrain underfoot. It was endearing the way that Horse came up and nuzzled me whenever I paused to think or look around.

That night we stayed over at a solitary hut. The hut stood low to the ground for warmth and was entered by crawling through a small doorway. It was occupied by a woman of about my own age called Yambo who was the third wife of a local government officer, and another woman who was his second wife. Since there were no men present I let down my hair and began to brush it (I never did this in front of men because I felt it was provocative). The women gasped when they saw the silky length of my blonde hair, and reached out spontaneously to touch it. They called it *grass* which I discovered was hair in pidgin and not an insult.

For supper we ate *kaukau* roasted in the fire, and because I had a saucepan we boiled some vegetables and dried meat. The vegetables (potatoes and cabbage) were grown by the women on ground which their husband had cleared for them, and their job was to plant, tend and harvest them. At harvest-time their husband would come to collect the vegetables for market. The only garden tools they had were crude digging-sticks. Their only clothes were the skirts and cloth shawls they wore. They didn't possess blankets for sleeping, and relied instead on the abundance of firewood to keep them warm. I made tea for everyone but as usual there was the problem of them not having any cups and they had to share mine. In return they gave me a fruit to eat; it looked similar to a banana but inside it was like a passion-fruit, pulpy and delicious-tasting.

I was worried that Horse would stray into their *kaukau* gardens at night (he knew how to dig for *kaukau,* and loved it), so I tethered him in plentiful grass close to the road.

It was impossible to tell at what time he was stolen, but when I went out shortly after dawn, he was gone. My heart pounded with fear as I dashed back to the hut to tell Yambo. She grabbed my hand and we ran down to the road to try and pick out his tracks. His hoof prints led back the way that we had come and were easy to pick out on the stony earth; he had been walking not galloping. Yambo pointed to the occasional prints belonging to a barefoot man, who she said would be the thief. I asked her if she knew why he had stolen my horse and she replied *'Man i laik kisim moni'* (Man likes to get money).

In a particularly stony stretch we lost the trail and climbed up to a higher point where the forest had been cleared back, to see if we could spot him from there. I longed to see his white back somewhere among the bushes but there was nothing. Dispirited, we returned to Yambo's hut and sent runners to find out if anyone had seen Horse that morning. The waiting was hard to bear even though breakfast helped time to pass. Afterwards, when I couldn't sit idly waiting any longer, I set off to try following his tracks again. After a couple of miles a boy came running towards me to tell me that Horse had been seen and led me to the hut where he was tethered. As soon as he saw me, Horse whinnied, the noise bringing the thief out of his hut. He was angry, and said that he had found my horse straying loose, and that I would have to pay 50 *kina* (£36) if I wanted him returned. He was holding Horse for ransom.

I began to bargain with the man and finally we agreed on 12 *kina* (£9). I hadn't expected to have to pay for him and had no money on me, but he let me take Horse away, and the boy came with us to collect the money. There was no question of my tricking the thief by not sending the money, because among these people one's word is binding, and I had agreed to pay the ransom. It was also a personal belief that if I double-crossed people, I would be deceived by others in return.

It felt good to be with Horse again, and as soon as all the money had been sorted out I thanked Yambo for her help and set off. Around the back of Mt Giluwe where the road reached about 9,000 feet (2,750m), I noticed a logging track leading up through moss-forest towards the mountain's domed peaks. Because of the morning's tensions I decided to go up the mountain where I could be on my own, away from the complications of other people.

After the mossy, spongey forest floor the track deteriorated to a very rough path. But the climb was worth the effort. Mt Giluwe's summits were set in a refreshing vast alpine tundra where we wandered for miles on top of the world. The mountain was a long-extinct volcano, and had some glacial formations that showed me how an ice-cap had once covered what was now grassland. The clear air, the vibrantly blue sky and the pretty deep-blue gentians that surrounded me restored my spirits. There was a snow flurry late afternoon but it was short and not serious. My main problem was lack of oxygen since the summit altitude was 14,500 feet (4,400m), which made us both quickly exhausted.

Coming down from Mt Giluwe we passed an odd-shaped peak called Clancy's Knob. There was a *dream-haus* near the summit, where men went to meditate and find out from their ancestors about the causes of any recent death (men's deaths that is, they didn't bother about women).

Today many people accept the idea that sickness and death can be natural, but they still maintain that many others die through sorcery. *Sanguma* are raised up by somebody with the power of evil intention, and in the *dream-haus* male relatives can discover the culprit's name. At the hut, a grass rope led from the hut to the summit of Clancy's Knob, for relaying the message. Usually one man climbs to the top to call the ancestors' attention, while the other stays at the hut to make a fire and roast some pig-meat. Part of the meat is put out to entice the spirits, and the rest is eaten by the men. Sleeping with a bellyful of rich pork should bring anyone a bumper-crop of dreams. One man sits awake all night to watch the sleepers and wake them when they twitch to ask them what they are dreaming about.

When the name of the evil-doer is discovered, sorcery is often used to perform a payback murder. Sometimes effigies (payback dolls) are made of clay wrapped in strips of soft bark.

The importance of the spiritual world is demonstrated in the various cult-spirits which are sometimes bought by villages from witch-doctors or sorcerers, as a kind of protection against evil spirits. No-one seemed sure where spirit cults came from but it is known that they were traded up from the south. The most famous is the Timp cult in the area north of Mendi, and when it ended (in 1973) there was a massive ceremony with ritual magic to force it out of the cult hut. The cult-spirit had been bought and installed for a seven year term after which time it had to be evicted lest it try to stay and cause trouble. Whilst it was inside the cult hut it had been cossetted and cherished with offerings of the blood and jawbones of pigs during every *pig-kill* or ritual feast.

At the eviction ceremony, the jawbones were broken by the men and thrown onto two big piles as an outward expression of the bones of the cult. The cult-medium then declared that its spirit had moved into an opossum which he had put into the hut, so the animal was sacrificed, and the next day the village held a mock-funeral. However, a spirit cannot *be* killed and now that the opossum had gone the spirit was at large in the village.

On the third day an hour before dawn the men sacrificed twenty pigs, and chanted spells while pouring the pigs' blood into a pit, to entice the spirit into the pit where the blood would keep him happy, lazy and quiet. At daybreak, in case the spirit had slipped out of the pit, they performed a ritual to blind the spirit, using oil poured through a sow's womb and mixed with women's menstrual blood; the most deadly of all poisons.

Then followed a *sing-sing* where 1,500 people in full *bilas* (body decoration) celebrated the end of a cult.

Villages became more frequent on the lower slopes of Mt Giluwe as we stumbled wearily down a dirt road beside a deep-slit river gorge. Rainclouds drifted ominously over the hills, coming closer and closer until they smudged out all the land-marks. When I couldn't even see the hill ahead of me I stopped to ask for shelter at some huts. It was a mistake. Masses of children ran towards us screaming excitedly, while all the adults seemed to be shouting at once. I was completely overwhelmed. The woman of the house tried to get rid of the children by hurling some water and handfuls of ash at them but it didn't work and I think that most of the ash landed on me anyway.

It was now pouring with rain but the children were undeterred and ran around outside the hut, shouting at Horse and throwing stones at him to make him prance. I quietened him, and explained to the children that they weren't being kind but they were so excited that they threw even more. I suppose that there was no malice intended but it was upsetting to see, and when persuasion and threats all failed to stop them I decided to ride on. I was soaking wet anyway.

To my dismay all the children followed me, many of them still throwing stones at Horse's legs and shouting 'Givim sixty!' (60mph). The road was too stony for us to outrun them and when I tried it they all ran behind, shrieking with excitement. Even turning Horse round to walk at them only scattered them temporarily; they soon regrouped behind us. I began to get angry. Heavy rain and night were falling, we would have to stop soon and I was worried that the brats would continue to tease Horse. In desperation I had a brainwave. They were nearly all schoolchildren returning home from the local community school. Their headmaster must be able to exert some authority over them, so I found out where their school was and rode there. The headmaster was a helpful and kindly Enga man who, when I explained the situation to him, made the children go home. The experience left me feeling despondent. The hassle of the children forcing me to go on when I wanted to stop and rest, was too much that day on top of all the other hassles. So far Horse had in a lot of ways been more of a liability than a help; he had created a lot of extra work for me on the river crossings and when he had been stolen, and I wondered if I had made the right decision.

The headmaster helped me to construct a makeshift stockade

in a grassy space between the school buildings, and he invited me to stay the night with his family. They killed a chicken for us all to eat, and I had to stop them from feeding all their *kaukau* to Horse.

The next day we continued on down the lower mountain slopes, with views over flat marshy plains encircled by lesser mountains. We passed a small lake, and paused to eat some sugar cane with a girl whose face was painted in intricate patterns of white stripes and circles. Wind sighed through tall shady casuarina trees as we went gently down and down walking and slipping on the wet red clay. I also met a woman smeared in the typical bluish-white clay, on her head and torso, that marked her status as a widow. She would wear the clay, renewed when necessary for about nine months. Round her neck and shoulders she wore scores of necklaces of *pitpit* seeds; they must have weighed about 50lbs (23kg). During the period of mourning, she told me that the necklaces would be removed one by one. She also had two stumped fingers, chopped off at the knuckles, to demonstrate her grief.

On rounding a promontory I found myself overlooking the Mendi Valley. From that height and distance I could see how the town of Mendi had grown up around the flat piece of land that was used for an airstrip; and how the small township sprawled in miniature in its bumpy surroundings. In the vicinity I could also see an outlying ranch (which I noted as a possible source of horse-shoes), and a detachment of the Australian army who were doing mapping and road-making. I unsaddled Horse for a breather and we rested on the promontory.

From the books I had read at Kiripia mission I recalled that even before the town of Mendi had been built, the valley had supported a dense indigenous population of 600 Mendi clans of warrior-farmers. When they were discovered in the 1930s they were still living in the Stone Age, having no tools or weapons of metal, only bone and stone. Their discovery by some gold-seekers came as a surprise to everyone because until then it had been assumed that Papua New Guinea's highland interior was sparsely peopled. Exploration was suspended during World War II, and administrative control of the southern highland clans was only established from 1950 though 'new' clans have been discovered as recently as 1977.

At noon we reached the hot dusty town. I tethered Horse outside the Post Office, posted some letters home then rode to the small Ministry of Information. When I asked about maps, I was shown all the Ordnance Survey maps ever drawn up, including some incomplete ones. One was simply an aerial photograph with areas marked 'obscured by cloud'. Everyone in the office was helpful, in particular a young Australian woman called Heather Dean who gave me advice on where to look for horseshoes. Before I left they very kindly let me trace the maps that weren't yet published and presented me with a full set of those that were.

The search for shoes took Horse and me six miles out of town towards an agricultural station, which I was told had a herd of horses and a man who knew how to shoe.

As we went in through the ranch gate a band of wild horses spotted us from afar and came galloping toward us over the hills. I urged Horse into a canter because the station buildings were still about a mile away, and I was worried that Horse would get difficult to control in among the wild horses; he had already noticed them and I could sense his tension and alertness. As they came closer I realised that the wild horses were being led by a stallion, and that we could not reach the safety of the station before he reached us, so I reined in and brought Horse to a walk. Before I could jump off his back the wild stallion reached us and closed in to attack. Both stallions reared up and Horse nearly threw me in the process. Their flailing hooves met as, squealing and lunging, they bit each other viciously on the neck. When they drew back for a fresh attack I jumped off and got out of the way. All I could do was to pepper the wild one with small stones to keep him at bay while I tried to restrain Horse. He was leaping around excitedly, longing to fight, and to win the brood-mares. However, armed with more pebbles I persuaded Horse to go forwards along the track and into the yard.

The farrier came out to meet me but unfortunately he had neither horse-shoes nor nails, so we couldn't even refit the current shoes, let alone fit new ones. None had yet worn out or come loose however, but they couldn't last much longer. It had all been for nothing!

But not quite, the farrier introduced me to the manager who

invited me to stay. I was given an empty bungalow where I straightaway set about lighting the wood stove to heat some water for a shower. The 'shower' was simply a bucket which I hung above my head so that water could spray out through holes in the bottom. It was glorious to have a hot shower again and I was thoroughly enjoying myself when over the noise of the water I heard voices and clatterings in the kitchen. I told whoever it was that I would be through in a minute and put some clothes on, but when I went into the kitchen it was empty. What was more worrying was that the food supplies I had left on the table were now scattered on the floor. I checked all the rooms, doors and windows but found nothing. Then I heard voices again. By this time I was quite perturbed. I picked up my long machete, and creeping stealthily along the corridor I flung open the door of the kitchen. There was a screech and a crash of plates as the culprit leapt in the air; it was a parrot.

He was red and green and, I discovered, could speak pidgin quite well. I burst out laughing, alternating between a desire to wring its neck for giving me such a fright and light-headed relief. Later we became friends and he shared my supper.

The next day I saddled Horse and rode back into Mendi. I disliked being in towns where I knew nobody, it made me feel lonely and empty, unlike the contentment I felt in the hills and jungle. But I was glad that Horse was with me. First priority was to find somewhere for him to stay. As Heather had tried to be helpful over the horse-shoes, I thought that perhaps she wouldn't mind helping again. In the event she did more than that: she invited both Horse and me to stay.

We were terribly happy there: Horse lived in the garden, and spent most of his time standing outside the back door demanding the cook's attention, or being petted by the children. Horse loved them all and whinnied softly whenever anyone opened the door.

11
The Huli Wigmen

While in Mendi I wasn't the only house-guest of the Deans. Ursula Savill, an English artist who had been commissioned to paint a mural in Mendi's hotel was also staying there and we soon became good friends.

One of my tasks while I was in Mendi was to do something about my broken camera but soon I found that there was not only nowhere in Mendi that could fix it, but nowhere in the whole of Papua New Guinea either. Nor was there anywhere I could buy one; it would have to be sent back to its makers in Japan. Knowing that it would be at least three months before it would be returned I was more than grateful when a friend of Heather's (Sue Favetta) lent me one of her cameras so that I would be able to continue to take photographs.

After four days we were ready to leave. Rested and refreshed, it was time to move on towards the Tari Basin and its Huli wigmen. The Huli portraits in Ursula's portfolio had re-inspired me, seeming to justify the Huli's reputation for being the most spectacular-looking of all the highland clans. The Tari Basin now lay to the north-west of us, about seventy miles in a straight line, though of course the mountainous terrain made straight lines impossible. My map showed a variety of dirt roads leaving Mendi, one of which was an old *kiap*-road about 40 miles long (65km) and going to Nipa in the direction of Tari, so I decided to use that route.

Late the next morning I saddled Horse and said our goodbyes, and after cantering down to the store for some fresh supplies we left Mendi. The old *kiap*-road led us across the wide valley and down to the Mendi river, over an iron bridge which had probably been constructed by the Australian army, and up into a steep mountain wall. A strong wind whipped the dust raised by

Horse's hooves into dustdevils which swirled away down the track. Black clouds rushed across the sky threatening rain. It took a while to get used to being on my own again after the companionship of Heather and her friends.

On a hilltop the Wildlife Department had stationed a cassowary farm. We stopped there in the afternoon, and were invited to stay overnight. I was fascinated by a close-up look at these ferocious birds. As soon as they saw me they strode aggressively up to the wire-mesh fence, jabbing their beaks against it and hissing angrily. One gave a weird gobbling roar of rage. He was an enormous six-foot tall specimen with glossy black feathers, a bald head that was covered in dark-blue skin paling to turquoise and topped with a large green horny casque, and a long, bald, scarlet neck that had blue dangling neck-sacks. No wonder people were afraid of them. The farm kept about nine cassowaries of both highland and lowland varieties, but as yet had had no success in rearing chicks from eggs. Andrew, the Wildlife Officer from Manus Island, described how he usually caught young wild chicks with nets so that they could be tamed before they grew too big and aggressive.

Other local methods of hunting them are by bow and arrow, or by trapping them with a sliding vine noose. The macho way is for a man to jump onto the cassowary's back from behind using his legs to pin the bird down, and forcing it to the ground. This is a dangerous sport.

Adult cassowaries were for sale from the farm. They were purchased by highlanders for use as *bride-price* (price of buying a wife) and for displays of wealth such as a cassowary *race*. In pidgin the word 'race' means competition; a cassowary *race* is a financial competition. As I understood it, each clan gathers all its assets together in order to buy as many cassowaries as possible. Then the two sides meet to display their birds and the *race* is won by the side with the most. After the counting, the cassowaries are usually killed, each man strangling his own. Their feathers are kept for *bilas*, their bones for daggers, and the meat is eaten by all.

The next morning I rose early and watched as the cassowaries were given a feed of *kaukau*. After my breakfast of *kaukau* and tinned fish Andrew's wife presented me with a small *bilum* she had made and decorated with seeds and feathers; it was just the right size to hold my maps, compass, tobacco and knife.

Horse dawdled as we trudged uphill between sheer mountains, slowly edging up the side escarpment above Mendi valley. The day was overcast and muggy, but there had been no rain for four days, a welcome gap in the continually wet weather.

As we detoured towards a village called Was, I became aware of a terrible smell. I had smelt that stench before but couldn't remember what it was. I asked two passersby about it and they explained that in the next village were two men who had been dead for ten days and were lying roped to horizontal poles held up high by supports. They wouldn't be buried until a compensation dispute was settled.

One of the dead was a young unmarried man. His village was claiming about 12,000 *kina* (£9,000) from the clan which had killed him; while the other corpse, an old man, was considered to be worth 4,000 *kina* (£3,000). Together this made what I considered to be a stunning amount of money to be raised by the apparently poor villagers who seemed to have so little, and even less to trade. But the men assured me that it was only money that was easy to borrow from friends and relatives. I was gradually discovering that the people of Papua New Guinea have a different attitude to money from the one I am used to. It seemed that their money was not related to the cost of living since they built their huts and grew their food 'free', and that any money they made was extra, to be used for gambling or buying prestigious things like more pigs, which could cost 600 *kina* (£450) each or paying compensation. And not all the people were poor — the economic development of the highlands was bringing good financial rewards to those who were willing to try out new ideas like coffee-growing, farming, etc., and the country's natural resources of gold, silver, copper, oil and timber, were only just being tapped. I had noticed the peoples' inflated concept of money on several occasions already, and concluded that it was truly a rich country.

If the compensation for the bodies was not paid, there would be payback deaths. In this society it seemed logical that payback and compensation should exist. Many clans were living in close proximity and there had to be a way of preventing bad behaviour, and murder. With payback traditions, each whole clan was responsible for the actions of its individuals; it was a way of maintaining peace and stability. Even the legal system accepted the validity of payback and compensation and one court recently had awarded compensation of 300 pigs.

The stench of decomposing human flesh got worse as we neared the village until I didn't want to ride that way any more. From the top of the ridge we started down towards the Lai Valley on a track which was clinging to a ledge along the cliffs. Rain came sweeping over the peaks so we hurried to a thicket of trees to shelter. The rain was torrential but short-lived and afterwards we continued going down to the valley-floor then along it beside the Lai River.

What I had not considered was that the rain would have flooded the innumerable streams which cascaded down the valleyside into the river. The first few streams were spanned by low-set bridges which stood only inches clear of the swollen water that rushed beneath the holes in their slippery and rotted planks. I dismounted to check each bridge before leading Horse across, making sure that he used the safest ways. Perhaps we became overconfident, because at the fourth one Horse slipped on the wet wood and trapped his hind hoof in a gap between the planks. Blood ran down his leg as he struggled to pull himself free. 'Gently, gently' I said trying to calm him, afraid that another hoof would slip causing him to fall and break the trapped leg. But I had no effect and he kept kicking until he was free. When we were safely on the far side we stood and trembled together. For a while I didn't dare to examine the wound which was now bleeding profusely and I watched helplessly as he put the injured leg gingerly to the ground, grunted with pain, and lifted it sharply again. Then he did a strange thing, he stretched the hurt leg out backwards and forwards over and over again, presumably to ease the soreness. When I looked at the cut I could see that it was quite deep but that no tendons had been cut or bones touched, so I just cleaned and bandaged it for him. When we walked on, Horse walked without limping.

Nevertheless, we took life easy in the Lai Valley. In several villages I saw piles of wood and stones laid out to signify that *Moka* was due. *Moka*, or *Tee* as the custom is also called, is the ceremonial exchange of wealth between neighbouring clans. The ceremony is a display by the home clan of their strength,

109

physique and their amassed wealth (pigs, cassowaries and *kina* shells), at the end of which they give their wealth to the visiting clan. There is great rivalry to see which village can give the most extravagant *Moka,* and in the lavishness of the gifts they demonstrate their superiority. There is no sense of generosity in the giving, it is merely an integral part of their economic system. Their system seemed topsy-turvy: we measure wealth by what is owned, they measure it by what is given away, and often they have borrowed extensively in order to give away more. Being in debt is regarded as healthy and bankruptcy brings status and prestige — but in a delightful way it made sense. Wide borrowing increases a man's ties, makes him form new alliances, and cement old friendships. The web-like mixing of everyone in debt with each other gives them a feeling of clan involvement and social unity. Each gift sets up a debt in return, which has to be repaid with extra when *Moka* comes round again. It seems an ingenious investment policy.

As I understood it the *Moka* works on a seven-year cycle, moving in a chain reaction through the mountains and valleys as each clan gives to their neighbours on one side, and receives from the other. When the *Moka* has completed its cycle and begins to return, the roles of givers and takers are reversed.

Fire-pit stones and pig-posts mounted up in the villages we passed through, and I met several men out collecting in their debts or looking for loans. Along the riverside were neatly arranged *kaukau* gardens, divided by rows of multicoloured cordyline plants of red, purple, green, and yellow. Their long leaves were specially cultivated for *arse-grass.* Certain colours were reserved for *sing-sing*-wear only.

In several villages there were *long-hauses* of approximately 300ft (90m) length built to accommodate a visiting clan during celebrations. Outside one village were some ruined *long-hauses* standing parallel to each other and looking overgrown and forlorn. They had a wonderful air of neglect with creepers and flowers springing up from their straggly thatch and tall green grass growing around them. Horse wanted to stop and eat so I unloaded the saddlebags and let him graze. While I was resting in the sun, enjoying the peacefulness of the place, a passerby came and sat by me and talked about the forthcoming *Moka.* He was having trouble raising his quota of pigs to donate to the *Moka;*

110

his wife's relations were lazy and weren't helping very much while his father was relying on him to impress the guest clan by giving more pigs than he had ever given before.

When I heard about a village which was holding the ceremony to fulfil the *Moka,* I went there. As I walked into the village the air was shrill with pigs' squealing and people talking, laughing and arguing. I edged into the throng. Several hundred people were assembled on the open ground between some huts, and leading from the huts were rows of wooden posts, each with one pig tied to it, squealing its protest. A few of the pigs were smeared with coloured ochres. The crowds of men were magnificently decorated with head-dress towers made of feathers in colourful patterns and topped by the long springy blue plumes of the King of Saxony bird of paradise. The plumes flicked back and forth as the men walked. They wore wide waist-belts of bark with a front apron and bunch of leaves behind; their skin was greased and ochred in parts, and on their chests many had large *bailer* shells. Their faces were blackened with charcoal, and banded red and white across their eyes. Not everyone was painted alike, some had red and yellow striped noses and variations on that theme. Luckily they were so intent on the pigs that I escaped much notice. It was a relief not to be the focus of attention for once and to be able to observe without being watched myself.

Pigs are necessary to most social transactions, including the settling of disputes or the buying of a new wife. Valued and loved, favourite pigs often live in the house and are fussed over like domestic pets; sometimes the piglets are even breast-fed by mens' wives. The use of pig-meat as food is secondary, except at times of feasts. After the pig-inspection the *Moka* ceremony moved slowly towards its climax. Sturdy warrior-farmers lined up in crescent formation facing out to the visiting clan, and with sedately rhythmic movements they danced to the beating of drums and the powerful rhythm of their own voices chanting. Some men carried ceremonial axes, or spears, which they pointed at their visitors. Then they backed away in a graceful knee-bending dance which showed off the strength and suppleness of their bodies. They marched in ranks and in unison, a picture of clan solidarity. Some women (probably the wives of pig-donors) were decorated with ochre to show that they had been responsible

111

for successfully raising the pigs. The giving away of pigs was done individually. Men walked along their lines of pigs, shouting in fast flowing sentences their reasons for making such gifts. Pausing beside each pig in line, the giver called out the name of its new owner, who immediately rushed forward, untied the pig and hurried away with it, anxious to get home before dark.

When all the pigs had been given away, there were few visitors left and everyone dispersed for the night.

On leaving the Lai Valley and the pig-festivities, Horse and I followed the road which climbed several thousand feet, emerging into a high-altitude wilderness where there was no sign of human habitation; there was just miles and miles of open forests of *pandanus* palms, white daisy flowers, heather, bracken, and leafy red bushes. It was wet and misty. Conical mountain peaks were obscured by cloud and merged into shades of grey, until it was hard to tell cloud from rock.

The narrow stony road crossed many streams with timber bridges of two parallel trees supporting widely-spaced cross-bars. At most bridges we had to stop while I chopped branches or found suitable wood to fill the spaces so that Horse could use them. It was tempting to take chances, but I couldn't risk Horse's life because of my carelessness. He was very cautious now and sometimes sniffed his way suspiciously along the rotted timber. When the loose logs on another bridge rolled beneath us, Horse jumped clear but the shoe which had been wrenched in the previous accident came slightly loose. To avoid the bridges whenever possible, we forded the streams but getting down and back up their steep banks was difficult and almost as hazardous.

A group of young men that had been following us for a while caught up with us at a bridge and stood looking at Horse while I put some branches in place. They accompanied us on from there, chatting idly more amongst themselves than to me and not being very helpful. I didn't like having them around and tried to discourage them but it was hard to make them go away in this stony wilderness. Eventually at a small path beside a bridge they announced that they were going home, and demanded my money and my *cargo* (saddlebags).

My first reaction was to dig my heels into Horse and to gallop away but a quick glance told me that the bridge ahead was in poor repair and I wouldn't make it. My stomach knotted with anxiety as I realised that I couldn't get away but taking a deep breath I made an effort to appear calm and reply slowly. I admitted that I had set out with ten *kina* but that I had bought some *kaukau* for one *kina*, which had left nine, and so I went on down an imaginary shopping list, stopping to subtract each item, sometimes pretending to get it wrong and deliberating my arithmetic with them. I spun it out as long as I could hoping that someone would come along the road. Meanwhile I had dismounted from Horse and taking my bush-knife out had begun gathering fallen branches to patch the bridge. There were four wide gaps to be filled; the men wouldn't attack me while I held the knife, and Horse was safe because I had already told them that he was savage and he would kick and bite if they touched him.

No one came along to help. I kept bargaining until the bridge was crossable. By that time the price was down to 60 *toea* (40p) and a can of fish. I led Horse across the bridge, but unfortunately the men turned on me before I had the chance to get on Horse's back. One of them hurled stones at us as another grabbed my *bilum* and someone else seized me by my arm. I was angry and frightened, and lashed out at them. Suddenly the situation reminded me of the children who had pestered me before and very quickly I decided to try a similar ploy. So making myself look as angry as I could, I told them that I would find their headman and tell him how they had behaved and that they had tried to steal from me. This had an immediate calming effect and after a great deal of hesitation on their side and anger on mine, they gave back my *bilum*. As I put it into my saddlebag I also sprang up into the saddle and urged Horse forward. The men tried to grab Horse's head but he bounded forward and we galloped away along the track. They chased us for about a mile, forcing us into a reckless river crossing, where the water was so deep and muddy that Horse only just managed to flounder across. When I was sure that the men had given up the chase we relaxed our speed.

We arrived late in the afternoon at Nipa and made straight for the High School where the teachers again welcomed me, and allowed us to rest for a day.

After I had related my story about the men trying to steal my *cargo*, the conversation turned to cargo cults. Cargo cults were a recurring feature in Papua New Guinea and two of the most famous I was told, were the President Johnson affair that I had already heard about, and 'Vailala Madness', which took place after World War I in Papua New Guinea's Gulf region. Like most cargo cults it happened because the New Guineans had watched aeroplanes landing and bringing cargo (machinery and weapons) which they had seen being distributed without any money being paid. They thought that the white men were following some magic ritual to bring cargo, and decided to ask for some for themselves. Thus they built makeshift offices where men sat and passed bits of paper from one to another in imitation of the white men they had seen. At the coast they built symbolic docks, and inland people cleared small rough runways so that cargo could arrive. One cult leader claimed that all cargo came from Papua New Guinea's ancestors and rightfully belonged to its people. He accused the whites of intercepting and stealing the cargo and instigated a ritual designed to redirect the cargo to his village.

When the cargo didn't arrive the people were ordered by their cult-leaders to demonstrate their continuing faith in the cult by burning their huts and killing their pigs. This began to happen and finally the government was forced to intervene. They didn't arrest the cult leaders because to have done so would only have strengthened their belief that it was a white man's plot. Instead they took some of them to Australia and showed them where the cargo originated, to prove that it was not magic.

From Nipa to Margarima, twenty miles away, we followed the Highlands Highway. It was mostly a dirt road, but on this particular stretch it had disintegrated into metre-deep clay mud and was closed to all traffic. We left Nipa early, and I urged Horse to go fast since I hoped to reach Margarima before nightfall. When we reached an eight-mile section of mud I dismounted. The mud was astonishing; it was thick, oozing and came up to my thighs. Several times I had to ask Horse to pull me back out of potholes. He wasn't enjoying the mud either but dense forest crowded the would-be road and there were no side paths, so he had to wade forward with mud up to his belly, as best he could.

We passed two Caterpillars and an assortment of trucks all of which were sunk to their headlamps in the mud with teams of workmen trying to free them. They were in a worse state than we were.

The road improved as it wound up over mountain ranges and down into valleys. At one river crossing a road engineer and some workmen helped me to rip off the sides of an abandoned truck to mend a particularly delapidated bridge. When we had all crossed safely, he invited me to stay the night in Margarima where he lived with his co-overseer, an old Scotsman. I cooked dinner for them but they got drunk and so I retired to bed. The men stayed up drinking and every hour or so one of them would burst into my bedroom, fling himself on the bed and ask 'Well, do you want sex now or not?' Fortunately they weren't aggressive about it and always left without much fuss.

I made a late start after a concilliatory breakfast of bacon and eggs, and Scots porridge. Horse had slipped his halter but was grazing contentedly nearby. I saddled him, shook hands with the men, and then we left. It felt good to be out in the mountains and away from them. I guessed that we were at about 7,000 feet (2,100m). There were occasional huts, where I caught my first glimpse of some Huli clansmen but these were not wigmen and it was the Huli wigmen that I looked forward to seeing. These men were meagrely decorated and their children had pot-bellies, tropical ulcers and runny noses. They didn't have the stamina to tag behind for long.

Then we were alone again, heading onto the Tari Gap, the vast alpine plateau leading up between the Doma peaks and Mt Ne, beyond which lay the Tari Basin where I hoped to see Huli wigmen. The air was thin and Horse puffed as he walked uphill. Tall dark mountains surrounded us with sides of sweeping grasslands dotted with islands of moss-forest. We kept to the stony road since the grasslands were swamp-grasses and very boggy, and we camped the night on the edge of an island. The night was cold but dry; I heard a pack of wild dogs hunting in the distance and hoped that they wouldn't come nearer.

Shortly after dawn the harsh cries of wauk-wauk-wok told me that birds of paradise were courting nearby. The noise came from inside the forest, specifically from a tree branch at head-height. A blue bird of paradise was displaying himself to a typically drab-coloured female; he was hanging upside down from the branch, his breast puffed out and his blue underwing plumage spread into fans. He was shaking his feathers, making them quiver and sending ripples of blue colour down them. He sang as he showed off, making an odd buzzing sound which encouraged the female to move closer to him. He waited without moving for a full minute, then moved in swift steps over to the female to mate.

I returned to my camp and revived the fire for coffee before leaving. We had all day to ourselves, walking beside small streams and along the top of banks where peat-bogs dripped over steep ledges into the roadside gulleys. Fern trees in the valleys stood up with branches curled into scrolls, imperceptibly unfurling. Strong hot sun beat down on us from an intensely blue sky. We reached 9,000ft (2,700m) at the pass, and began the descent. Moss-forest gave way to a big open-spaced forest where the trees were dressed in the reds, golds and purples which here denoted springtime. Leaf-colour seemed to be back to front, with the leaves emerging in reds in the spring, and turning to green by the autumn. Tree-trunks were pale and blotched with orange mosses. Raucous birdsong came from a black bird of paradise, whose long white tail-feathers floated out behind him in flight.

My first view over the Tari Basin was obscured by a blanket of thick grey cloud which spread over the basin beneath us like a lake, encircled by mountain-tops. When we got down into the cloud everything around us was dripping wet and the mist was like a fine rain. As the morning progressed it grew gradually darker until in the afternoon the blanket broke up into thundery clouds and dispersed in the wind. As the stony road descended the lower mountain slopes it became a firm red clay track and suddenly we were free of slow tedious walking. Horse enjoyed the change and he cantered gaily along with his head held high.

In a village Horse snatched a few *kaukau* cuttings and some women rushed to get him some more so that they could watch him eat. So we paused while he guzzled, and it was then that I caught sight of my first wigmen. Their wigs were shoulder-wide and shaped like upturned boats or mushrooms, and they were decorated with yellow everlasting daisies and bird plumes. Their faces were framed by thick black beards, and one man had entwined soft ferns into his beard. They were colourful and magnificent.

The men had been engrossed in playing cards when I arrived

116

and were gambling heavily on them. This seemed to be one of the most popular ways of using money and I wondered if it had become merely an extension of their exchange customs.

Seven miles from Tari we came to the High School and went in to meet one of the teachers, Miss Moira, who turned out to be a young American with a heart of gold, and a full set of blacksmith's tools! Neither of us was very experienced at shoeing horses, but we agreed to give it a try in the morning. Meanwhile, she offered a cow paddock for Horse, and for me a hot shower, refreshment, food, and a movie at the school that evening.

It was an American suspense movie. Moira was in charge of the projector and of the censorship, censoring it as it went along by blacking out any sex scenes as soon as they flashed on and continuing when she guessed that the scene was over. I agreed with the censorship because the local people's morals and values were generally much higher than those portrayed by American moviemakers, and the films could encourage them to think that all white women are promiscuous and enjoy sleeping around. Perhaps my attitude is selfish and the censorship denies them their right to this kind of entertainment, but for me as a woman a lack of censorship creates additional danger and on several occasions I have been hassled and threatened for sex, usually in towns where the western influence is strongest. The suspense part of the movie included a dramatic rescue by hang-gliders; everyone watched entranced, feeling every last pang of fright and suspense; none of us had seen a movie in a long time and it made us more susceptible.

After a leisurely breakfast Moira and I collected Horse and began trying to re-fit the shoe which had come off. The shoe itself was slightly twisted so we hammered it flat as best we could, then filed the hoof to match. Nailing it on was less easy and we had to take care not to let any one of the nails slip into the delicate part since that would have lamed him. In fact Moira and I made a good team and we did a professional-looking job.

From the High School I rode to Tari where I was hoping to find Ursula, (the artist whom I had met in Mendi) who had invited me to stay at her bungalow near Tari. It was a very small town with a Catholic mission, *kiap* office, airstrip, and some trade-stores. We branched away from the town on a rough sandy

117

track and after several miles we arrived at Piwa agricultural station with its few bungalows, *kaukau* gardens, and a herd of pigs. In one of the bungalows lived Ursula. We settled in, and somehow it became home. It wasn't that anything reminded me physically of home; travelling round meant that home was simply a state of mind, and it often came in unexpected places. Having a base to travel from, I used my time to explore the region thoroughly which was a pleasant change from linear travel. But I didn't put my saddlebags away, I always took them with me so that I could keep my options open and not be forced to return at nightfall if I didn't want to.

Tari Basin was vast and encircled by distant towering mountains. Around Piwa the land was undulating and green, sliced with red-earth roads and paths. Wigmen were repairing parts of the roads. They worked with spades and digging-sticks and just wore their casual everyday wigs. People were surprised to see a horse, and were amazed by his size, and the fact that he was carrying a rider and cargo. When Horse cantered along they shouted *'Luk im run'*, and from behind their huts many people peered out with their mouths opening and closing in astonishment but with no words coming out.

Along the road, even if we were walking slowly, people would run for safety; sometimes they hid behind trees or ran up roadside banks in panic, then turned to look at the animal with expressions that flickered between disbelief, fear and delight.

While riding around the Porami ridge one hot sunny afternoon we were accompanied for a while by an elder Huli who strolled along playing pan's pipes (many bamboo tubes bound together). He blew softly and tunelessly into them, just interpreting what he saw in terms of music. On his bowed head he wore a magnificent wig decorated thickly with red daisies and a central star of beer-bottle tops.

As we returned to Piwa I heard a mournful wailing and high-pitched keening that led to the funeral of a young man. He had died from cerebral malaria, which had recently accounted for many deaths in Tari. Apparently the malaria came to the basin when the Highlands Highway was built over the Gap and the mosquitoes had bred in the stagnant puddles alongside the roadwork. So much for progress.

The dead body was smeared with pig fat and the mourners

118

were daubed with white ochre. Unlike face-painting which was precise and defined, the ochre worn for funerals was smeared on messily to denote grief. They buried the body in a grave which had a six-foot deep ditch all around it, to protect it, and they lined the sides of the grave with pointed wooden stakes. By tradition, the body would be dug up after a year or two when only the bones remained and the bones would be taken back to the person's land.

We could hear the wailing all night from Ursula's bungalow; a ringing 'o' of lament, that was an infinite line of vocal sound with whooping solos over the top.

Next morning we got slightly lost and came across a silk-worm project run by two Asians. They were rearing thousands of silk-worms in large trays spread under some bright lights. All I could hear was the noise of steady munching as thousands of jaws tore at fresh supplies of mulberry leaves and the voices of the two men giving me a brief lecture on the subject. The caterpillars eat day and night, quickly growing to seventy times their original size, and shedding their skins four times. After a month they are three inches long and ready to stop eating and begin to spin their cocoons of silken thread. When the cocoons are complete they are killed in a hot oven before being soaked in basins of hot water to dissolve the binding gum. A single thread of silk is too fine to be used on its own so usually four cocoons are unravelled together on a wooden reel and twisted into skeins. More skeins have to be added before the thread can be used for weaving. I thanked them for showing me round and went back out into the sun.

At noon Horse and I picnicked and rested on a grassy river-bank. I swam, or rather lay in the fast-flowing water, using a rock as an anchor and feeling like a piece of riverweed rippling under-water. It was a blazing hot day; the water was icy and kingfishers were diving for fish.

The following day I packed another picnic and we set off towards the north of the basin. We paused at Hoyabia church mission for morning coffee, and out in the hills we stopped to watch three wigmen fashioning pan's pipes out of bamboo. They used bamboo tubes of about one centimetre diameter, cut to various lengths, and they bound seven tubes together with bark-string. They said that the pipes were part of any normal man's walkabout, to be carried with him and played from time to time as he walked along. Often they used them to gain time for thought during a difficult situation. Their best musician tried out the new pipes, and corrected their lengths until he achieved the sounds required, which combined into a sort of harmony. He wore a plain wig, its edges trimmed with strands of wool, and fronted by the spread wings of a parrot. In typical Huli style he wore *arse-grass* and a frontal apron of fibre-fringe. A cassowary bone dagger was tucked into an armband, and down the back of his neck hung a long hornbill's beak. As he played the pipes his notes blended with wind rustling through the tall grass and the humming of bees.

The road ran along hill ridges to Tibiribi hamlet where the pipe-makers had said there was a *pig* and *cow-kill* in process. When we arrived the killings had finished and some old weathered wigmen were starting to skin a cow, and prepare three pigs for the *mumu*. Other wigmen completed the pit by lining it with hot stones which they carried from the fire with huge wooden tongs. Slabs of meat were laid in the pit, followed by layers of *kaukau* and greens. The pit was sealed with earth, and packed down to trap the steam inside. For this occasion many of the men wore red face-paint on the end of their noses and around the rims of their eyes. It made them look fearsome and grotesque (which was probably its intention). One man had decorated his whole body with white-clay handprints. Some spivvy young men from Tari had brought beer, and when they got drunk I thought it a good idea to leave. It was a wise move because they tried to catch up with me, and ran behind Horse for a couple of miles (their stamina surprised me) before they gave up.

Living at Piwa meant that I didn't have to allow time for making camp or finding a village each night. I enjoyed the temporary feeling of having a home and having somewhere to turn towards at dusk, and as we cantered back to Piwa I felt contented and completely in tune with Horse and the travelling. When we got there I put Horse into an overgrown field, and watched Ursula treating him to a bucket of *kaukau*. Then we went indoors to chat about the day's happenings and light the wood-stove and start to cook supper. Sometimes we would have music on, and then we would enjoy a gentle evening — me wrapped in my writing, while Ursula painted portraits of wigmen.

Horse and 'Horse Lady' (as I had become known) visited Tari itself several times. The *kiap* there was an Englishman called Ben Probert, who had spent twelve years in Papua New Guinea and done a great amount of foot-patrolling in the Tari region. His advice and information were extremely helpful to me. Another attraction in Tari was a bakery! One of the Catholic sisters had taught a Huli how to bake bread, and now he sold it hot from the oven. I could never pass that bakery without going inside. Our food-shopping was usually done at the market where crowds of people would gather to look at Horse, hugely enjoying his efforts to steal nibbles off the sugarcanes I strapped to his saddlebags.

Ben Probert had told me where to look for Kolete, the sacred place that the Hulies believed was their point of origin in this world, so I set off to visit it, taking the road to Koroba, and branching off at Komo. Roadworks were in progress, and road-signs of warning said *Draiv esi, ol man i wok long rot* (Drive slow, some men work on road). The road went uphill, giving views across flat marshy plains, and went higher until we could see far across the Tari Basin to Doma's peaks. At Tagari river I detoured to an immense waterfall. It was an awesome place; the torrential water sounded like thunder and the whole valley-head was dripping and misty with spray. We crossed a gorge and from the bridge, I looked down on the black rock cliffs below. Tall *klinki* pines peeped above the other trees in the forest, and we met a group of boys whose faces were painted in vertical halves of white. I think that they were initiates learning how to look after themselves in the open. Their face-paint would inform people of this, so that they would leave the boys alone and not offer food or shelter to them.

At a small village market I bought a pawpaw (for twenty cents) and some root-ginger (to brew with tea). Kolete was not far and two young boys accompanied me for the rest of the way. To reach the sacred place we had to get across a deep stream. The boys found a long pole to span the stream and two thin poles to use as walking-sticks which we jabbed into the river bed as we walked along.

The Hulies believed that their ancestors had come out here from an underground world. Some of the caves had interlinking

121

passages with red ochre daubed on the walls. But somehow the place was disappointingly ordinary, without atmosphere and I couldn't imagine people emerging from the rock. Of course the ancestor myths do not represent factual history, but I expected more. However the boys seemed very respectful of the place, and they urged me to leave before dusk; obviously their imaginations were better than mine.

Beyond the western edge of Tari Basin was the Levani Valley. This was the sensational 'hidden valley' found in 1954 by John Zenhender and his expedition. Despite many obstacles he successfully entered the valley and it was announced that it contained a new race of people who had never before had contact with the outside world. However it was later discovered that the inhabitants were Dunas and little different from those outside; and an easier way into the valley was found by some mineral prospectors. I followed their disused mining track up the mountain-barrier then transferred to a dry streambed which led rockily upwards. The route down into the hidden valley was rough and unrewarding, while the valley itself was marshy, gloomy, enclosed by cloud and oppressive. I wondered why I had visited it, but this was swiftly followed by wondering why I needed a reason. However it was a depressing place to be, so once I had taken a look around a village and had seen some of the people, I returned to Piwa.

Somehow, rather than making trips out of the Tari Basin, I enjoyed just being in the basin itself because it was the heart of the 'land of wigmen'.

The daily routine of make-up was something I had long-forgotten until I watched the face-painting of a young Huli in a village near Piwa. We were sitting in the early sun outside some huts enclosed behind a fighting-gate. Helped by an old grizzled man, the Huli first applied a base-coat of pig grease. The old man then stirred up some yellow ochre and, using a brush of reed-fibres, he carefully painted the yellow over the top half of the young man's face. The eyes he outlined thickly in red. It seemed a far cry from the make-up I had known of beige foundation-creams and brush-on rouge.

Next the old man began painting patterns of dots round his

companion's nose and chin. Hulies regard make-up as a complex art, and by wearing it they demonstrate their physical and emotional well-being (much as women wear makeup in our society). Highland women sometimes wear face-paint but mainly only when they are of marriageable age; it is primarily a male art. Highland men seem to produce nothing else of artistic value (no artifacts, statues, etc.), and it appears that all their creative ability goes into self-beautification.

In addition to displaying well-being, the face is used for decorative symbolism, to convey information, ideas and emotions. The patterns and the decorations *(bilas)* also give news of recent alliances and deaths so that an expert can tell the person's home village or *arse-ples* by knowing the clan patterns. These patterns of parallel stripes, snake-like scales or interlocking diamond designs have an established name and format: the raindrop pattern for example is called *waep nomor.*

The old man went on painting. The lines of dots now ran round the young Huli's eyes and down his nose, and his chin sported blue spots on white ochre. I laughed when I thought how hard we tried to achieve 'the natural look'. They use dramatic effects and bright colour combinations, since they believe that brightness has the power to attract wealth. Red in particular is supposed to bring wealth, pigs, and women. The face-paint was not washed off at night, it was usually left until it wore off naturally over several days.

I asked the old warrior in pidgin if he made his own paints and he said that although trade stores now sold cosmetic paints, most people still preferred to make their own. White, blue and yellow clays were gathered from specific riverbanks, then dried and crushed to powder. Red clay merited special treatment to make it brighter: it was wrapped in leaves and cooked slowly over a fire to make the inside portion of the clay turn vibrantly red. Before use the powders were mixed either with water, or with pig's fat and women's breast-milk.

At social gatherings like *sing-sings,* fights or *pig-kills* the purpose of *bilas* is to create mood and signify the unity and prosperity of the clan. It is not used for disguise, as in cultures that use masks and spirit figures. Neither is it kept for special occasions only; it is an everyday thing, especially in Tari, where no self-respecting man likes to be seen without some form of *bilas.* I remembered a time when I had felt the same way, and hadn't liked to be seen without make up, but I think I used it more as a mask to hide behind.

The morning mist was rising, drifting up the valleys towards the mountain peaks. Beside us the thatched huts were steaming as the women lit fires in them and the village came slowly to life. When the young man was satisfied with the quality of face-painting, which he examined in a piece of broken mirror, he turned his attention to the arrangement of his wig. It was a typical wide mushroom-like wig, built on a cane framework; a complete unit which he simply wore on his head like a hat.

Boys are not allowed to wear wigs until their initiation period, when they also learn the meanings behind the patterns. Their first wig is made from their own hair-clippings, often including donations from certain male relatives. To make the wig some of the hair-clippings are stitched with bark-thread onto the cane framework, and more hair is continually teased in (using a bone needle or a short stick like a knitting needle), until the wig becomes solid. Tree resin or pig grease is used as a setting lotion.

This man's wig was embellished with yellow everlasting daisies and the upper beak of a hornbill. For the final touches he inserted a nose-quill of one white feather, and twined some strands of trailing moss through his beard. His wig finished, he stood up, dusted off the bunch of leaves hanging from his waist, and went off, ready to face the day ahead.

For myself also it was time to face the future. My visit to the Tari Basin had a feeling of completeness and I decided that Horse and I should leave the basin and the province of the Southern Highlands, and go to explore some of the other highland provinces. I wanted to go to the Enga Province, a comparatively turbulent region, known for the roughness of its mountains and warring instincts of its Enga clans. Ursula told me that clan-fighting had broken out recently and urged me to take care.

12
Enga Tribal Warfare

I was sad to leave Ursula and after saddling Horse I set off for the Gap. On route we passed several groups of wigmen sitting playing cards and gambling in villages. We turned east at a junction beside a monstrously ugly mock-gothic church, made of artificial materials and painted a shade of pastel green which matched nothing in nature. To the side of the white limestone road were clear streams and buddleia bushes in mauve blossom. A group of women caught up with me, grass-skirted and bare-breasted with babies and piglets clutched in their arms. I liked their company and we talked happily about a forthcoming marriage until a lot of children joined the parade and the whole thing got too noisy.

Horse and I left and came to rest on the shoulder of a mountain overlooking the basin. A small column of vertical smoke rose in the stillness; the only sounds were of a bell tolling at a church mission, a waterfall, bees searching for nectar, wind rustling in the trees and Horse chomping grass. There were thunderclouds above us over the forest, and low clouds sweeping the tree-tops. Spots of rain fell, but luck was with us and they didn't turn into a storm. We reached the end of the forest and went up into the boggy grassland with its archipelago of moss-forest islands. It was late, and the sun was sinking as we detoured down a spongey path to an island and made camp round the back of it. I always tried to make the camp as invisible as I could so as not to attract attention at night; not that anyone else was likely to come along (even hunters were usually afraid of the dark), but just as a precaution. Horse stood tethered close to me happily munching *kaukau*; there was no pasture and the land was too boggy for him to go free. The noise of the waterfall led us to water, where I sat and watched the sun go down.

Shortly after the sun had set a full moon had risen. At that altitude the clarity of air made moonlight bright enough to read by. The night was cold but my sleeping-bag was warm. Horse slept within nudging distance of my hammock, occasionally waking me with blasts of warm breath on my face, as his muzzle brushed my skin.

At dawn I was woken by some wild dogs approaching us. They stopped when they saw us and stared. Their necks were longer and thicker than domestic dogs and their ears were hooded; they were tan-brown and had brushy fox-like tails which had a white tip. After several tense minutes they turned and ran away.

Soon after dawn Horse and I walked on. I enjoyed being on the Gap, partly because of its desolate atmosphere and bleak sweeping slopes, and partly because there were no people or signs of habitation to show that humans existed. It gave me a tremendous sense of freedom to know that I didn't have to identify myself as a person or justify myself to anyone; I was free to be just part of the land and sky.

A reminder of the world of humans and technology came with a jolt when a light aircraft flew low over us on its way through the Gap. The pilot was navigating by land not by instruments, and flying low because the place was notorious for the clouds which could suddenly close in and reduce visibility to zero. Accidents were not uncommon and when they happened the wreckage could lie hidden in the forest for years. A recent single-engined plane flying from Mendi to Tari had never arrived and when a search was made for it a twin-engined plane was found instead which had crashed several months before.

My waterbottle needed refilling so, leaving Horse to graze, I made my way over to a stream. Suddenly the ground gave way to bog and I was up to my knees in mud and still sinking. I looked around for something to grasp hold of and managed to grab a tussock of grass by leaning forward and straining to reach. By this time I had sunk to my thighs. For a moment I felt panic, realising how totally alone I was and that if I did get into serious difficulties either here or at a river there was no one to help me. But the thought of dying drowned in a bog struck me as being pathetically absurd, and after a struggle I managed to crawl out on my belly. Fortunately my water-bottle wasn't lost, but I was absolutely filthy and had to wash my clothes. I dried them later, draped over Horse's back in the sun, using him as a clothes-horse.

From the Gap we descended to Margarima then took the old road to Kandep, heading north through undulating mountains clad in yellow clay and tall *pitpit* grass. On the way we passed a village getting ready for a small *sing-sing* and I stopped to watch the preparations. A group of girls were sorting out their *bilas* and proudly showed me their multiple strands of trade-store beads and many types of shell ornamentation. Although they had never seen the sea, highlanders had for thousands of years acquired shells via well-developed trade routes: large cowrie-shells *(koma koma)* and little ones *(giri giri)*, tiny round *tambu*-shells, mother of pearl, *bailer* shells and the most valued of all, *kina* shells.

Kina shells were a unit of currency before money was introduced. They used to be worth about £20, but when the missionaries came in they brought hundreds of shells with them and flooded the market, reducing the value to about £12. They are frequently used today as a part of a *bride-price*. In a girl's life, I was told, *kina* shells change hands three times: at birth, marriage, and death.

Certain other treasured items of *bilas* are often handed down through generations and become valuable as exchange goods because of their age and rarity. Other items have value because they can only be obtained by hunting or trade.

Tethered by the huts I noticed a pig which had white ochre lines painted on it. One of the girls said that it was her mother's pig, and that it was not due to be eaten at this *sing-sing*. The lines on the pig's body were part of a spell, the outward expression of the mother's desire for her pig to grow fat in the drawn areas.

The pigs for the *mumu* were slaughtered but some of the meat was being distributed in raw chunks to the visitors who put it in their *bilums*, to re-distribute among their relatives and friends when they got back to their own village. This created the debt of further feasts in return.

Beside the empty ground-oven sat men with yellow-ochred hair, and flat hats of ferns or mossy caps and bird feathers; several men smoked bamboo pipes with a twist of tobacco. It would be many hours before the *sing-sing* began, so Horse and I continued on our way.

The rolling hills became steeper as the land sloped down to the Margarima river. In front of us was an old timber bridge that not only sagged in the middle but had more than seventy per cent of its cross-planks missing, and those that were left were askew and slanting all over the place. I unloaded the saddlebags and carried them across the bridge, returning for Horse and preparing myself for another icy cold swim. The river was deep and fast-flowing and we had to swim hard to make it to the other side. Fortunately the water was crystal clear and we could see where the rocks were and avoid them. We rested on the grassy river-bank and dried off in the sun. There were several other bridges, mostly small, nearly all in total disrepair, and therefore useless for Horse. The alternatives were either to jump across or wade, which we did according to their width.

Leaving the rivers behind us for a while we climbed up through rough mountains and into Enga province. A wet mist had come down and I was glad to stop for the night at a small community school. Horse grazed free. I stayed with the head-master and his wife, and spent a talkative evening sitting on woven-reed floormats which were indicative of the marshland area I was approaching. I wasn't yet fluent in pidgin. However, despite the fact that pidgin is ridiculed by western academics and educationalists, who condemn it as baby talk, I was finding it to be a highly expressive language. The headmaster asked me if I was tired, *'Yu laze?'* to which I replied *'Mi laze tru'* (very tired).

It was tiring to spend many hours a day on horseback, and frequently I would walk alongside Horse to stretch my legs. Our daily routine included several rest-stops for us both to relax, but I found it difficult, always feeling the need to be alert to our sur-roundings and keeping an eye on what Horse was up to. It was hard work to travel with a horse since I had to look after both of us. Having no-one to share the tasks meant that I had to do them all myself, with the added complication that I am allergic to horses. However this is something which I have put up with for years and which I knew would gradually go away the longer I was with him.

Yet I wouldn't have wanted to travel the highlands in any other style, and despite the hard work I knew that by setting out with Horse I had made the right decision; his strong legs made the journey possible and his companionship made it a pleasure.

The cargo ship *Tombatu* on which I spent three weeks travelling from Surabaya to Jayapura, on my way to Papua New Guinea. These are some of the 800 head of cattle that were taken on board at Kupang. Note the upended oil drums which were placed as stepping stones across the corrals.

My guides, Kom, Arak and a local man resting in the hills near Sisimin on part of the two-week walk between Oksapmin and Lake Kopiago. Arak, in the middle, is wearing cordyline leaves as *arse-grass*. Each man carries his own bow and arrows.

A Hewa man making rafts which would keep us afloat in crossing the Laigap river. The rafts were made of three logs tied together with vines. Two vine loops were made to slip over our wrists to help us hold on to the raft, leaving our legs free to swim.

Above: Myself riding Horse, the Arab stallion with whom I travelled for 1000 adventurous miles.

Below: Duna men at Kaugona eating the pulpy red *pandanus* which tasted rather like tomato ketchup.

Below top right: Two Huli men selling *kaukau* at the market in Tari. *Kaukau* is the staple food of the tribes people; it tastes like a sweet potato and is usually roasted.

Below bottom right: Myself camping in the Tari Basin. I didn't carry a tent and, when not sleeping in a hut, I enjoyed many nights sleeping out in the open in my hammock.

Top left: A Huli man standing by a fighting-gate at the entrance to his village.

Top right: A muddy part of the Highlands Highway — the only road between Mendi and Tari.

Left: A Huli wigman, bearded and with a *pitpit* stalk through his nose.

Below: The mountainous terrain around Mt Wilhelm. The huts were windowless and smoke from the cooking fires seeped out through the thatched roofs.

Above: A Mendi woman with a load of *kaukau* that is carried in the string *bilum* from her forehead. The spade was a luxury — many women had only crude digging-sticks.

Below: Two Goroka men at the Highland Show. Their white body decoration was painted on using a splayed stick dipped in ochre. Note the bark belts, *arse-grass* of cordyline leaves and cassowary plumes in the hair.

Above: Numerous necklaces of Job's Tears (*pitpit* seeds) are usually worn by widows to show mourning and are removed one by one according to custom until the mourning-period is over; these Henganofi women are dressed in mourning for ancestors killed in battles.

Below: A highland warrior with two wild pigs' tusks through his nose, cowrie shells and parrot feathers in his hair, and tufts of croton in his armband.

Above: Male *bilas* with ochred face, and bird of paradise quills and a shell through his nose.

Above: Female *bilas* with necklaces of kina shell, trade-store beads and dogs' teeth.

Below: Myself talking with some warriors at Goroka. Their eye-catching head-dresses are of cassowary and bird of paradise feathers.

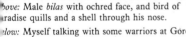

Above: The traditional ceremony of the lining-up of pigs in Maprik region. The man is beating each pig while calling its new owner's name. Note the *haus tamboran* and painted ancestor-faces.

Above: For the yam festival at Kuotngu small yams are decorated with faces made from dry burrs edged with kapok fluff. Yams are grown and harvested by men in secret, away from women.

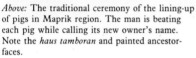

Below: Antn beside the Sepik river 'cooking' his new canoe. After the canoe has been hollowed out using axes, the wood is heated by flames to shrink and seal it.

Above: Some typical family huts, in Swakop on a tributary of the Sepik, built on stilts because the land is flooded for six months a year. The huts are made of ironwood, palm leaf stalks and palm leaves; a notched pole leads up to the doorway. Huts contain extended families of 10-30 people. The canoes at the riverside have carved crocodile-head prows.

Below: Crocodiles being farmed near Pagwi. They are valuable for their skin, although the skin of farm-crocodiles is not as strong as that of wild ones. Crocodiles are kept at the farm for several years, until large enough for slaughter. Their meat is sparse and not valued (apart from the tail-meat which is sometimes considered a delicacy), and tastes rather like lobster.

Above: Myself in the dug-out canoe among water-lilies on Blackwater lake. My luggage is in front of me, covered by a woody piece of *limbum.* I spent nearly four months paddling down the Sepik river and on its tributaries. You can see the improvised clay and tin patches where I made repairs to the canoe-side.

Below: The young initiate caught in the *haus tamboran* and forced to undergo the skin cutting ceremony as a punishment. Because he had not been prepared for it he felt more pain.

Below: An initiate after the scars had healed showing the pattern of scars around the nipples (representing crocodile eyes), with lines down to the crocodile's 'mark' on his stomach.

During the evening when I went outside to check Horse's whereabouts I found two elderly clansmen looking at him. They said that they had heard about the horse and had come to see him with their own eyes. After returning indoors I mentioned the incident to the headmaster and he replied that stories about Horse and 'Horse Lady' had spread far and wide. He said that in our own way we were becoming part of the country's history, and that our travels would become a legend.

The next morning started misty. A small energetic troupe escorted me from the school for a while along the narrow road.

It rained all afternoon and Horse and I got drenched as we rode over a mountain pass into a wide bowl of marshland. We followed the marsh shoreline then went up to another mountain pass. A watery sun began shining, and from somewhere in the distance we heard singing. As it grew louder Horse started sidling and prancing with excitement. A few bends later we arrived at a village where everyone was helping to build two new *long-hauses* (like the *long-hauses* I had seen around Mendi). Everyone was working; the sound of men busily chopping came from the forest; rows of young men were beside the forest cutting *kunai* grass for thatch; a group of women were sitting weaving walls and mats of mountain-bamboo, and everyone was singing a traditional chant which went back and forth between them all. A friendly argument sprang up over what kind of animal I was riding. Most women agreed that it was a bull, until a young man arrogantly declared that it was a horse.

One of the village elders explained to me that *long-hauses* have a seven-year existence. After they are built they are not used for the first year. In their second year they are used for a *pig-kill*; in year three they host a small *sing-sing (sing-sing nuting)*; year four, the lining-up of pigs; year five, a big *sing-sing*; year six they lie fallow; and in year seven they host an immense *pig-kill* at which the *long-hauses* are burned to the ground.

Building then starts again, and as we could hear in the nearby village, the cycle would move forward. It was like a calendar, marking events and giving people some frame of reference for time.

I loved listening to the old men of the villages and felt honoured that they gave me their time and shared their folklore

129

and history with me. Yet it also gave me a problem: the information that they gave me was not necessarily correct and not being an anthropologist I could not judge its accuracy. I also had to bear in mind that people often said 'yes' to a question when either they hadn't understood it or they thought it was polite to agree with me. Sometimes I found that the information differed from, or wasn't mentioned in books and publications, but I don't think that meant it was automatically wrong. All I could do was to try to check it as much as I could, but doubtless there were times when I misunderstood what they said or got things in the wrong order.

From that happy, welcoming village we went down into another huge marsh-basin ringed with mountains, and with lakes dotting the flat expanse of feathery *kunai* grass. Flocks of wild geese by the water were alarmed at the hoof-beats and they took flight. Gusts of rain, cold at this height, swept across the exposed land causing me to shiver in my anorak. A few cold wet hours later, spent along the shoreline of the lake, took us across the marshes on a man-made causeway. It was a long heaped line of rocks, with bridges running over flows of water. Because the first bridge looked alright I didn't check it out and Horse got a hoof trapped in one of the gaps and had to pull himself out. I ran clear as he leapt for safe land, but I swore at myself for allowing the episode to happen.

My heart sank as I examined the next bridge on the causeway. It was impassable to Horse unless I could find twelve stout pieces of wood; and the area was treeless. Swimming was out, and Horse naturally refused to return to the last bridge. It seemed we couldn't go forwards or backwards. Icy rain had been pouring down for some time and I was freezing cold. Cold dribbles of water had started running down my neck and I didn't know what to do. Stuck on a causeway in pissing rain, soaked to the skin, hands and feet numb with cold, I was tired and despairing. I shivered as hard as possible to try to get warm, and wished we were somewhere else.

It took me a frozen half-hour to pull myself together and slither down the bank into the mud and reeds to where a piece of wood stuck out. I pulled at it but it was held fast in the mud, so instead I rocked it until it came fractionally loose. Stepping deep into the

130

water to get better leverage on it, I had a pleasant surprise — the water was much warmer than the air outside. It wasn't enough to thaw my numb fingers though and they kept sliding off the wood. Finally I stood triumphant with one piece of wood and carefully slotted it into the first of the twelve spaces. One down, eleven to go. After six pieces of wood I couldn't find any more. It was late afternoon, the rain wasn't easing up and now it mixed with the tears running down my face. Again I searched for wood. In the warm oozing mud I found some old posts. I don't know how long it took to make that bridge good, but it felt like an eternity.

We reached the third bridge and I looked at it bitterly, it was in a worse condition and longer than the two before and the wood I had brought from the second bridge was not nearly enough. In the dark rainy evening, I felt drained and despondent. I looked around desperately for alternatives and noticed the mudflats by the causeway were drier than they had been before so I went down for a better look. Horse would be flank-deep but he should manage to wade across. It was a messy crossing but successful.

Our trial was over. We walked on in the dark until thankfully, we reached an Apostolic church mission near Kandep.

The mission was run by a kindly Australian couple who gave me warmth and comfort, a hot meal and a soft bed. They said that a few months previously the causeway had been under five feet of water.

Missionaries in Papua New Guinea were a mixed bunch, and although all the ones that I had met so far were sympathetic, considerate people, I had heard some very odd rumours about some of their works and teachings. (A report written about the misdeeds of missions was so libellous that it wasn't published in Papua New Guinea.) Many of the problems seemed to be caused by extremists and do-gooders who had plenty of religious zeal but little empathy with the people. The organisation that seemed to come in for the most constant criticism was the Asian-Pacific Christian Mission whose missionaries apparently felt that it was their duty to tell the people that their ways were barbaric, and that their traditional belief systems were devil-worship. They discouraged the lowland tribes from carving statues, saying that they were worshipping false idols, and that carving made them 'forget God'. Dancing was banned — especially sexual dances —

131

since it was considered incompatible with Christian life. They taught people to be ashamed of their traditions, their culture, and their nakedness. I met one young girl who told me 'You can see I'm a Christian because I'm wearing Christian clothes'. She had abandoned her traditional clean grass skirt for a ragged, torn, and dirty European dress.

At breakfast the Grants with whom I was staying, mentioned that the Mendi Valley Rodeo was about to take place; it seemed odd to find a rodeo in Papua New Guinea where there were so few horses. It was an annual occasion, the big event being the Great Cross-Country Race, with prize money of 200 *kina* (£150). When I asked what kind of people took part they said any kind from ranchers and cowboys to Catholic missionaries. I had never taken part in a rodeo, but considering how fit Horse had become in nearly two months of travelling, it occurred to me that he might be as fast and surefooted as the best. One of the events that also tempted me was the Bronco-bucking competition.

We had been heading north toward Laiagam and Wabag; but Mendi lay not very far to the south-east of us and since the rodeo was taking place in about a week, I decided to head for there instead.

Despite the trials of the causeway the previous day, I set off the next morning feeling great. It was sunny and even the biting, cold wind couldn't get us down. I looked down at the map and saw the contour lines representing the mountains and looked up to see them printed a quarter-million times enlarged in the terrain around me. I saw myself as a moving dot in this landscape of white limestone, craggy cliffs and circular marsh-bowls, while close by me were clumps of beech trees with young red leaves, *pitpit* grass with its maroon feathery plumes and masses of wild lupins with their pretty purple and white flowers. The track was clay, its geology showing in its colours — of sienna to pink, of brick red to orange and yellow — which told me about the heat and volcanic activity in milenniums past. We cantered for a while then Horse stopped to graze clover.

As I thought about the mountains I felt a sense of completeness, and it occurred to me that my journey with Horse might not last very much longer. I was beginning to feel restless for new experiences.

It was early afternoon when I decided to stop for the day. We grew tired quickly in high altitudes (we were about 8,000ft (2,500m) up), and Horse needed plenty of rest to make him fit for the cross-country race that I had decided to enter. Our stopover was at a small community school. The headmaster was out fishing, but when he came back, I didn't take to him at all. He was a shifty-looking Enga, who I doubted had done a day's work for months. He lent me an empty hut which belonged to a teacher who hadn't bothered to turn up for the school-term.

The thatched hut became home for an evening. It had a fireplace and sawn-off oil drum as a stove, and a school desk and chair. Outside the open door was the marsh-bowl, a lake, and Horse. I pulled the desk outside into the shade of a big tree garlanded with passion-fruit vines in flower, and caught up with writing my diary. For some reason I felt wonderfully content.

Morning assembly for the school children (or *skul munkies* as they were called) was held beside the flagpole in front of the thatched classrooms. The assembly comprised a small straggly group of thin dark-skinned boys wearing a collection of leaves and loin cloths, singing what must have been the national anthem. Bursts of song, with staccato endings, echoed out over the lake marshland. After they completed some rather ragged-looking marching exercises, I left them and went to the nearby village market to buy *kaukau*.

It was a mistake to take Horse into the market area. All those little piles of fresh *kaukau* tubers spread neatly on the ground, were too much for him and he simply went berserk, leaping forward scattering them left and right, and taking bites out of as many as he could. People shrieked and ran to hide. When calm was restored I bought all the damaged *kaukau* and some extra as well. I was happy to buy plenty since if Horse was going to enter that race he would need to build up his strength. Probably the other horses would have been fed with oats.

Occasionally we met Engas on the road; the men were bearded and wore *kina* shells round their necks, while their stocky brown bodies were clothed with wide bark belts with front-flaps and bunches of *cordyline* leaves; the women's faces were tattooed in patterns of lines and dots on their noses and foreheads. There was one word they kept saying in their excitement when they saw us approach; the word was *tua*. I had heard it so many times that

I asked its meaning: they translated it as 'She is' or 'She comes'.

A pass of 10,000ft (3,000m) lay ahead and we went slowly up into the tall range of mountains which marked the border between the Enga and Mendi clans (and was also the border between Papua and New Guinea). Sometimes we paused to rest, and from one rest-spot I saw some rapid movement in a distant valley. The wind was blowing the wrong way for me to hear what the noise was all about so I back-tracked to take a look. As I approached I could hear shouting, chanting, yelping and occasional battle cries though I still couldn't see anything. After looping up round a hill we emerged on a spur of land overlooking the valley, and there before me I saw an astonishing sight.

A tribal bow and arrow fight was in progress; two groups of men were gathered at opposite ends of a valley and in the middle was a melée of running figures with bows and arrows. There seemed to be an invisible skirmish line between them to which the warriors ran to call insults at each other and let loose a few arrows. Their marksmanship looked poor and I saw no one get badly hurt though one man got an arrow in his buttock as he was running away. By now I had identified the two tribes as Engas and Mendies. The Mendies were closer to me and could be recognised by their face-paint which comprised wide white or yellow bands of colour painted round their eyes like masks. Their opponents must have been Engas because although they were too far away to see clearly, we were in Enga territory. But it was sunny and the action was a mass of darting figures who charged forward in small groups from each end of the valley yelping with excitement, and jumping from side to side as they prepared to fire. I watched some Mendi warriors as they fired and noticed that they didn't even stay long enough at the skirmish-line to take aim before firing, they just loosed an arrow and retreated. After firing several arrows they went running back to the valley's end and rejoined the noisy knot of comrades who stood well out of arrow-range.

Loud whoopings, shrieks and the shouting of insults were followed by an extra insult as some Enga warriors ran into the skirmish area then turned and slapped their buttocks at the Mendi clan. More Enga warriors ran forward and fired a volley of arrows which fell short of their enemy.

Suddenly it began to rain. Warfare was abandoned; no one

wanted to get their plumage wet. Taking off their *bilas* they hurried home to their villages — the fight would be resumed another time. I don't know how long the fight had lasted since I had arrived after it had begun but I had been watching for about half an hour. It had been an exciting sight and I was pleased that I had had the good fortune to watch it going on.

Tribal fighting is not uncommon in the highlands, it is a custom and it has formal rules rather like a sport. It is seldom that people get killed. Fights happened because pigs were stolen from another clan, because of murder, or accidental killing, or for payback. Before a battle, a council of war is formed (comprising elders and leaders, and excluding the headman who is responsible to the government, which rules that fighting and warfare are illegal), to decide the time and place of battle. The battle is not started until both sides are ready. In a recent large outburst of Enga tribal squabbling the government had intervened with helicopters and tear gas, but the warriors claimed that they had kept the helicopters away by shooting arrows at them.

The bigger the fight, the more *bilas* and decorations the warriors wear. The one I saw was obviously only a small fight since their decoration was fairly subdued.

Their arrows would be of the war-type, not the same as those used out hunting, and I remembered how Kom on my long walk had explained the different uses of his individual arrows. The Enga war-arrows are said to be tipped either with bone from women's vertebra, or 'magic' bones from ancestors; while the Mendi war-arrows are tipped with bone from the forearm of male ancestors, so that the ancestors can guide the arrows and kill the enemy. Their bows are made of strong blackpalm.

After a fight with killing there is a victory dance for the winners, while the losers go off to mourn their dead. Payback would then be due to avenge the killing; a life for a life.

It didn't seem strange to me, I felt at one with the country and accepted the warfare as a tribal custom; it was not any stranger than their other customs, and in fact it had less impact on me than my daily interactions with warrior-farmers in their home villages.

The rain had already soaked me so there was no point in sheltering and I carried on riding to the 10,000-ft (3,000-m) pass.

135

It rained solidly for two days during which time we continued to have problems crossing the numerous streams and had to resort to wading most of them. It was a cold, wet, dispiriting time.

Somewhere near Mendi we took the wrong road. I didn't discover the mistake until some villagers told me *'Mendi behind-im yu'*. We began by re-tracing our steps but got caught behind a slow-moving procession of highlanders carrying ten pigs, which were slung upside down from poles carried between pairs of men. Some other men were carrying leaf-wrapped packages; they were *bilassed* and occasionally they burst into spontaneous dancing along the track. The track was too narrow to be able to pass so I asked them where they were going; they were on their way to a wedding and the pigs and packages were an instalment of the *bride-price*.

I dismounted and walked to stretch my legs, and got into conversation with the bridegroom's brother. He carried a moneypole, embellished with a hundred *kina* (£75), but he said that it wasn't worth as much as a pig since money didn't last so long. I asked about the price of an average wife and he replied that it was between twenty to thirty pigs — though recently a government official had paid seven new Toyota trucks.

Whatever the price, he explained, it was usually more than a man could afford. This forced him to borrow heavily from his friends and relations, which was good because it increased his ties and knitted him solidly into his clan. *Bride-price* also made the bride's family help and encourage the bride to become a good wife, since if she was sent back the *bride-price* would have to be repaid.

Our procession reached its village destination with Horse and me still caught up in its midst. I watched as they put the *bride-price* out on display and it was inspected, and finally accepted by the bride's family. The leaf-wrapped packages each contained a *kina* shell that had been rubbed with red ochre, which I was told was the correct way to present a *kina* shell. With the acceptance of the *bride-price*, the marriage was sealed; there was no religious ceremony. Pigs were slaughtered for the wedding feast, and much of the meat was put to cook in the ground-oven, lined with hot stones and charcoal. Sweet potato, red *pandanus* fruit and edible ferns were piled on top, and the pit was sealed with banana leaves and earth. Meantime the young men and women had donned more decoration and begun dancing. They danced in separate male and female groups. I watched the women as they swayed with the drumbeat, slowly bending sideways and rocking on their heels until they had turned to face the opposite way. Their faces were painted with dramatic white stripes, and hanging above their bare breasts were pearly *kina*-shell pendants and reams of bead necklaces. The bride, was standing to one side. Her skin shone black with a mixture of tisago tree oil and charcoal from the fire, and she wore a short bridal skirt (also oiled and blackened), and a black headshawl of bush-fibre.

Since neither of us was dancing I wandered over to say hello. She was a shy girl, but she told me that she had just spent a month living with her mother-in-law and getting to know her new relations. The dancing gained momentum; the men were moving fast, and singing rude songs to the young women, who shouted back some suggestive comments. The women had linked arms and were jumping up and down, their chanting rising to crescendoes.

The arranged marriage, the idea of which is greeted with some horror in our western society, seemed to make sense here where the society is less mobile and where generations of families have lived together in close proximity for years. Marriage to them is more of a social contract that takes into account wealth and status and the needs of the family in the wider sense. There is less emphasis on physical attraction and it is considered important that a wife is able to work strongly and to bear children.

The duties of a wife do not generally include cooking or bed-making. Men don't usually allow women to cook for them because they believe that women are unwholesome, and that contact with women is dangerous to male strength and health. A bridegroom was expected to protect himself from his wife by using magic spells to ensure his safety during sex; it was also believed that loss of semen made a man weak. It seemed like a simple way to avoid over-population. I had also read that there was a taboo on sex while a man was making a tool or weapon; they believed it would be weak and easily broken. Part of the reason for all this was belief that women control the evil *sanguma*, and that they are therefore to be feared.

137

However among the young men and women this was not apparent as they continued to dance on into the evening. Some women asked me if I was married and when I said no they said *'Ah, mi sori'* and made clucking noises of sympathy. I tried to explain that I simply wasn't ready yet to be married and that unlike their girls who married in their teenage years, my people often married later. Personally I have nothing against the idea of marriage, but I am aware that if I had married earlier I would probably never have made either the African or this trip; it left me realising how happy I felt in my travels.

The bridal couple didn't join in until late in the evening, and then they led everyone to a hut to dance the courting ritual which was known as *turnim head*. The hut was dark and smoky and lit only by a small fire. Unmarried men sat cross-legged in a row on the floor, and sang romantic songs in nasal tones to call the young women to them. The women came in and knelt opposite the male of their choice. Pivoting gracefully on their knees they rubbed noses with the men, and turning cheek to cheek they rolled their faces together, crooning. They swayed backwards and forwards repeating the performance, alternating between the two men diagonally opposite. Some of the girls had flowers fringing their faces; others had put fragrant leaves in their ears which blended with the smell of cheap perfume; while their face paints were reputedly mixed with love-magic. Only unmarrieds could take part in the *turnim head*. Sometimes they would stop for a break, and then some of the dancers would leave to make room for new people to continue the dance through the evening.

When they were finally exhausted the men and women separated and retired to sleep in their respective huts. In another hut I lay dozing in my hammock contemplating other weddings I had been to, from the magnificent to the lowly, and, as lowly went, pigs included, I felt today's wedding had been one of the best.

13
The Mendi Rodeo

We reached Mendi the following day. Horse recognised the town and without needing guidance he went straight to Heather's house, and parked himself in his favourite spot outside the back door. Heather gave us a lovely welcome and insisted that we spent the two days before the rodeo with her so that we could rest, and get ourselves cleaned up. The children helped me to bathe and groom Horse, and beneath the mud, his white coat shone with health and vigour. A cut on Horse's fetlock was not too serious so I just cleaned it up and put ointment on it; it didn't seem to hurt him at all. I also had some minor cuts and grazes which I attended to but my main worry was the rain; it had now been raining for a week, and because the cross-country course was likely to be a mud-bath I began to have second thoughts about taking part.

But there was a more important problem to think about first. When my visa had been about to expire I had sent my passport to Immigration in Port Moresby for extension, asking them to post it back to Mendi Post Office. The passport should have been waiting for me the last time I was there, and the fact that it was not here this time meant that something had gone wrong. I made enquiries by telephone to the Immigration Office, and from what they didn't say, I gathered that my passport was lost somewhere in the system. The problem wasn't the type that I could ignore; it was a serious offence to be in Papua New Guinea without a valid visa.

All this boiled down to the fact that I would have to go to Port Moresby. It would take months to get there on horseback, and it would certainly be too far bearing in mind that I had to end up with Horse at Kagua to give him to Father Albert. To travel a long way with Horse just to do an errand is quite a different matter from travel for its own sake. Horse could have been left on a ranch somewhere until I came back, but I knew that was not how things would turn out. Over the years I had come to understand that things didn't happen that way, especially when travelling and that it was better to be free of ties so that if something interesting happened I could explore it and not be held back. I also disliked going backwards I always liked to go forwards to new territory and new experiences and so the decision was made: the day of the rodeo would be my last day with Horse.

The day of the rodeo arrived and it was *still* raining. Early in the morning I saddled Horse and rode out five miles to Oiarip Agricultural station, where the rodeo was to be held.

Corrals had been set up near some buildings and a bunch of wild horses was herded into one of them. The main corral was ringed by a crowd of people and along its top bar nine feet high sat many more, most with brightly-coloured umbrellas. Adjoining corrals contained cattle and some very large bulls, which were divided by the fence which led the animals into a line of buck-shutes. The steer-riding contest had just started.

Cowboys both black and white worked at organising the buck-shutes, and as the rodeo progressed I saw that its competitors varied in Papua New Guinea's own inimical style: there were coffee-plantation bosses and workers, cowboys, ranchers, some seasoned rodeo-riders, Catholic mission folk, VSA and peace corps people and me. I was the only female participant and had entered myself not only for the cross-country race but a bronco-bucking event as well. Despite the rain the atmosphere was noisy and festive.

A variety of horses were tethered to posts and rails so I led Horse into a wide grassy space to avoid any trouble — I wasn't sure if it was wise to bring a stallion to a social event. He snorted and stamped a bit, but mostly he just stood staring goggle-eyed at the other horses; he hadn't seen another horse since he had fought the stallion.

None of the steer-riders managed to stay on for long. An Australian cowboy and a lay-missionary made the best attempts, though with the latter the steer fell and broke a leg. I watched them intently and tried to pick up tips for later.

The next event was the flag race; horses and riders galloped back and forth across the arena retrieving flags, skilfully making quick turns with agility and speed. Several of these horses would be in the big race, and had probably been fed on oats for weeks. I began to have butterflies.

While the bending races were going on I went to inspect the cross-country course. It was certainly cross-country; it ran up and down hills, through tall tussocky grass that hid pot-holes, over ditches, patches of bog and boggy streams. The rain had turned the ground into a mud bath, but people I spoke to said it wasn't too bad. I thought that they should know best.

When I returned, the archery competition was in progress. I remembered the Engas I had seen fighting, and how their arrows had missed or fallen short, and I was intrigued to know if they shot more accurately at a target than at each other. Only about six arrows hit the target.

Another local event was the wood chopping contest, and here there was no messing around as sturdy highlanders with hard-muscled shoulders wielded their axes with devastating swiftness. Some men had decorated themselves with ochre and feathers in their hair, and everyone entered into the spirit of the competition.

Then the loudspeaker announced the big event, the Great Cross-Country Horse Race, and I found myself with fourteen others cantering towards the start. The start was on the crest of a hill. We lined up, and the starter called 'Ready, Steady, Go.'

The horses surged forwards in a straggly bunch and thundered away over the boggy hills. Mud splattered everywhere. I wasn't doing too badly until I dropped back to steady Horse to approach a slippery, angled bank. The leading horse reached the bank, and fell, causing the horse directly behind to fall over him and somersault awkwardly. I heard the crunch of his neck breaking under the impact. Within seconds another horse had crashed as well so I swung Horse off the course to circle until a way was clear for us to get back into the race.

We galloped up the next hill, overtaking a horse on the way, rounded a curve and went down an appalling slope of tussocky grass with treacherous pot-holes and crumbly ledges that dropped into pockets of bog. Neck and neck with another horse we hurtled downhill towards a muddy stream, and saw four horses floundering shoulder-deep in the muddy track. We approached them at a gallop. I could feel Horse hesitating, uncertain whether or not to run over them, so I swerved to look for another place to cross. The rider beside us had no such qualms — he rode his horse straight across the backs of the mud-sunken horses, but he missed his footing on the bank and fell into the mud. There was no point in my stopping to help, I wasn't strong enough, so I did the next best thing and rode for the finish to get help and ropes sent.

Rain was still lashing down. We took a run at the stream, only to land saddle-deep in the mud on the far side. Thrashing frantically and sinking with every step, I wondered if I should get off and try to pull him out. Suddenly Horse found a firm foothold, hauled himself out, and we were again galloping in bounding leaps across the rugged hills. Horse was surprisingly responsive as we jumped a gully, ploughed through more marsh, and raced into the final straight. I could see more pockets of bog across the straight but we splattered our way through them without difficulty to reach the finishing line.

I don't think that more than a handful of horses finished the race; we were fourth or fifth. There was no jubilation at the finishing line, just a worried crowd of people pressing for news of fallers.

The sadness at the news of the dead horse was shared by everyone at the rodeo. It could have happened to any of the competitors and we were sorry.

However, the atmosphere was soon lightened by the greased pig event and the dog race which followed it. Only three dogs finished the race; the rest ran in circles and started fighting with each other. More horse events were followed by a lively tug-of-war in the mud and rain. Then came the bull ride.

Bulls stood mean-eyed and menacing behind the bars of the buck-shutes. A rope round the girth was all each cowboy had to hold onto and I watched as each in turn lowered himself onto a bull's back, twisted the rope tight, and raised his other arm high to signal he was ready. As the shute opened the bulls bellowed with rage and charged out into the corral, heads low, bucking furiously. I watched how the riders tried to use the grip of their knees as a pivot for their body, and how they left their feet swinging free to balance them. I felt another flurry of butterflies when I overheard that the bronco-bucking would be even fiercer.

The sound of roaring and stamping filled the air. One particularly large bull, a humped Brahmin, threw his rider and then charged at the rails. Despite the barricade the crowd shrank back, and as the bull trotted round the corral, snorting and shaking his heavy horns, the crowd peeled back from the rails in a wave of perfect synchronisation.

A small band of wild horses waited restlessly in a side corral, and when the bull-ride was over, they were herded, with some difficulty, through the gate into the buck-shutes. For the bronco-bucking, the rodeo committee decided that stock-saddles could be used, though of course it was forbidden to hold onto the saddle. I was told to hold the halter rope in one hand, leaving the other hand free. The qualifying time would be eight seconds. My name was near the bottom of the list, so I had plenty of time to study tactics and feel nervous. The horses were brumby stallions and unbroken colts; some of them didn't buck immediately but it was pointless to wish for that, since the stopwatch only recorded the time when the horse was bucking. My name was called; I had been allocated a fiery-looking chestnut stallion.

I felt composed as I climbed over the shute rails and held myself poised above his back while someone tightened the cinch. I noticed how every muscle in the stallion's back was tense with anger. Lowering myself gently I settled deep and firm into the saddle, my feet seeking the stirrups and taking care not to touch the horse's sides lest he leap into action too soon. Taking hold of the halter rope, I signalled with my free hand that I was ready.

The shute-gate rattled open, the stallion hesitated for a second, then he sprang out into the arena. Suddenly it was real, he was bucking like crazy, the jerking jack-knifing of his movements jarring and wrenching my body in every direction at once. A sharp twisting thrust nearly dislodged me, and I doubled the grip of my knees as I tried to remember what I had just learnt. In the whirling confusion of my mind I noticed that I hadn't yet fallen off, and I felt strangely relaxed. Only a few seconds could have passed; mud was spraying up from his savage plunging hooves, and through it the crowd was a vague roaring blur.

Then inevitably I lost my balance and, knowing I was about to fall, I kicked my feet out of the stirrups and let go. I felt a flying sensation, and landed unhurt in deep mud. People said I was laughing as I staggered from the arena.

I won third prize and certainly I was laughing when I went to receive the ribbon and prize. The crowd was cheering wildly, roaring applause; an unforgettable moment.

What a rodeo.

But my happiness was short-lived — the end of the rodeo spelt the end of my adventures with Horse; my loyal companion with whom I had been through so much. I had seen Father Albert at the rodeo and arranged to meet him at the end. Now we stood side by side looking at Horse — he reluctant to take Horse from me and me dreading the moment when he would be loaded onto the cattle truck and driven away. Father Albert tried to console me by describing his farm and the cattle and goats and herd of mares that would be Horse's new companions. But he could see that he was only making me sad and gently led him away to his truck. I noticed all the fresh mud on Horse's coat and the movement of his long white tail as he flicked away some flies. My eyes stang with tears as I watched Horse disappear out of my life. But I didn't cry until later that evening when in my pocket I discovered the last remaining *kaukau* which I had forgotten to give him as a goodbye present.

14
Transitions

The band which played at the Rodeo Ball offered me space in their bus going to Goroka, which was in the right direction for Port Moresby. Another good reason for going to Goroka was because the Highland Show, an annual gathering of clans, was due to be held there the following weekend. The musicians were good company and the long journey east on the Highlands Highway passed pleasantly. But inside me was a feeling of loss, of being parted from Horse, my friends and a region which I had enjoyed. Going from the familiar into a new unknown made me a little apprehensive. Goroka was only a small town, but for me towns were more daunting than the jungle. Fortunately I had one contact there, a friend of an acquaintance, with whom I went to stay.

He was called Bruce. He had a dog called Bruce, and a horse called Bruce. Bruce the horse had recently strained a tendon while playing polo-crosse, so he had been replaced by another horse, also called Bruce. Bruce took me to watch one of the polo-crosse tournaments, and I could see why the horse had been injured. The game was possibly the most violent that I had ever seen; the riders used the horses much like fairground bumper-cars and showed no respect for their animals at all. They tackled each other at full gallop, they thwacked each other's horses in the face with their crosse-sticks, and even when they fell they still hit out seemingly trying to disable the opposing team.

At the previous tournament there had apparently been more casualties than people left unscathed: one person broke his neck, several had broken arms, others had head injuries resulting from head-first dives into goalposts, three people were bitten by a bad-tempered horse and another was kicked by one. It was all part of the game.

None of the riders I met ever rode up into the lofty mountains which lay along three sides of the horizon — they didn't ride outside the club's grounds because it was considered too dangerous. I said nothing; I was just a listener. Most of the riders were expatriates who worked on coffee-plantations and other local concerns. I recalled it being said that the expatriate population of Papua New Guinea is made up of three types: missionaries, mercenaries and misfits. The term mercenaries isn't used in the military sense but means being there only for financial reasons (salaries are high). Misfits, yes, many of us were misfits. For myself, I missed being out in the mountains and I felt lost without Horse. Later that evening, on the radio, I heard the sad news of a plane crashing into a mountain in the Tari Gap killing all six passengers on board. One of them was the newly-elected premier of the Southern Highlands Parliament for whom there would be a year of mourning before a new premier could be elected. The second news item was that a member of a search party for the crashed plane had been killed when she had got out of her plane to wipe the windshield and walked into the propellor. When they gave out her name a chill went down my spine — she was a friend of us all in Goroka.

I had to shake myself out of a depression.

My visit to Goroka coincided with the Highland Show, an annual gathering of many highland clans which had begun in the 1950s as a means of bringing the people together on a festive occasion to promote goodwill between them and try to discourage fighting. The show was always a success, and attracted up to 40,000 clansmen.

I spent two days at the show, mingling with crowds of warriors and watching the arena events. In all, I met people from about thirty different clans: those from Watabung had bold, heavy features with thick beards and wore animal skins; from Oumba-Kana came men with blackened bodies, and headbands of white feathers; from Bena came proud robust girls lavishly decorated with shells, fur and beads; while another group of oiled and blackened men wore black leaves, with clay fire-bowls on top of their heads sprouting tall flames that made a dramatic and startling picture. A third black-bodied group came from Lufa and wore wreaths of plants on their heads and carried black spears. They gave a demonstration of their fighting-dance later in the day, jabbing the spears aggressively into the ground and yelling taunts and insults at other clans, until they pushed their luck too far and an actual fight broke out!

Witch-doctors stood aloof and were easily recognisable in their sinister capes of black feathers and necklaces of teeth. Occasionally pairs of men played bamboo flutes together. The flutes were up to a metre long, decorated with burnt geometric designs, and were held to the side like flutes, but with one hand placed over the end to alter the sound. Several people recognised me from a picture that had appeared on the front page of the national newspaper, of Horse and myself at the rodeo. I heard Horse Lady whispered many times in the crowd; expatriates and New Guinea nationals waved and called greetings.

When the Kukukuku warriors arrived all the clans shrank back in fear. They are the most notorious killers in the highlands and are noted for their homicidal customs. They are said to smoke-preserve dead bodies in a cane basket held up on a pole, sometimes in a line of baskets against a cave or cliff wall near Aseki. On occasions, some Kukukuku wear necklaces of human finger bones. These warriors wore cloaks of bark (pounded soft with stones), and they carried stone war clubs. Their home lay to the south and was almost completely isolated by its ruggedness. In 1970 during friction between clans there was evidence of mass slaughter and cannibalism.

The most well-known group at the show was probably the Mudmen of Asaro (they had performed in London!). They are proud assertive war-like people who because of their dense population often have land disputes. Their balloon-shaped headmasks of clay were reputed to have originated many years ago just after the village of Asaro had lost badly in a battle, and the warriors needed a new tactic for their payback attack. They made some large bulbous masks of clay and coated themselves in the same grey clay. When the enemy clan saw these apparitions, they thought the mudmen were ghosts and they ran away in terror. Some Asaro head-masks had long-stalked ears, or were globe-shaped with peaked foreheads, and decorated mouths. They looked as if they belonged in a science fiction movie.

I rested beside a group of Wabags where one of the men was mending his wig, using a small twirling-stick to tease the hair back into position. Long bone spatulae protruded upwards from both sides of the wig to which he pinned two broadleaves that reminded me of ears.

There were no Huli wigmen from Tari because the highway was still closed. A man from Nipa told me that the Scottish road-engineer I had met had been beaten-up by some Hulies. They had tried to get through the muddy section to go to the funeral of their premier (the one who had died in the plane crash), and when their vehicle became bogged down in the mud, and the engineer had refused to allow the Caterpillar to pull it free, they had attacked him. Since he seemed to be universally disliked, perhaps this was natural justice.

Despite the absence of the colourful Hulies there was evidence of much face-painting, and some elaborate body-painting. Two men I met were painting each other in patterns of snowflakes; using a split-splayed twig, dipped in ochre, to stamp each snowflake on the skin. Other men's bodies were covered in white-ochre and striped with brown wavy lines of parallel finger-trails; another distinctive group was coloured in halves, lengthwise in black and tan.

Resting, I sat and watched the colourful tribes go by, wearing head-dresses of feathers, wigs of various types, headbands, *kina* shells, hornbill beaks, masks of *pandanus* trunk covered in green moss, or primitive black wood masks. Included in several head-dresses were modern effects like beer bottle tops, red paper, pictures and shiny tin foil; the edges of the wig were trimmed with cotton wool or Christmas tinsel. Highlanders were like magpies in the way they collected shiny things.

Axes, tomahawks, spears, bows and arrows, clubs, and cassowary-bone daggers were carried by the men. The air smelt of rancid pig-grease. Hagens and Mendies were chanting and yelping. Frog-people wallowed in muddy puddles left by the rain. Young women were decorated to the maximum and their naked chests gleamed with oil. Dances were thrusting, swaying, circular, stomping. Display was the order of the show.

Inside the arena the groups played their music and danced to the crowds in the grandstand. Outside the arena they stayed with their village friends, milling around or resting in groups on the grass. A group of Henganofi on their way to the arena parted the crowd as they trotted through. Six men abreast headed the column with hundreds of pale Job's Tears covering their heads, faces, shoulders and bodies. The crowd (myself included) flowed into the space behind them. Suddenly the column turned and began trotting back at us forcing us to get out of their way. Their eyes glinted behind the pale seeds as they trotted back and forth, prancing in excitement and warming up for their dance-routine.

There were some superb displays of dancing in the arena but somehow they seemed less real than those backstage. Two days of display between clans vying with each other for acclaim was quite a spectacle and by the end I felt totally satiated by the sights and sounds — the music, the chanting, the colours and the dancing — that I had seen and experienced.

Goroka was not very far from Mt Wilhelm, the tallest mountain in Papua New Guinea at 15,000ft (4,500m), which I thought would be fun to climb even though it was quite a few miles in the wrong direction. A road went most of the way, so setting off with my backpack, I walked along hitching as I went. One ride took me to Asaro, the village renowned for its mud masks, where I was approached by the village fool who was dressed for *sing-sing* and painted in thick yellow ochre. The villagers helped me by calling him away. Lunatics were not outcasts, and were usually looked after by their home-village.

A Land-Rover carrying the government's Minister of the Media gave me my next lift and took me to a small village that marked the turning to Mt Wilhelm. A *pig-kill* had just taken place and while I waited for another lift I watched the now-familiar sight of people leaving with pieces of raw pig wrapped untidily in leaves. Finally an open-backed truck came along and stopped for me. I rode in the back, sitting perched on my backpack and clinging onto the truck for dear life as we bounced along on the rough dirt road and skidded around hairpin bends. At times the edge of the road fell away into sheer cliffs down to the gorges and ravines a thousand feet below. Slab-sided escarpments showed how the earth's crust had been broken and forced upwards. Although the journey was uncomfortable I was at least being rewarded by some of the most dramatic scenery I had seen so far.

We passed huts and garden settlements perched on mountain shoulders with their *kaukau* gardens cultivated on the slopes at

70° angles. The truck was a sort of bus service; it stopped to unload and load people and cargo, innumerable times at these remote dwellings. At one, we stopped for half an hour while the driver off-loaded a parcel of sacks, a chicken and some oil-drums full of kerosene, and took on some full sacks of dried coffee beans (grown locally as a cash crop). I got out to stretch my legs and take a closer look at one of the huts. It was square and its walls were of two-tone woven bamboo; the rooftop had a row of spikes along the ridge.

The passengers re-boarded the truck and it drove on along the road. Sitting in the back I was among some colourfully dressed women who chattered gaily in *ples-tok* (place-talk, which here was the Simbu language). But they told me in pidgin that I should get out at Kegusugal, the highest village on Mt Wilhelm after which the road descended and continued to link up some other outlying coffee-growing hamlets. It took three hours for the truck to reach Kegusugal but I had enjoyed the ride and was sad when it was my turn to get out.

It was too late in the day to start walking up the mountain trail so I decided to stay overnight in the village and set out in the morning. A smiling woman named Maria invited me to stay at her hut.

Early the next morning I set off to start the climb up Mt Wilhelm, taking the path from the village to the airstrip which, at 8,000ft (2,450m) was the highest airfield in Papua New Guinea. As I climbed into muddy moss-forest I felt weak from the altitude (it took me at least a day to acclimatise), and sometimes my legs buckled under me. After four hours the path led out of the forest into alpine grasslands and then up into the lower glacial valley. Walking through a spacious forest of fern trees, I looked up through the scroll-shaped branches to see lacy leaves making patterns against the deep blue sky.

To get out of the valley I climbed up beside a waterfall, and entered into another glacial valley. There was a lake in the valley and an island in the lake. The island had stunted, crooked trees that made angular silhouettes. I passed two climber's huts (both unoccupied) but I wasn't ready to stop and instead continued up beside another waterfall into the top glacial valley.

I stopped to camp by a lake at what must have been about 13,000ft (4,000m), and it was freezing cold. It was difficult to find firewood, because there were no big trees up this high, and the bits of dead wood which I found were rather damp. However I had matches, and was by now skilled at making fires out of damp wood having had plenty of practice over the past months, and soon the fire was burning well, using its own heat to dry out the dampness. After supper I banked up the fire and settled down to sleep on the warm ground beside the hot embers. My plastic rainsheet formed a good windbreak to shelter me from the icy wind. Long before dawn I woke up shivering and reached out to re-stoke the fire. When flames appeared I put a pan of water on for coffee which took an age to boil and even then was only warm because of the high altitude. After a rather unsatisfying luke-warm cup of coffee I packed up camp and hid my gear so that I could climb the summit without having to carry my backpack. As dawn came over the peaks I watched the lakes below reflect the changing sky, as it turned from grey to pinks and yellows. It was idyllically peaceful but bitterly cold.

I rambled back down to my camp and sat resting there. The lake water was now a deep turquoise, its still surface mirroring the rugged mountains that surrounded it. The sense of aloneness (not loneliness) was total and in my diary I see that I wrote 'Why does someone sit alone on a mountain top and hold council with the rocks and clouds rather than with people: What storms would I catch if I cast my nets? And what misty dreams do I hunt in the skies. Maybe I should go and live like other people.' Fog closed in during the late morning and the remainder of the day was really cold.

The next day I went back down Mt Wilhelm, walking, running and feeling better with every downhill step as it brought more oxygen. Late that afternoon I reached Kegusugul, the village where I had stayed before, and some children led me to Maria's hut. She was just leaving for a friend's wedding at a neighbouring village and invited me along.

A *pig-kill* had taken place that afternoon, and the *mumu* was being opened as we arrived. Breadfruit leaves and succulent pork (though slightly stringy) were offered to us, and when the feasting was over the bridegroom's relatives began to sing. They were sitting in separate groups; one for the bride and one for the groom. Both of them belonged to Simbu clans. It was customary to marry within the clan-group because this kept intact the family property. My friend and I sat with the bride's group, which comprised her grandparents, mother and father, sisters, brothers and cousins.

After the groom's family ended their song the bride's family sang back to them, and they took turns to reply to each other's *sing-sing* with more songs; single voices chanting stories, with a chorus between stanzas. As the sun went down and darkness fell it began to rain and we had to dash into the shelter of the huts.

As my eyes adjusted to the light of a kerosene lamp, I discovered that my companions included the bride and her parents. We all sat on the floor and a few men lit their bamboo pipes of tobacco. The bride's mother began talking to her daughter, reminding her for the last time about things she would need to know: how to keep pigs and cultivate a garden. Her father interrupted: *'Yu no kan sleep tumus. Yu get up long wok.'*

Over the hours many other people came to give the bride advice about her new tasks or her change in status. Sitting cross-legged by the smoky hearth, their faces lit up by the glow from the kerosene lamp, they talked earnestly in soft voices. In the background four old women sometimes sang a chorus, their reedy voices chanting 'oh mira, mira-mira' which someone told me was not a word but a sound of happiness.

By tradition, the bride could not leave with her husband that night, so he went back to his own village and would return for her in the morning. At two o'clock in the morning I fell asleep lulled by the smoky warmth and the four old women still singing their quavering harmonies.

Next morning after I had helped to see off the bride, I set off to hitch-hike back to Goroka. Several hours later, as I was being driven on the Highlands Highway, I saw a column of thick black smoke which was clearly not a bushfire (whose smoke is pale), and as we rounded a corner I saw flames and other spirals of smoke billowing from some distant huts. The Australian driver who had given me a lift stopped there out of curiosity and we both went to see what was happening. From a blackened clearing where charred remains of huts were left we could see that the local trade-store was burning. Further away was noise and more smoke. Some Simbus with bows and arrows hurried to join the fray while their womenfolk stayed to survey the damage. They said that the cause of the burning was a group of drunken men from a neighbouring Simbu clan who had looted the trade-store then set fire to it and created a fight with the inhabitants. We left them discussing the form of payback which would be due.

By mid-afternoon I was back in Goroka, and went with Bruce to the Horse Club. Bruce's replacement horse had been a failure since he simply refused to play, so he had bought a new horse (called Bruce). He was seventeen hands high, and I took him for an exhilarating gallop round the race track. In the Flying Club bar that evening I pricked up my ears when I overheard a story about a pair of white-coloured Arab stallions that had been shipped over from Australia by a ranch near Goroka to improve its herds. The boat had reached the port of Lae safely where the two stallions were transferred into a cattle truck. It was a long journey to the ranch, and when they arrived the rancher found that his two Arab stallions for which he had paid a lot of money, had been replaced by two old brown stock-horses.

That was back in 1975. It seemed likely that Horse was one of the 'missing' stallions. It was the owner before the Bells, who I had been told was a rough, tough Australian *kiap*, who had started the tradition that Horse must always be given away and never sold. Perhaps he had had something to do with the change-over of horses and his conscience had got the better of him.

I turned my attention when Bruce came over to introduce me to one of his friends, a helicopter pilot who was scheduled to fly to Lae the next morning. The pilot told me that Lae was not far from Port Moresby and that since the helicopter would be flying empty, I was welcome to a lift.

I sat in the co-pilot's seat and watched as the land fell away in a series of steep ridges beneath us. We flew low and slowly above the treetops. It was exciting, flying up to the top of each mountain and over into the nothingness of space as the land dropped steeply away.

In Lae I felt totally lost. To try and control my confusion I went for coffee at the town hotel, and there I met the Slattery family who took me under their wing and invited me to stay. It was a lovely evening: we ate an enormous supper, watched movies on video, and I slept in a waterbed.

Port Moresby, where I was heading, was an hour's flight from Lae, by small plane. As we flew between the big mountains of the Owen Stanley Range, 13,000 ft (4000 m) the pilot pointed out two Catholic missions — Woitape and Taipini — both of which sat on summits amongst breathtaking landscape. The original missionaries and their supplies were carried by mule from Port Moresby, but today the missions have airstrips and use light aircraft.

Port Moresby and Lae are two major cities (by Papua New Guinea standards), and you would think that modern technology could have engineered a road between the two; but there was no talk of one being made in the foreseeable future. Apparently the land is too rugged, the landslides too frequent, and the jungle's growth too rapid for a road to survive. When the Japanese had taken control of the northern coast during World War II and had tried to turn south to take Port Moresby from behind they managed to cut a trail most of the way but even they were finally defeated by the harshness of the jungle and mountains and were forced to retreat. The trail they had cut was named the Kokoda Trail, and is sometimes walked by hikers as a personal endurance test.

On arrival at Port Moresby airport I left my luggage and went straight to the Government Headquarters to try and find my passport. The Department of Immigration was optimistic that it could be found. They sent me to another office, who sent me to another office, and so on until I arrived back at the starting point (though the round had been interesting, not least because I discovered that I had become a national hero as the 'Horse Lady'). So I went to see the chief of the Department, who was a charming man, and said he would find my passport within twenty-four hours. As to the question of extending my visa, considering the slow way I travelled, he would be happy to authorise an extension for as long as I wished (within reason).

The problem of where to stay in Port Moresby was solved when I remembered that an English dentist (Paul Newell) lived here whom I had met on his vacation in the highlands. Paul had offered me a spare room at his house.

Port Moresby was different from the rest of Papua New Guinea and somehow it didn't seem connected. I noticed the sticky humidity of the sea air and the fierce heat of the sun on the dry, dead, vegetation. Water rationing was in force, and there were periodic electricity cuts. The reservoir which provided water for hydro-electricity was nearly dry; the city had expanded faster than its services.

The local Motu population were unlike the stocky bearded highlanders — these were tall and sophisticated coastal people. Many tribesmen lived in Port Moresby, working in the town or in the copra and cocoa plantations along the coast. Particularly striking were the tall, coal-black-skinned men from Buka Island.

Young men from all over the country were drawn to Port Moresby by the lure of money, girls, fast cars, and smart clothes. Naturally a few did succeed, but most young men failed to attain their goals and became disillusioned, just drifting around Port Moresby living in squalid shanty suburbs and growing dissatisfied and angry. Many of them become *rascals* (the pidgin word for thieves and robbers). It wasn't safe to walk in the town after dark, even for two people. Muggings, robbery and housebreaking were common. The security precautions at some expatriate houses were extreme and reflected the seriousness of the problem: barbed wire, locked entrances, killer dogs and burglar alarms were a common sight.

One night a thief broke into Paul's house and came into my bedroom and stole some things without waking me. Among the things he stole was my handbag, although he didn't take all the contents. He had not been hurried and had taken the time to go through my papers and discard those which he didn't want. He left my diary and note pads, my driving licence, and my passport (recently returned). Everything else could be replaced (even the traveller's cheques were re-issuable after theft); I was grateful for his thoughtfulness.

I still missed Horse, and when thinking of the mountains leading from Port Moresby up to the beautiful setting of the Taipini mission, I longed to ride there. I made contacts at the Race Club (the only horse-place in Moresby) and mentioned my idea. Someone offered to give me a horse. It was a brumby stallion which had been caught with forty other wild horses in the cocoa plantations just up the coast. The herd had been rounded up, corralled in barges, and shipped to Port Moresby, ending up at the Race Club. All those worth making into riding-horses were accepted but those that were too difficult were rejected. The stallion was one of the difficult ones but he was nice-looking, dark palamino-coloured and had a small compact body. I began trying to train him, working with him daily on a lunge-rein and putting a saddle on his back.

To find information about mule-trails I went to the Catholic mission. The father told me that the trails definitely no longer existed and that they had been demolished long ago by landslides and were now overgrown by jungle. That wasn't the news I wanted to hear. I decided to think things over, but meanwhile continued my work with the small palamino horse. The main problem I had with him was his dislike of being ridden. The second time he threw me I hit the ground and his hind feet came down on my ribs. The result was three cracked ribs. So that was that. There were some things which weren't worth doing, and riding that horse to Taipini was one of them.

To heal my cracked ribs I spent three weeks sitting quietly, being careful not to cough or laugh (both were painful), and taking excessive care not to sneeze. I profited from the three weeks enforced leisure by writing some features for the national airline, the only trouble being that the payment was an air-voucher, not real money, and I couldn't see the point of flying over the land by plane when I could be down there travelling in my own way. The writing was something I enjoyed doing and was something that I considered quite separate to the travels themselves — I enjoyed both for the individual and different pleasures they gave me. It was almost a luxury to be sitting down and writing, to be able to take stock of what had happened so far, without the rigours of travelling itself.

Of course I didn't manage to sit still for days and evenings too. There were parties every evening in Port Moresby. Some people claimed not to have spent an evening at home for a year. Most parties were made up of the same people, re-grouping every evening in different disguises; enjoying themselves in a frenetic way. And I enjoyed it too because it was a sharp contrast to the four-and-a-half months that I had spent in Papua New Guinea so far.

One weekend I went sailing in Paul's new catamaran which we managed to capsize three times in the harbour. But an equally usual 'sailing' experience in Moresby was to attach your boat to your car and, without bothering to take it to water, sit there and drink beer all afternoon.

Another weekend I went to a race-meeting. There were about five race horses and five jockeys who just kept swopping mounts and entered almost every race.

For a while it was fun to be a celebrity in town, but soon I grew restless; it was time to leave. It was time for me to learn something new, to see something else, and do something different. I wanted to try paddling a dugout canoe down the Sepik river, which is a big river and is actually rated among the world's greatest rivers in terms of annual waterflow. My ribs had mended quickly and were not painful any more. The fact that no foreigner (let alone a woman) had ever tried to paddle down the Sepik made me curious to see what adventures it would hold.

Part Four

The Canoe Journey

15
The Crocodile Hunters

A small plane took me to Wewak, a town on the northern coast and not far from Vanimo where I had entered Papua New Guinea. The first thing I did when we landed in Wewak was to go around the aircraft hangars and find out if any supply planes, government charters, or helicopters were flying to the Sepik region. It didn't matter where any of them went so long as it was around the upper portion of the Sepik river.

My luck was in; I met the mechanic of a supply plane which was chartered to go to Ama patrol-post in two days time. On my map he showed me that Ama was in an empty green-shaded area bordered by the international frontier with West Irian, the May river and the Sepik's source up in the mountainous interior where I had walked when I first came to the country. Ama's remoteness filled me with anticipation, and the mechanic directed me to an office where I bought a ticket for the flight.

Because the flight was in two days' time I telephoned an Australian family whose name had been given to me to see if they could put me up. The FitzGibbons collected me and took me in as part of their family. It was nice to feel so much at home, especially just before setting out on a journey. The two days were useful for sorting out my backpack and buying some last-minute provisions such as salt, corned beef, rice, sugar, coffee and tea, plastic bags, flashlight batteries, flick-lighters and beads (to give as gifts), also fishing line and some hooks. There would be no shops along the Upper Sepik.

The plane to Ama was delayed for several hours, though really it had no specific time, it ran when ready. The official was worried about the weight of baggage and delayed things for a while and since the day was gruellingly hot, it was a relief to board the little four-seater plane. The co-pilot's seat was allocated to me (for the third time), and when airborne we opened the windows to enjoy the cool fresh air. We flew just beneath the clouds, which gave me a good bird's-eye view of the immense and dense rain-forest. No trails were visible anywhere. The Sepik valley is flat and wide, perhaps eighty miles wide, and runs west to east between the coastal hills and New Guinea's mountainous backbone. From the plane I saw the river's course, which twisted and curled like a big brown snake, and sometimes looped back on itself. I could see how the river was slowly but inexorably changing course, leaving behind many horse-shoe shaped lakes known as ox-bow lakes which reminded me of the pilot who had told me the crocodile stories, and that the lakes are the crocodiles' breeding place.

The plane banked north away from the river and flew inland to Ama. There was a forest-clearing just large enough for an airstrip and a few thatched buildings. I couldn't see any canoes and didn't expect any since Ama was inland; but having seen how its vicinity was encompassed by swampy ponds and rivers I felt sure that I would be able to buy one nearby.

At ground level the heat was oppressive, but I knew that I would have to get used to it. Step one, I decided, was to get acclimatised and to absorb my surroundings. I was one of the few people there and as I strolled around and down some short paths, I was surprised to pass a Bowman who wore a penis-gourd. Back at the station I went to visit the officer in charge. He was a black *kiap*, and he was helpful and efficient. I explained that I was planning to buy a canoe and paddle down the Sepik; the idea startled him at first but he agreed that a canoe was essential for travelling in this area since the streams and rivers were used as 'roads' and even his men went on patrol by canoe. The government canoe was in a stream nearby and he said that I could use it to go to a village on the May river where I would be most likely to buy one of my own. Then he sent for two local men who would be my guides and bring back his canoe. I thanked him. It was a good start and I was pleased that things were going well. While I was in the office some women came in to ask if there would be a *sing-sing* the following month on Independence Day; they wanted to *sing-sing* on the airstrip, but the *kiap* explained that there was a law forbidding *sing-sings* on airstrips! When the office closed the hour was struck on a big wooden *garamut* drum and the national flag was lowered.

The three of us left early next morning, walking for several hours along forest paths. It was a hot sweaty day, and I was grateful that I had the guides to carry my heavy backpack. We found the government canoe moored in a narrow stream with the paddles hidden in the undergrowth. It was a thin and wobbly canoe, and as I sat in the middle I wished I had had the forethought to wrap my luggage in plastic. The men paddled from each end, standing upright to paddle with their long carved blades.

The stream which twisted through the jungle was narrow; vegetation reached out to close over the water, and in turn the stream fought back by flooding and eroding the banks. Many trees had fallen into and across the stream but the boatmen had bush knives to help hack our way through. The bush knives also came in handy for sharpening the paddles which we stopped to do. The idea that a paddle needs sharpening had never occurred to me before, but once it was explained that a blunt paddle wouldn't cut the water, it seemed logical enough. As we paddled along one of the men mentioned that he had a canoe he wanted to sell, and I replied that if after I had seen it, it looked suitable, then I would buy it. He asked me several times to buy it, and became quite persistent, but I remained firm — I knew exactly what I wanted, a canoe which was small and easily manoeuvrable, and I was prepared to see several before I bought one.

It was a long, tiring day. Finally we emerged onto May river (a tributary of the Sepik), at a point somewhere near my guide's home village.

He brought the canoe and a paddle to me in the morning. The canoe was far too long and unwieldy for me, yet I heard myself saying *'Yes, kanu i gudfela, mi laik buyim disfela kanu'*. He suggested that I tried it out and I said no, I knew it was the right canoe for me and I didn't want to try it. Then I gave him the money.

While I was talking with his friend on the bank I noticed the man surreptitiously climb down the bank into the canoe, so I moved closer to observe him. He took some leaves from his *bilum* and began making signs on the canoe floor; his mouth forming words as he muttered things under his breath.

All day I felt worried and heavy; I didn't want to do anything, not even try out my new canoe. This was so unlike me, I couldn't work it out. Whenever I looked at the canoe the idea nagged me that something was wrong. The most obvious thing wrong was that it was too big for me. In the end I got so bothered that I started asking others if it wasn't too big. They all said of course it was, but when I said this to the man who had sold it to me he simply said *'Wori bilong yu'* (that's your problem).

The next morning I spoke to the headman and showed him the canoe. After one look he said that it was obviously far too big for me, and from the conversation which followed I guessed he suspected that sorcery had been employed.

Everyone agreed that the man must take back his canoe and return my money. When he was confronted with this he became extremely angry so to appease him I bought from him a red-wood paddle that had a primitively carved handle. Once this was sorted out the headman arranged for me to buy a small but fairly sturdy canoe from one of his wives. This was much better — it was a typical wooden dug-out (made by hollowing out a length of tree trunk), with chiselled sides worn smooth with age, and a prow that was carved into the head of a bird-crocodile. The price was 15 *kina* (£11).

I put my backpack in the middle of the canoe and sat at the back; it was just wide enough for me to fit comfortably. Villagers gathered on the banks to see if I could manage it so I said my goodbyes and set out downriver at a slick pace just to show I could. Soon my arms were aching, but I didn't want to slow down until I was sure that I wasn't being followed. I checked the river behind me at every bend, and even though it was empty each time, I kept going fast.

When eventually I felt safe, I relaxed. Now I began to realise how strangely I had been feeling and acting over the past day. To some extent I believe in magic — acknowledging that although there are many invisible forces which we cannot perceive we cannot presume they don't exist. It is sometimes suggested that 'primitives' who live in harmony with nature possess natural powers, and I am sure that the man who sold me the first canoe possessed them.

The sun shone from a clear blue sky and the forest on either side of me rang with birdsong and the chirring of cicadas. Kingfishers dived for fish and two big turkey-hornbills whirred heavily overhead, their wings sounding as if they were tearing the air into ragged shreds.

The outer bends of the river were covered in swamp-forest, tangled with a hanging network of lianes. There were breadfruit trees, sago palms, trees with umbrella leaves, and others with big rounded leaves like many-fingered hands; the forest floor beneath them was under water, and swampy. On the inside of the river bends was *pitpit*, with its familiar 'Job's Tears' seeds. A rat swam into the openly-spaced *pitpit* and wove between the fat stalks, holding its face above the water. As I watched the rat's progress I became aware of something which I had been trying to ignore. Several times already I thought I had noticed logs, which weren't there when I looked again. Now I saw another and it was regarding me with glinting malevolent eyes. Certainly I knew that the Sepik is famous for its crocodiles, but somehow I didn't expect to see them so early in my journey.

The midday sun blazed down and, despite the fact that I was wearing a sunhat, my brains felt fried. I paddled idly, wishing I knew how to steer and paddle in one movement; the canoe went its own way, and often it veered so far off course that I couldn't prevent it swinging in complete slow circles. But it didn't matter; the current was gentle and there was enough room for mistakes.

There was no sign of human habitation until dusk when I came across a group of four large huts on stilts, whose occupants gathered outside and looked at me with blank astonishment. Children fled screaming in terror to hide behind their mothers' grass skirts. Some men came forward and I shook hands with them. Several of them could speak pidgin and I explained that I wanted to stay overnight. They still looked baffled, but gave me space inside one of the huts. The huts were high above the ground with floors of palm trunks and walls of palm-leaf stalks. Their most interesting feature was the ladders leading to their front door; they were simply long poles notched into steps. One household was clearly not-at-home, because their pole was turned slippery side outwards.

When I went to the river to wash my face the women warned me that the water was deep. I stood there watching as one of their children came paddling a canoe across the river; he was about four years old, and I marvelled at the early age children learned to swim and handle a canoe. I took a small step into the water to find it was only toe-deep (useless for washing), so I took another step, and fell in up to my neck. The comedy of it made me laugh and as a result everyone became more relaxed.

Their evening's food wasn't plentiful, so I cooked a pan of rice and tinned meat which we shared. They also cooked some *saksak* (sago meal), by adding water to the coarse flour and simmering it into a jelly-like grey substance. It tasted how I imagine a jellyfish would taste.

Mosquitoes were numerous and they whined hungrily outside my mosquito net all night.

Where the May river joined the Sepik I planned to turn right to go downriver, but the canoe got caught in a back-spinning current and I found myself being pushed upriver instead. So I went with it. The up-current was short-lived and I couldn't paddle against the main flow of river, but by cutting corners and catching circling eddies I made fair progress. I wasn't intending to go far upriver, I just wanted to see what it was like beyond a huge sweeping bend which seemed to go on forever. But it was discouraging when the current kept pushing the canoe into the reeds and I was soon exhausted. When it spun out of control again and went nose first into the tall grass, I stopped to rest there and discovered an open channel just wide enough to take the canoe. Feeling stronger, I followed the channel. It was a relief to be away from the current. At the end of the *pitpit* lay a swamp-forest. I had some chalk inside my pack so I took it out to mark the trees I passed, since getting lost would be too easy.

Paddling through the swamp-forest, I was at a level beneath and among the grotesquely gnarled roots covered in mosses and giant ferns. As I threaded my canoe between enormous trees garlanded with dark creepers and arching sprays of blue orchids, dim greenish light filtered through the leafy canopy high overhead. Low branches were enshrouded in cobwebs. The stillness was intensified by the whine of mosquitoes and the screeches of parrots. Humid, sweating forest; it smelt of stagnant water mixed with the perfume of flowers. It gave me strange and eerie feelings. The shallow water, coloured ruby by decaying vegetable dyes in the ground, glowed like red wine where sunlight dappled it. Reflections were interlaced with ripples. At times the water was only inches deep and when my canoe ran aground in the murk, I had to use a pole to push it free. Once from the corner of my eye I saw a crocodile slinking away.

The forest thinned and I emerged into bright sunlight sparkling on what I recognised as an ox-bow lake. There was another canoe on it but it looked as though it was empty. Squinting against the dazzle I made out the heads of two men, standing chest deep in the lake. I paddled cautiously closer and parked below some shady trees. The men moved slowly and silently. I watched and waited. It was a long time before anything happened, then suddenly one man ducked under water and came up holding a wildly-thrashing creature. He put it in their canoe and the other man raised a bush knife to kill it. Then they resumed their walk in the lake, towing the canoe behind them into a wide patch of water-lilies.

My curiosity was burning, but so was my throat, and rather than approach the men directly, I decided to make a fire and brew tea. When they noticed the smoke the men came over, and I offered them some. Inside their canoe were two dead crocodiles, both about four feet long. And that was how I made friends with some crocodile-hunters.

I stayed with them for several days; they had constructed a bush shelter in a lakeside clearing, and I hung my hammock nearby. Every night we went out to call crocodiles. The men called them by slapping the water's surface with flat bits of *limbum* (palm leaf pod), flapping it to make a distinctive spluttering noise. While one did that, the other cupped his hands over his mouth and made a *'nuark-nuark'* sound. It sometimes brought crocodiles to the surface, and once I heard a crocodile reply with the same *'nuark-nuark'*. The men used a flashlight to spot their prey and a ten-foot (3-m) long harpoon to catch them. The harpoon had eight long, sharp prongs and a carved handle topped with a tuft of feathers. A bush-fibre rope connected the men to their harpoons, and once they speared a crocodile, they pulled in the slack until it was beside the canoe. Then the first man thrust a pole at it (giving the crocodile something to attack and distract it) while the other killed it with an axe. There was some skill in this since crocodiles are seemingly armour-plated and the axe had to find the most vulnerable patch at the back of the neck, just behind the skull.

When I shone my flashlight around, I saw the lake as a universe with glittering red eyes everywhere, like galaxies of red stars. After about an hour the moon disappeared behind a veil of cloud which thickened until the sky went black and lightning flashed sporadically. The men decided to call it a day and as we paddled back, they explained that crocodiles were man's ancestors and that original man was born from a crocodile, which had also formed the earth. When he discovered that he was alone, the man cried and the Sepik river sprang from his tears. I asked my companions whether they really believed this, or if they knew that it was folklore, and one replied *'Nogat tru, im stori tasol'* (Not true, just a story).

I slept in my hammock which was slung high and out of reach of any wandering or curious crocodiles. The men slept on the ground — doubtless they knew what they were doing — but I was glad that I had my hammock.

Our morning's chore was to skin the catch from the previous day and night. The men let me join in since there were three crocodiles to be done and I assured them that I could do the job. So we laid the crocodiles on the grass and using sharp knives we each started to work, first slitting them along the backbone, then across the neck behind the skull and finally from the front legs to under the neck. After the initial cuts we flensed the skin back with the knife, cutting as we did so the strong white sinews which secured the skin to the flesh inside. When skinning the legs, we left the feet with their long clawed fingers intact.

I am no expert at skinning reptiles and it was slow, meticulous work (clumsiness could ruin the skin's value), but I didn't mind dissecting them; it gave me a chance to study them at close quarters. With the skin removed I could appreciate the formidable strength of their sinews and muscles. One of the men showed me how there was an additional pair of opaque eyelids that slid across to protect the crocodile's eyes under water, and also that their throat and nostrils had closable valves which enabled them to submerge with half-open mouth gripping their prey, without flooding their respiratory system. I was particularly fascinated by the mouth: there was no tongue (which came as a surprise), and I could see how their needle-sharp teeth which

168

overlapped outside the mouth meant that their jaws could only go up and down and not chew. The teeth were too firmly implanted for me to extract any, which was a shame because I wanted one as a souvenir. My companions said that it would take months of drying in the sun before the teeth would come loose from the skull. One of the men took off a large tooth that he wore on a string round his neck and showed me how it was hollow so that a new tooth could grow up inside it ready to replace the outer tooth when it broke. When he saw my interest he presented it to me as a gift.

At midday we roasted some tail steaks which tasted superb, very much like lobster. The rest of the meat was cut up for smoke-cooking. The skins are bought by traders who call occasionally at the villages and pay about 100 *kina* (£75) for each 22-inch skin, which is measured round the girth not lengthwise. It is not legal to buy oversized skins, so the big crocodiles are protected from being hunted. The hunters made little impact on the numbers — they had to work hard just to get a few each day and anyway crocodiles are plentiful. Each adult female of the salt-water species lays forty to eighty eggs a year and those of the fresh-water species about twenty-five eggs each. The eggs are oblong with white yolks, and they look and taste similar to chicken eggs. Both fresh-water and salt-water crocodiles live in the Sepik; the latter grow up to thirty feet long and are fairly ferocious, but the fresh-water ones are smaller and pretty harmless.

In the afternoons we paddled round several lakes, baiting the traps (like lobster-traps) and hooks with rotting meat. In daylight the men used a different method to find the crocodiles — they simply walked on the lake bed waist deep in water and felt with their feet for scaly bodies. Sometimes they said that they could feel a crocodile swim past and brush against their legs. The men's movements were slow and deliberate, confident that crocodiles would not attack unless angry or hurt. When one of the men found a body he reached down and put his hands round its muzzle. Without any fuss the second man helped him lift the crocodile out of the water into the canoe, and kill it. This is what they had been doing the first time I saw them.

In the late afternoon I usually canoed to a secluded pool of deep water for my daily bath. I never stayed in long though not wanting to push my luck. For me these were lazy days spent travelling nowhere, just accompanying the men on the lakes, or floating in my canoe among the waterlilies and dragonflies. I enjoyed seeing the many exotic birds such as the white cocka-toos, parrots, and *guria*-birds (earthquake-birds, named because they always shake their long plumes vigorously when they sit down), seemed to be everywhere.

When the time came for my friends to return to their village, it was time for me to return to the Sepik. After these few days 'holiday' I felt excited and eager to explore whatever lay ahead.

I returned to the river by following my chalk-marks, though I was confident enough to follow a few streams into the forest on the way. I loved the swamp-forests, and the people in them, who, living away from the main Sepik, still used stone axes, and were often naked. Some of the men wore penis-gourds and necklaces of teeth, and I learned that they usually had several gourds that would be worn on different occasions — the most ornate being worn for initiation ceremonies.

Villages were scarce, but I could tell which streams led to dwellings because fallen trees in the water would be notched just sufficiently for a canoe to pass. Elsewhere, where trees had fallen over the water I had to push the canoe beneath them, either by laying flat and pushing with my hands, or sending the canoe under while I climbed over. My bush knife was invaluable. Sometimes people I met thought that I was an ancestor, *('yu bilong tumbuna')* and they called me 'mama', not because I am a mother figure, but because they believed that their ancestors were white-skinned.

Even on the main Sepik villages were scarce. Mowi was the first proper village that I found and because it was raining the villagers took me into a *haus-wind* (open sided shelter), where they all sat down to observe me. I asked if someone would sell me another paddle (my red-wood one was proving too short), and I bought a six-foot (2-m) one for 1 *kina* (75p), which was old and strong but wasn't carved. I took out my knife to begin carving but an old man beside me said *'Mi laik wokim disfela',* so I gave the paddle to him and he began to carve. The old man talked as he worked, and his fourteen-year-old apprentice sitting beside him, watched him intently. Often during the rainy afternoon the master got tired and simply dozed off, and then the apprentice would carve the less important marks and hand back the paddle when the old man woke up.

Under the stilts of a nearby hut a boy was beating rhythms on the ends of four hollow bamboo tubes of different lengths; the sound he made was a melodious whoomping hoot which was almost surrealistic. Space age noise in a Stone-Age culture. This thought reminded me to ask if anyone would sell me a stone axe, and three were offered to me. I looked at them closely — the axe heads were made from black obsidian chipped into shape and set in long-handled forked branches. I chose the one that felt best for me and gave the other two back. It was nice to be able to gather cargo and not have to worry about the weight.

The air smelt of fermenting sago, and I watched as some women efficiently hauled a heavy sago palm out of the river using bark ropes. The sago palms are left in the river for a year after they have been felled, at which time they are ready for *skrub-im*. The women's knee-length grass skirts flicked from side to side as they walked round examining the tree. Its fronds and thorns had been cleaned off previously and now the women began to strip away the bark, using their axes. Beneath the bark was a mass of pale fibrous pith. This pith would be pounded and washed, then sieved through a strainer of coconut fibre. The pulp which remained would be repounded and washed until it turned purple-grey. When dry it could be stored and used as required. This was the *saksak* which made the glutinous jelly that formed the basis of their diet.

It was still raining. The old man woke up, and remembered he had killed a pig the previous day so he told his apprentice to bring us some roast pork.

During the day almost everyone in the village had come to say hello, and late afternoon when the remainder returned from working in their gardens, they came too and asked to hear the story of my travels in Papua New Guinea. We crowded into a big hut, all squeezing in as best we could and I started my story. I was about halfway through when suddenly there was an explosive cracking splintering noise and the whole house lurched and began to collapse. Its stilts had buckled and broken under the unaccustomed weight of so many bodies. People flew in all directions as the house thumped to the ground, but we all managed to

171

scramble outside before the roof caved in. Fortunately no one was seriously hurt, although a few had some nasty bruises and grazes.

Another empty house was found for me to stay in, and an army of young boys was assigned to cater for my needs. They fetched and boiled water, and cooked me a tasty supper of fish, sago and a pithy plant coated in red juice. Before falling asleep I wrote my diary, and watched the dense cloud of mosquitoes dancing in the candlelight outside my net.

16
The Upper Sepik

In the morning, eight little boys made me a novel bacon-and-egg breakfast of pig's ear, and a boiled crocodile egg with some charcoaled sago. They also filled my water bottle with hot strong coffee which I drank as I floated downriver. The coffee stayed boiling hot all day if I kept the flask in the sun. For water, I drank from the river like the local people, though I couldn't imitate their scooping it with their fingers, flicking it in the air and catching it in their mouths in a lapping action. The Sepik river water was always muddy; some days it tasted muddier than others.

I followed the big brown river's meandering course through the forest; its current swung slowly from side to side as the river bent. I learned to watch out for the hairpin corners where back-spins of current met the downflowing current and made the surface turbulent, and for the sudden troughs caused by deep currents hitting the banks. Because I was down at water level the roughness looked worse than it actually was; the Sepik is not a fast or furious river and the rim of my canoe stayed at least six inches clear of the water.

Yet, as each day passed, I grew aware that the Sepik was becoming wider and stronger. The inner sides of the hairpin bends were now studded with many whirling eddies, all spinning separately and at different speeds (as the pressures on them altered). I still wasn't very good at controlling my canoe, since I hadn't mastered how to paddle and steer in one stroke, and when a tributary entered the main river I crossed to the far side to avoid the turbulence. I guessed that this was the place the old wood-carver had warned me against. He had said that if I got caught up in it a *sanguma* would come and take my arms, then my head, and the rest of my body and somehow change me. The *sanguma* puts the person back in one piece, but when the person goes on his way, he is unaware of the difference or of what has happened.

The day was hot. The sun blazed down from the blue sky, but a cooling breeze blew upriver. The air rang with the sound of cicadas, and large yellow and black butterflies danced in front of me. I splashed water on my face; already my face and arms felt very sunburnt and my hands felt rough and calloused. A solitary white heron *(suan)* flew past me, low over the water. Occasionally I followed short-cuts across hairpin bends, where the river was gradually forcing a new route. Coming out of one such channel I saw the same white heron, still winging effortlessly along the main river.

Then I saw what looked like another short-cut, and I headed for it. I had to paddle forcefully to cross the main current to avoid being swept past the entrance, and I reached it before I could look inside. The canoe sped inside and to my horror I realised that I was in a dead end with the current being forced tightly round on itself. My canoe wumped as it was tugged below and I was drawn into the seething circling pool. A dead tree was also circling afloat, and it scraped the canoe several times. I just couldn't get free of the tree's branches, and despite paddling at full-strength my canoe was pulled around continually and I seemed powerless. I tried not to panic telling myself that things would be alright so long as I didn't capsize. Then a thick branch of the tree caught the prow, and I crawled forward to push us away. But I didn't have the strength — the branch was being forced down and made heavier because the whole tree was rolling slowly as it circled. In desperation I grabbed the bush knife and hacked at the branch; it cracked open and my canoe was freed just in time. With a strength that surprised me I fought clear of the rest of the tree, and caught the current as it escaped from the inlet.

Feeling rather stunned, and very relieved, I floated downriver. Maybe that was the place the old man had referred to. I checked my canoe for damage and noticed a small crack along the side. Water was beginning to seep in already and it became urgent to get to the next village to patch it up.

It was fortunate that at the next big village, Inioc, there was a mining camp depot, and they had a few rusty nails, some putty, and some tin cans which I flattened and cut to make patches. The only problem was that when I beached the canoe to dry it out, its wood cracked in the hot sun. The new crack ran half the length of the canoe, at water level. There wasn't enough putty to fix both cracks but someone took me to a bank of good-quality clay which the locals used for their canoe repairs. While patching the canoe I was surprised to see that although its sides were quite thin, the underneath was very thick and solid. I also noticed several badly damaged and water-rotted places — I hoped it would last for the whole voyage.

Many villagers came to offer helpful advice and the *luluwai* (headman) came to commiserate and sold me two *garamut* drumsticks, ornately carved into a mixture of men and crocodiles. In the early evening some widows, unattractively plastered in yellow ochre, sat down to watch me. They had ochred heads, hair, shoulders and long flat empty breasts, but as the sun went down over the river their bodies glowed in the golden light.

The next morning when I left Inioc, I noticed that the river's level had fallen about half a metre overnight. People said that it was still unusually high for a dry season. Unfortunately the repair along the watermark hadn't dried, and when I sat in the canoe water seeped through the crack in places. To help keep the clay dry and keep it out of the water, I sat on the opposite side. It made the canoe look lopsided, but more importantly, it kept the crack above water.

I had been travelling for little more than an hour when suddenly I became aware that the river ahead was blurred by a grey cloud about three feet deep that drifted just above the water. As I got nearer I could see that it was a thick layer of fluttering insects, which on closer inspection I could see were like grey, winged earwigs. I hoped fervently that they didn't sting or bite, because there was no way of avoiding them. As I paddled my way through them I discovered that they were behaving in an odd way. They were flapping around at water-level, flying upwards then diving at the water and levelling off to skim along the surface. Whenever one lay motionless, another would bump him into action. They seemed to be struggling. Among the dull-grey flies I began to see other fluffy yellow ones and slowly I realised that the grey ones were in metamorphosis. They were splitting their old skins by friction against the water, and shedding them in flight, emerging as pale yellow winged insects with an inch-long swallowtail. The air was so thick with them that I could hardly see the prow of my canoe and my paddle hit some every time I pulled the blade out of the water. Occasionally a fish jumped up to catch one, and a fish-eagle swooped around catching a few too.

Later that same day I passed some men out fishing. They were standing motionless in their flimsy canoes in the fast current, spears poised, and scanning the depths for fish. I drifted along contentedly and at one stage was overtaken by a line of gulls perched on a floating tree trunk; a uniform line of birds just out for the ride.

In the afternoon I reached Tauri, a village of huts on stilts set in a grove of tall coconut palms. The people gave me an empty hut to sleep in; it was beside some men's huts and heavy drumming resounded from beneath one of them where they were pounding their *garamut* drums fast then slow. One of the women explained that the men were showing their sorrow over the deaths of four hunting-dogs which had been killed in a fight with a wild pig. Later on, they brought a dish of food to me: *saksak* and green leaves boiled into soup with the bodies of a handful of those fluffy yellow flies. I thought of my morning's experience; it was odd how life turned out.

My progress downriver was unhurried. Independence day celebrations were in progress and would last three days, so each morning I paddled until I reached a village with festivities. At Oun there was an archery contest for uninitiated boys. Their target was a banana flower at sixty feet (18m). The boldest boys stepped forward first, jauntily fitting bamboo arrows to their blackpalm bows, but none of them really stopped to take aim, and only the bullseye was scored. Most of the arrows didn't even touch the flower. It puzzled me that they didn't take aim and I recalled that neither had the warring highlanders in their bow and arrow fight.

From Oun, I paddled to Kubkain, which was located on a rocky knoll sticking out into the river. The inlet by the hill was a mass of whirlpools, some of them strong enough to overturn a canoe, and I had to go in, in order to reach the canoe 'parking-lot'. A crowd of people caught sight of me as I approached. I hoped that I wouldn't make a fool of myself but managed to reach the bank without spinning or hitting too many other canoes. I parked mine beside a 'cadillac', a big canoe whose prow was carved into a magnificent crocodile's head with tendrils of palm-leaf hanging from its jaws.

Celebrations were already in progress. I arrived in time to hear the end of the headman's speech, saying that no fighting was allowed this year, and that if any broke out he would deal with it more severely than the previous year. There was to be a series of football matches in the afternoon and a *sing-sing race* (musical competition) in the evening.

Some missionaries were responsible for introducing football to the people and had got teams together from four separate villages. They had donated the ball and some oddments of footballers' clothing. Two players had shoes, one had just socks, and three had one sock each; as they ran the socks slid down and flapped around their ankles. Several players had dark glasses, one with only one glass. The field was so uneven that the ball often bounced in odd directions and the players' passes were so enthusiastic that the ball frequently got lodged in trees or went into the crowd. Young children were responsible for chasing the chickens off the pitch. I sat beside a reserve player, who told me that his team had hardly practised because their village was flooded and they didn't have enough dry ground to make a football field. When the floods subsided to knee-deep the players would begin practising again.

The first match was Kubkain vs Swakop. Swakop, I was told, was an evil place with four spirit houses. In the interval I was given a cup of hot sweet tea, and some boiled sago maggots to eat. They didn't look at all appetising but I ate one out of politeness. Its head was crunchy and its body was soft; I swallowed it quickly to avoid tasting it.

Later to my surprise I noticed three white faces, one was the Catholic father who had come to visit his mission, and two were sisters from a language institute (SIL). The sisters asked me to join them beside the football field and we talked about their work which involved creating written languages out of the local dialects, and then translating the Bible into those dialects.

There were no goals scored in the first two matches, and someone suggested widening the goal posts, but the idea didn't catch on. The tournament lasted until the light faded, and after the winners (Kubkain) had been applauded the teams all went away to wash and change for the evening's *sing-sing race*, at which I had been asked to be one of the judges.

It was dark when the young men re-appeared in their *bilas* and the first group climbed onto the bamboo stage. When the lamps were lit, the men burst into action. Blackened shiny figures beat drums, strummed ukeleles and jumped up and down on the stage making the whole platform bounce crazily. I didn't know how to react and for a moment I wondered what on earth was going on and what I was doing there. The absurdity of it all nearly made me laugh aloud. The dancing was so energetic that the stage had to be reinforced before the second group could go on. When all was safe again the leader of the second group stepped forward to introduce them, and in his nervousness he not only forgot what he was going to say, but was unable to remember his group's name either.

Their act was even more energetic than the first as they leapt around pounding an assortment of wooden drums, bamboo drums, tin cans and a motley collection of string-instruments. In a frenzy of musical energy they used the stage like a trampoline. It was all slightly mind-boggling. I gave them eight points out of ten for effort, but my highest score was given to Swakop, who looked particularly dramatic with white-rimmed eyes, two flat shells attached through the nasal septum and pearly *kina* shells round their necks. Their music was vigorous and their bouncing on the stage so enthusiastic that they frequently fell over each other.

The evening was a great success, even though a fight broke out at the end when the judge announced the results. Calm was restored fairly quickly and most people went home to sleep, though a few of the old people grouped for a traditional, more mellow *sing-sing*.

When Independence Day festivities finished life went back to normal. I floated downriver with a mug of coffee, and watched the morning unroll around me. The first people to pass me were a line of ten men standing up in their canoe and using paddles taller than themselves to propel them along. Their canoe sped through the water under the power of all their muscles and I caught snatches of a war-like chant as they went. They were one of the groups from Kubkain, so we exchanged greetings, but I didn't encourage them to hang around.

Shortly afterwards another canoe came along, containing two men whose chests and backs were scarred with raised bumps. The men stopped to say hello, calling me *Sepik meri* (Sepik woman), and when I asked about their scars they said that the marks symbolised a crocodile's scaly body. Its eyes were cut round their nipples, its front legs went down the men's ribs, and its back went over their shoulders and down their backs and thighs. We chatted briefly then parted. They were from the mountains behind Ambunti, where initiation included this skin-cutting ceremony dedicated to crocodiles. I drifted on into the morning.

From behind me came a raft of six canoes held together by people's feet hooked over the rims. On it were about twenty adults and children who were surrounded by baskets of food, fish and cooking pots. One canoe was filled with coconut sprouts. At the stern of each canoe was a clay firebowl, with wood burning permanently for cooking purposes and to dry out tobacco leaves. Some old women were paddling gently and smoking cigars of tobacco rolled in a banana leaf. Other women were busy cleaning fish, deftly gutting them and washing them clean. A flock of gulls flew round them hovering and diving for scraps.

We travelled together for a few miles, before they invited me to their village of Swakop, a short way off the Sepik. I remembered the footballer telling me it was an evil place, that the Swakop men refused to accept government law or interference in the affairs of their village, and that they didn't like strangers. But clearly I was invited so I decided to go. It was late afternoon when we turned into the black-water stream to the village. The sun's rays slanted through the trees, silhouetting the dark paddlers through the thick smoke from their firebowls.

When we arrived at the village the people installed me in a shaky old hut set slightly apart from the rest. Undaunted I decided to go for an evening stroll around the village. On foot it was impossible to go far because the ground was mostly flooded, so I wandered around instead by canoe. The huts were on tall stilts, and the tops of their ladder-poles were magnificently carved. The spirit houses were built at a leaning angle, tilted forward, and a group of naked men sat in front of one playing some *garamut* drums. The drums were made from large logs, hollowed out through a narrow slit. Their sides were carved, and they were played with a long sturdy stick, the top of which was thinner than the bottom and carved.

Local women were forbidden inside *haus tamborans* (spirits houses) throughout the Sepik. It was said that if a woman even so much as looked inside one, she would die soon afterwards. As in most of the Sepik cultures, people at Swakop believed that the world of nature was dominated by the spirit world. Everything had a spirit or *masalai*, and every spirit had its own personality and individual powers. People took care not to offend the spirits, which could express moods like anger and pleasure, and could affect a man's failure or success. Communication with the spirits was possible in music and dreams, or by calling them up.

There was a strange and strained atmosphere in the village and some people looked at me in a hostile way. I followed the women's path (they had their own) and detoured around the spirit huts, taking care to abide by their rules and beliefs and to avoid upsetting them in any way. Unlike the *guvmen* (government) or missionaries I wasn't here to impose my laws and beliefs upon others. By showing respect I also found that I was given respect in return, and perhaps was safer than I might otherwise have been.

I left Swakop without incident, and chased a flock of wild ducks for miles downstream. Instead of paddling the same route out, I followed another branch of the stream for three hours, then met the Sepik. It looked wider and more powerful than before. With every tributary that entered the Sepik I noticed increased strength in the river. I enjoyed the way the river's character changed continually: today it was very broad and shallow at first with islands between the river channels, then later it narrowed and became more powerful, as it looped through the forest. One moment there were some blue hills far ahead, next they were behind us, then in front again; it was confusing. Off the bends were small back-spins of current. Sometimes the canoe seemed to brake as it hit eddies, other times it leapt forward or sideways and then my paddle zipped emptily through the water, like it was thin air. It was a joy to have nothing better to do than to feel the textures of whirlpools.

I was not afraid of getting lost, feeling sure that where there was a current the channel must rejoin the main river. I also had a map of sorts. It was an out of date flying-chart of northern New Guinea which had been given to me by a pilot's wife, although in fact it was only half of the chart, and the other half was missing. But the Sepik river was well-shown on my half, and not only were many villages marked by name, but dotted lines showed where local short-cuts went across the necks of river-bends. Not that these were always reliable — over the years the river's course had changed — and I was discovering that it now bore little resemblance to the map, which I updated and corrected as I went along.

Three white cockatoos flew overhead squawking to each other, as I threaded my way between more islands, with trees on them that had multiple roots like tentacles. The blazing sun got hotter and hotter until I noticed thunder clouds brewing and thought it was time to look for shelter. I stopped at a group of huts called Yassan-Two, where the people spoke a different language and had different customs from both Kubkain and Swakop even though they were just a day's travelling from each other. Another difference I noticed was in the canoe-prows; each region or village seemed to have its own style of crocodile head. Some were rough and scaly with grisly jaws, others were smoothed flat and looked wily. But the designs weren't mandatory, and individuals were free to create any type of prow. Just before Yassan-Two I had been passed by an old lady whose canoe-prow was carved into a bird's head with spiralling eyes, and a large open beak holding a seed.

For supper that evening I ate boiled water-weeds, fish, and yams; it was a nice change to have yams instead of *saksak*, particularly since the recent heavy unseasonal rains had washed many of the yam gardens away and created a shortage.

That night the threatened storm broke, and in the morning my canoe was half-full of water. The canoe was like a rain-gauge, telling me how much rain had fallen overnight. I didn't take my canoe out of the water at night or turn it over, because it is not the custom to do so unless they are being stored. Ordinarily they are parked in lines at the river's edge and tied with string or bark-rope from the canoe-prow to poles that are stuck upright by the bank for that purpose.

I set about bailing the water out of my canoe using *limbum*. The pod's base was flexible and strong and was ideal for scooping water from the canoe's rough hewn floor. To mop the wood reasonably dry most people used a wad of soft absorbent leaves, but I had a piece of cloth. My 'canoe rag' was a possession that was greatly envied, since cloth was extremely rare and therefore valuable. It had begun its life as a length of hand-made batik cloth from West Africa, a present from my brother Toby who worked there. I had used it as a sarong until it had become too faded, as a windbreak and sunshade on *Tombatu* for a month and now it was my canoe rag; it was still one of the most useful things I owned.

After Yassan-Two I had been told to look out for a short-cut across a long river-loop but I missed it, and on seeing two women setting their fishing nets, I went over to ask them the way. They shrieked and fled when they first saw me so I had to wait and smile in their direction for a while in order to encourage them back again. After a moment they came out of hiding and called to me, *'Yu stap meri?'* (Are you a woman?). *'Na ya save pul-kanu!'* (And you know how to paddle a canoe!) *'Mi stap meri olsem yutufela'* (I'm a woman like you two) I replied, watching as they absorbed the fact and their expressions changed from bewilderment to delight. At last one of them paddled over to me. As she pulled up alongside she offered me a fish. Unfortunately for me, if there is one thing I am squeamish about it's holding a live fish but for their sakes I tried to look pleased as it flapped and squirmed in my grasp.

On our way back to the short-cut, my canoe swung off course and turned in a full circle. The women clucked angrily at the way I was paddling, and came over to teach me the proper way. Paddling Sepik-style wasn't just a movement of dipping your paddle in and out of the water, it was a clean circular motion where the angle of the blade cut through the water and controlled the steering. It took a while to grasp but as I built up a steady rhythm I discovered it to be a springy motion because the blade's angle flicked the paddle up and created its own momentum. My control began to improve.

The short-cut was narrow, twisting and fast, and it ran between fifteen-foot (5-m) tall swamp-grasses. Half an hour later we emerged onto a calm lake. Another stream led us back to the Sepik and the women's village. One of them proudly showed me the seventeen baby crocodiles her son was keeping until they were big enough to sell to the skin traders downriver at Ambunti.

Ambunti was not far, but the women warned me to watch out for a sharp bend and bottleneck in the river that made the journey potentially hazardous; apparently the water there was so rough that many canoes had been overturned in the past. To appease the crocodile-*masalai* who inhabited its double set of whirlpools I was advised to throw some *buai* (betel-nuts) into the water.

I saw the right-angled bend and opposite headlands clearly in advance, and moved my canoe into the centre of the river. The bay was large enough for the current to come round back on itself. As I approached the headlands I recognised the glassy smooth middle patch that had fooled me before but I felt hyper-alert and well in control. Suddenly the smoothness changed to a barrage of currents going backwards then turning and sweeping forward. My canoe was surfing on a swell, until the water heaved sideways and we got swept into the turmoil. The whirlpools were superb sport — I dodged between them, hit a few and was pushed into waves that spilt into the canoe. As I raced along, I paddled faster and faster until suddenly we were through the bottleneck and back into calmer water. We had got through unscathed.

Late in the afternoon I arrived at Ambunti, and got a strange welcome from the SIL mission. I had brought with me a message of introduction from the two sisters I had met upriver, who had suggested that I stay in their empty guest house. But the couple here couldn't seem to grasp the situation and kept repeating that because I wasn't part of SIL I couldn't stay, though they would rent me the house for eight *kina* (£6) a night. That was preposterous, so I walked off. The woman came after me on a bicycle and invited me to stay at their house but it had all been so weird I decided against it. I climbed back into my canoe and paddled down to the Catholic mission instead. Everyone was away, but on the hill above the mission a kindly villager lent me an empty hut.

What I saw of Ambunti I didn't like. There was a beer bar and the men had a noticeably different attitude to me. During the night I was woken by someone knocking on the door. I ignored it at first but the person refused to go away and started shaking the door. Fortunately I had barricaded it earlier as a security precaution. When it still didn't stop I called out 'Who is it?' and after the door was rattled even more fiercely for a while, a male voice whispered that he wanted to come in and talk to me. Whoever it was was obviously drunk and I told him that he could visit me to talk in the morning. He whispered again and when I didn't reply he began hitting and rocking the stilts of the hut to wake me. I felt sure he was only trying to frighten me so having got over my initial nervousness I decided to yell at him loudly and very crossly. His husky agitated response showed that he feared being discovered so I shouted again and eventually he went away.

I was glad to leave Ambunti the next morning. Once afloat, life resumed its tranquillity; the current was gentle and I sipped coconut milk from some fresh coconuts which I bought in a village nearby. After Ambunti the river became more populated as I left the Upper Sepik and reached the portion of the river known as the Middle Sepik.

I had been on the river for about four weeks when I reached Pagwi and since my legs needed stretching I decided to explore inland for a few days. I parked my canoe where it couldn't be seen from the public canoe-park and tied its rope securely to a thick root on the bank, then taking my backpack I set off on foot.

17
Yam Festivals
in the Maprik Region

From Pagwi there was a dirt road leading inland to Maprik, where I spent a night, and the following day I walked east from Maprik, it felt good to walk.

Rain began falling as I walked through a village called Kuotngu, and the guardian of a *haus tamboran* invited me inside to shelter. His name was Noah and he told me that I had arrived in the middle of the yam festival. This explained the numerous racks in front of me, piled high with yams wearing *bilas* and topped with yam-masks. Painted masks were made from bamboo cane woven in the form of a face. Other yams had heads made out of burrs implanted with white feathers which gleamed in the dusty half-light of the old *haus*. A fire burned at the entrance inside the palm fence which hid the *haus* from prying females or children. It surprised me that I was allowed in, although I had heard that this area attracts many anthropologists and visitors, so perhaps the traditional taboo had been lifted.

Like most *haus tamborans* of this particular region the *haus* shape was a triangle with one obtuse angle at ground level, sloping the *haus* forward to resemble the upper jaw of a crocodile. It was thatched to the ground and the centre post inside was carved with grotesquely distorted lifesize men. On the floor there were three big *garamut* drums, the biggest was an immense 10 feet (3 m) in girth.

I stayed with Noah and his family but I didn't see much of him because he was still busy collecting yams to try and fill a second hut. The cultivation and harvesting of yams is men's work and is done in secret away from their women.

At dusk the rain stopped and the sky cleared, giving an odd glow to the twilight. A group of men with hand drums went to a swept sandy area in front of the *haus tamboran* and began calling the village to *sing-sing* to celebrate the yam harvest. It was a powerful call, with every stanza ending in a Hee-ooh shouted at the top of their lungs.

A woman arrived and sang a high solo back to them with the men in chorus behind her voice. From two yam-huts came the rhythm of *garamut* drums being played by pairs of men with long beaters. People gathered and started an ambling dance-step, forming wheels within wheels, that spun in opposite directions. There was no moon yet; the ground was lit only by flickering fires. Lightning flashed sporadically, and fireflies fluttered in the grasses. The rhythm of the drummers reminded me of an old manually-wound gramophone as it gained and lost speed in turn. Men chanted and women replied in song, their singing losing height and speed in time with the drumming.

A central hub of men squatted with drums, and eight additional drummers circled around them with chanters circling in opposite directions. Women in the chorus made a sauntering circle, most having a *bilum* strung from their foreheads, inside which was either a baby or some yams. The women stopped and formed a knot while singing to the men. The drumming changed its rhythm so that it fell behind the singers, each drum falling further behind the other. Over the hours the rhythm grew stronger and more intense; the drumming lasted throughout the night.

At dawn some men began the lining-up of yams. A bamboo frame had been built round the *sing-sing* area, and they stood the yams upright against the frame. The smallest *mamis* (yams) were brought out first; they were scarcely two feet long, and had faces of burrs fringed with feathers and kapok. A tall bamboo stick on the end of the frame was used as a measuring stick and had notches in it recording the lengths of each year's longest yams; several had reached 7 feet (2 m) and their all-time record was 12 feet (4 m). There were 280 yams in total, and when they were all arranged against the frame, the whole village turned out to admire them. I particularly liked the effect of some yams painted in ochre patterns and splendidly *bilassed* with yellow paradise plumes, shells and masks. These special yams were slung from poles so that later they could be taken in a procession to a neighbouring village.

Meanwhile, relatives and friends from other villages drifted in during the morning to join the festival. Some of them brought quantities of tobacco leaves and *buai* which they tied to the measuring stick.

At breakfast-time we rested under the palm trees and ate boiled yams served in halves of coconut shells. There was much talk about a fight that had broken out during the night and it was decided that the guilty ones would have to give a pig to the villagers as punishment. While we were still eating, a man emerged from the yam-house; he was carrying two spears and strode along the rows of yams singing to them in a solemn monotone. One by one, the *Big-men* of the village joined him, pacing up and down the sandy clearing, speaking vehemently to the yams, and praising the harvest. Afterwards, almost all the yams were given to women as gifts.

During my walk in the Maprik area I saw many curious *haus tamborans*, one of which had been recently used for an initiation ceremony. Its entrance was through a small tunnel, from which I emerged on hands and knees into the hut through the carved open legs and protruding womb of a wooden female crocodile. The initiates were 're-born' through the crocodile. In another *haus-tamboran* I saw some strangely distorted statues, among them a life-size carving of a woman, naked and reclining, primitively carved but so respected that men stopped to scatter lime powder on her ochred wooden body. In a yam-hut another sight caught my eye; in among the yam-masks I spotted a yam topped by a plastic doll's head. Its blue eyes, yellow hair, and pink skin looked totally out of context.

After I left Kuotngu I followed a jeep-track for some way and then a sandy, cold, clear stream which took me past several villages, and to a shallow gorge where I stopped to picnic. There I watched flashy, black and yellow butterflies feed on nectar in red hibiscus flowers. I detoured up a hill to visit two tall *haus tamborans* facing each other 30 feet (10 m) apart. The fronts, made of stitched bark and painted with ancestors' faces, were typical of the area. One of the villagers named every face and showed me inside where there were some statues, some weapons, a hanging drum, and many cobwebs.

A track of damp mudstone led me away from the village through trees laden with mosses, tree-ferns (stagshorn) and orchids; it was cool and shady. Low cliffs and small mudstone caves dotted the landscape and I stopped to bathe in one of the many pools formed by the eroded mudstone on the stream bed. The track ended at a village with a small lake set amidst banks of palm trees. Up through the village and into the mountains beyond there were two more lakes; the top one was a *ples masalai* (place of spirits). It was a long thin valley-lake with small canyons either side of it and an atmosphere made exciting by the wind, which blew hard, and whistled straight through the place. Also in the hills around Maprik were the scattered remains of war-machines from World War II. I saw a bomber which had crashed in the trees, now overgrown with weeds.

One village I passed through was the home of a former cargo cult leader who had encouraged everyone to give him a box containing a little money, saying that after he put it all in a special place the boxes would become filled with money. Apparently though he had just collected it and spent it all himself and today, I was told, he is an M.P. in the central government. But perhaps the most disturbing rumour I came across was at Wingei village where I had stopped to see the ceremonial opening of two new *haus tamborans*. Men kept coming up to me in a furtive way, taking me aside, and asking in whispers if I knew anything about a crucifixion that was to take place near Maprik at Christmas (they thought Christ died at Christmas), and what the phrase meant 'to be fit to carry the cross'. It was obvious that some of the less responsible missionaries had been at work, and when I was shown a tattered copy of an apostolic magazine I could understand what had happened. In it was a report of their visit to the Maprik area of Papua New Guinea and I copied down this excerpt:

'As many as five church services were held each day, and the happiness over each day's harvest (of new souls) was invigorating to us. We distributed our English literature, and those who knew any English would translate to everyone else. The need is great for our literature to be translated into the pidgin language so people can read it.

'We would like to portray to you the childlike faith and love that lives in the hearts of our members ... Each one desired to bring us an offering. Food was provided for us after the services but our hectic schedule forced us to eat briefly and leave.'

To me, this was not what missionary work was about: to fly into a community and tell the people that their indigenous beliefs are wrong and sinful, and then fly out again, seemed irresponsible and uncaring in the extreme; no wonder there was such confusion.

All day in the village I heard drumming coming from the two new *haus tamborans*; the *haus'* faces were still hidden behind palm branches which would be torn away at the morrow's *sing-sing*. Sandy courtyards, fenced off with palm, prevented women from seeing what was happening. Drums and voices sang short and low, long and high, like an inverted sigh. After a supper of wild pig, *kaukau* and greens, I went to sleep listening to the drum-beat rolling down the hill.

At dawn I woke to the squealing of pigs as they were towed or carried to the *haus tamborans*. I slipped into my clothes and went up to the *hauses*. Nothing much was happening, except for a naked man dancing in front of one of them and so I went away for breakfast. My host tried to persuade me not to go back to the festivities because they were not Christian. His new beliefs told him that he must never take part in traditional belief ceremonies; such things were devil-worship.

As I returned to the *haus tamboran* I could hear tempestuous drumming from behind the palm-frond fence, and see branches that were pushed through the fence being rustled and rapped on the ground. Other sticks were pushed through and drummed against *limbum*. This heralded the unveiling of the *haus tamboran's* face; the palm-leaf cover was torn away to reveal a customary reddish bark painting of two ancestor faces beneath a sun. It had rows of carved moon-shaped faces underneath.

Women were allowed to dance in front of the *haus* in the morning; when they formed a straggly line and pranced towards the unveiled face then backed away and advanced again. Men rattled sticks ferociously whenever they got too close to the fence. The women were holding bunches of large heart-shaped taro leaves, and were wearing grass skirts and for some reason they looked like flower nymphs. The men's chanting sounded triumphant, their low growling rising in a crescendo to long oh-oh-ays, and interspersed with grunts from the rows of pigs slung on poles at the edge of the sandy *sing-sing* ground. A man with a red-ochred face and a nose quill of bird bones was inspecting the pigs for fatness.

The *sing-sing* increased in force when a line of men arrived holding each other by the waist, their shoulders and heads bowed over each others backs. Next a group of drummers arrived, all crouched over each other in a solid moving mass. Their faces were painted in sections of colour rimmed with other colours. Their mouths were covered by beadwork discs edged with double boars' tusks, and a beadwork strap which hung like a beard down their chests. They formed a monstrous musical body, throbbing and pulsating in time to the drumming. Staying entwined, they took their place at the head of the line of crouched dancers and led them circling inwards in spiralling loops which turned back on themselves, the line moving in snake-like slithering coils.

Afterwards came the lining-up of pigs when eighteen of the fattest, still tied on poles, were laid in two lines in front of the *haus tamboran*. Some of the pigs were so heavy that four men were needed to carry them. The air was filled with their squeals of rage and indignation as they were moved. In the silence that followed one of the men went along the rows calling the names of the people who would receive the pigs as gifts; he was accompanied by a man with a large stick who thwacked each pig to make it squeal as it was called. After each pig was hit everyone responded by chanting o-o-o-o-o on a high note.

The men were highly decorated for this ceremony. Their shoulders, backs and chests were covered in crossed cowrie-shell straps, paradise feathers and armbands of shells; their jaws were blackened, and bordered with white dots; a wide yellow stripe was painted like a mask across their eyes, and on top of their heads they had headbands and *bilas* or head-dresses.

After each pig had been allocated to its new owner the owners ran over to them and began beating the pigs with their sticks. The crowd laughed as the pigs grunted and squealed. Next the men heaved the correct pigs and poles onto their shoulders and with muscles straining, they hurriedly left the area. Other people arrived, and with long spears they savagely jabbed the ground where the pigs had been lying.

At the second new *haus tamboran* on the hill's summit a similar ceremony was taking place. This *haus* was as splendid as the first, though opposite this one was an old *haus tamboran* which was *unbilassed*. Its ochre decoration was peeling and little was left except the paintings of three ancestor faces with zig-zagged halo head-dresses like the ones being worn that day. I was told that the old *haus tamboran* was named Minja, and the new one opposite was called Nau. To the side of Nau was a small shelter where a pig was taken to be killed and butchered. Its body was divided into hunks and most of them were put into the *mumu* for supper. After we had eaten the *Big-men* sat around telling stories.

The drums continued all night like the muffled thudding of horses' hooves on plains of baked clay.

18
Held Captive as a Spy!

Two weeks later I arrived back at Pagwi only to discover that my canoe had been stolen. I had left it in a safe place, or so I had thought, and it hadn't occurred to me that anyone would try to take it away. No-one else seemed surprised however, and I was told that canoe-stealing was common in Pagwi. Although most people were sympathetic, they said that it was unlikely I would ever seen it again. Suddenly it seemed that my canoe-journey was over. I knew that I didn't have enough money to buy another canoe because I had noticed how prices had risen as I had moved downriver. In this less remote stretch of the Sepik wealthy tourists were prepared to pay forty *kina* (£30) just to hire a canoe and motor for one day.

I couldn't believe that it had gone and that the end had come. The realisation was devastating. I blamed it on progress corrupting tribal morals, on the 'road' that brought beer to villages, the missionaries, and anything else I could think of. When I stopped feeling so angry I decided to do something practical about it. My canoe had to be somewhere and I wanted it back.

I began by asking the locals for ideas about where I should look and although at first no-one could or would give me any information, finally I met a man who said that he knew where to look but we would need a canoe with a motor to get there. So I contacted Pagwi's *kiap*, and having explained that my canoe was very distinctive with its bird-crocodile prow and those botched clay-and-tin patches, he agreed to let me use his canoe and motor, and sent me off to the local police-post for some petrol. The police-man (John Miangi) and his family were lovely people, and let me stay the night with them.

Early the next morning we took petrol cans to a big canoe with an outboard engine. The man who had said he knew where to find my canoe turned up and soon we were speeding along the river. On reaching the village he was looking for, we cruised slowly past all the canoes at the riverside, until right at the end I saw mine. Because so many thieves lived there John said it would be impossible to find the culprit, so we simply untied it and left. My canoe was mine again, and a fresh stage of my journey opened out ahead.

It felt good to be paddling my canoe again, and although I still had much to learn about canoeing I no longer got pushed into the reeds by the current; in fact I was discovering how to use the canoe as an extension of myself and growing more skilful with it.

Just downriver from Pagwi there was a stream entering the Sepik from the Chambri lakes, but it was choked solid with salvinia. Salvinia is one of the fastest-growing weeds in the world. Its tangled mats of fuzzy leaves and long tendril roots caught round my paddle and made progress slow and difficult. From there on, the river was dotted with small breakaway clumps of salvinia, and at one point when I was trapped between a clump and a whirlpool by the bank I had to race it to get through.

A village came into sight, with a big *haus tamboran* which looked like an ark on stilts. The gables at both ends leant outwards and curved up to long points, and along the ridge was a row of spiked sticks. Hundreds of carvings were stacked among the stilts under the *haus,* and they were all for sale. I got out to take a closer look and found totem poles, flutes and drums but the prices were far too high for me. They were obviously made for the tourists.

I didn't feel like staying the night at that village so I paddled on in the stillness of the evening. The sun was setting and a full moon had already risen; the water reflected the red and gold of the clouds. Drifting midriver, I put on my sarong and dived out of the canoe into the water. It was a lovely way to bath, swimming and drifting down that vast river.

I climbed back into the canoe, dried and changed, and as darkness fell I arrived at a solitary hut. It was ramshackle and half-collapsed and at first I thought it wasn't lived in but I was wrong. A friendly teenage girl appeared who said that it was her family's house and she took me inside to meet her parents. They invited me to share their supper of nail-fish and its eggs, greens and a thick pancake of *saksak*. Afterwards we talked about the father's carvings that were piled high under the hut. He said that carving involved making an image come out of the wood to give life to the wood. Soon I was listening to stories of *masalai* and about *taim bilong tumbuna* or the old days. After several hours I turned in. I was tired from paddling a long way and from the excitement of recovering my canoe that morning.

Breakfast was fish and *saksak* pancake, after which I went with the daughter to collect the night's catch of six fish from her nets. Most were nail-fish (named because of the sharp spikes on their fins), and she broke their spikes rapidly before they could do any harm to us. We exchanged gifts before I left: I gave her a necklace of coloured glass beads, and she presented me with a *bilum* that she had made herself, and a small carving from her father.

When the river separated into two channels around an island, I went to the right and had almost reached the second stream from Chambri (intending to go up it) when I met hordes of women in canoes. They paddled over to me and when they were alongside their hands reached out and gripped hold of my canoe, their faces wreathed in smiles of delight. They called me *'Sepik meri'* (Sepik woman) and said that they had heard stories of a white woman and canoe but had not believed it was possible. Their canoes clustered around mine like the petals of a lotus-flower, and in this way we all floated downriver, as the women sang songs about their happiness at having discovered me.

They had been collecting fish from their nets, and were cleaning the fish as we drifted along, attracting gulls and some tawny hawks which swooped with outstretched talons to grab fish-entrails from the water. The women were still singing. They took me to their village close by, and I stayed with a large powerful woman and her nine children. In total about sixteen people lived in the house: grandparents, parents, children, and children's children. Each sub-group occupied a space in the hut, and although there were no wall-divisions each space was a separate unit complete with cooking fire, smoke-rack, mosquito-net, and some decorated wooden hooks which hung from the rafters and held baskets of food to protect it against rats. Because of crowded conditions in the big *haus* I was given a small empty hut behind it.

In the evening, I was sitting by the river quietly writing in my diary when a young man came up to me and demanded to see my passport. He was abrupt and loud, and I could sense, was going to make trouble. Unfortunately for me, I didn't have my passport — I had left it in Wewak because I had been worried that I would lose it if my canoe capsized. It hadn't occurred to me that I might need it. I told him this but the young man shouted back that I was lying. He said that I was a spy; I must be a spy because I was on my own; I couldn't be a tourist since tourists only travelled in groups by motor-canoe. Also he had seen me writing some village names on my map, and marking in the changes of the Sepik's course. Other voices were raised aggressively, shouting that foreigners without passports were spies, and soon the shouting rose to a clamour. Finally they told me I was under arrest and took away my canoe so I couldn't leave.

They wouldn't reason with me; they were too excited over having caught a spy. (In third world countries the word spy includes anyone who is in the wrong place at the wrong time.) It was crazy and very threatening. Using considerable persuasion I managed to calm the situation and temporarily restore sanity, but it kept flaring up all evening as every young bighead in the village came to interrogate me.

During the course of events I lost my temper several times; it was all so ridiculous and stupid. But I knew, too, that somewhere along the line I had mishandled the situation and therefore it was partly my fault. If I had gone about it differently there might have been no trouble, but it's hard to handle every situation right. That night they put a guard outside my hut.

Life was not all bad. On the morning after my arrest I woke to the music of bamboo flutes in the air. Their song was low and mournful, overlaid with high-pitched plaintive notes. I listened while brewing some tea over the fire in the big hut. The music wafted in through the palm leaf walls and up through the slatted palm floor. The women were sympathetic to me. Theresia, the matriarch of the family, was sitting near me on the floor. She was a large person, with a flamboyant character, smiling face, and teeth stained red from chewing *buai*. Without *buai* she told me she wasn't happy, but fortunately her supply was plentiful. She gave me a nut to try, and laughed heartily at my expression of disgust when I bit into it. It was incredibly bitter but I persisted and chewed it to a pulp. Theresia then handed me a decorated round gourd containing white powder. It was powdered lime and when she mixed it with the *buai* and *daka* (pepper vine) it turned the juice bright red. It was an intoxicant but I didn't chew enough to get high, because it was so bitter.

Theresia accepted a cup of tea, and added six spoons of sugar. She was busy working with a pile of freshwater mussels, to make more lime for her gourd. After cleaning the mussels she put the shells on the fire, and cooked them until the fire burnt out. My attention was caught by the fireplaces, the fires were all set in big clay firebowls, two foot in diameter with a low front and high ornate back. Each firebowl was embellished with clay points and engraved designs.

As Theresia collected the shells from the firebowl, and began to crush them into a fine white power, we were interrupted by a group of men who barged into the hut and demanded to know my identity. It irritated me to have to explain yet again that my passport was in Wewak, and in an attempt to shorten the procedure I suggested that their government would be angry with them for arresting an innocent person. This made them stop and think, until one of them pointed out that he had heard on a friend's radio (years ago) how one spy had already been caught and they had been warned to be on the alert for more spies and to arrest them at once. Apparently that 'spy' had been a freedom fighter from West Irian, who had fled from the Indonesian troops, crossed into Papua New Guinea, and made his way down the Sepik river. In the Middle Sepik he had been caught and arrested, because he had no passport. I pointed out that clearly I was not an Indonesian, but the men disagreed, saying that since they didn't know what Indonesians looked like, I could be one.

Now that I had discovered where their 'spy-mania' was coming from, it made the situation a little less threatening. I was glad that I understood pidgin (which was almost the same as in the highlands) well enough to comprehend what was going on, though I still couldn't speak it fluently and this added to my frustrations.

Despite all, I knew I was among friends. Theresia kept a firm hand on events and used her influence to protect me, often sending the men about their business. Also she had found out where my canoe had been hidden.

For the evening meal Theresia taught me to make *parems,* which were the staple food here. They were made from the same coarse sago flour as *saksak,* but mixed with a few drops of water and patted into a thick dryish pancake. The pancake was 'fried' in a clay frying-dish, which was heated until it was burning hot. No fat or grease was used, and the *parem* was 'fried' direct on the clay. The heat of the fire and dish put me in a lather of sweat; I could never have cooked two meals a day like that.

Parems tasted much better than boiled *saksak,* and when browned on both sides they were almost delicious. To go with the *parems* we had baskets of freshwater prawns and crayfish.

That night I was woken around midnight by the sound of bamboo flutes. I got up, dressed, and followed the sound towards a dilapidated *haus tamboran.* Dogs barked as I neared the hut, and Matthais (Theresia's neighbour) came out to see why. He was pleased to see me and said that he would get permission for me to enter the hut. He disappeared back inside, then beckoned me in.

In the dim light of the fire I could see that four men with bamboo flutes six feet (2 m) long, were playing in pairs, each couple facing each other and shambling slowly in a circle, with the flutes held out to opposite sides waving slowly like bird wings in flight.

Along the hut's rafters were many long flutes, some were ancient having been handed down through generations, and others had been captured during fights with other villages. Matthais told me that when a flute's owner changed, the new owner had to learn its song. Each sacred flute has the power of one song, and certain magical songs could only be played on one specific flute. Many of them had big wooden stoppers, intricately carved into shapes of birds and men.

Two short flutes were selected and their players joined in the moving circle of music. Things livened up, the song changed, and the men playing short flutes began to prance up and down, leaping like frogs and blowing sounds into the flutes, each line ending with a weird Ho-ho laugh echoing out of the end.

I was so absorbed by this that I didn't notice a young man come in through the palm-fringed doorway, until he stopped in front of me and said '*Yu mus dai, nau yu bin lookim insait long haus tamboran, bye yu dai finis.*' To my surprise the older men told him to shut up, and I gave it no more thought. But it occurred to me later that if I had allowed it to prey on my mind and had accepted the inevitability of death, as a village woman would have done, then I could understand how people gave into the superstition and let themselves die. In this type of magic, it seems that it is the power of suggestion, and the belief that it will happen, which makes people die.

Matthais had agreed to start teaching me wood carving, but the morning was spent waiting for him to come back to his senses. He and his friends had played music all night, drinking steadily and chewing *buai*, and by the morning they were stoned out of their minds. It actually produced more interesting music, so I listened to it in the breeze and went instead to visit Matthais' father, an old and wrinkled man, who reckoned he was about 100 years old, and remembered back to *tumbuna*.

So I passed my days under arrest happily enough. One night I spent hours trying to outwit some geckos which were stealing from a bunch of fruit I had hung in the rafters. Geckos are small translucent lizards with adhesive toes that enable them to climb walls; they make a loud clicking sound that sounds like ge-cko. Actually they are friendly reptiles but they stole my fruit despite my hanging it from a long thread.

Another night I woke up because my hut was shaking. I assumed that the man guarding my hut must be doing it for some reason so I yelled out at him to stop. Instead the shaking got worse until the whole hut was lurching and swaying and I was forced to get up to see what was going on. When I looked out of the window I saw an amazing sight. Not only were all the huts shaking but the trees and land too. I heard a splash as a portion of the riverbank and a tree fell into the river.

The earthquake lasted for several minutes (later I read that it had measured seven on the Richter scale), and was followed by dark clouds and heavy rain. It was as though the end of the world had come.

The next morning, after surveying the damage of the previous night the spy-cult flared up again, and I set about trying to persuade the village elders of my innocence. It wasn't easy at first because not only did they have no concept of what a spy is, but they couldn't understand travel for travel's sake, either. In the end I told them that I was writing a story about the Sepik and its people, which I wanted to take back to my own country, and tell to my people. The elders approved of this and having agreed that I was not a spy, said that I could go.

Later that day Theresia's daughter went downriver and stole my canoe back for me and shortly afterwards, I set off to visit Chambri Lakes. It felt good to be free.

At Chambri Lakes the combination of my newly-restored freedom and the natural beauty of the lakes made me high spirited, despite the salvinia which choked the waterways and made the going hard work. If I paddled with enough speed straight into a small carpet of salvinia the canoe could push its way through, otherwise it was forced to a halt. Creepers, reeds and grasses were growing on the older salvinia; some chunks were so solid that they had become floating islands. A few years ago there was no salvinia here, nor anywhere in the Sepik, now it was multiplying so fast that Chambri and everywhere downriver was severely affected by it. Trying to find open channels, getting stuck and lost, in a water world of green weed and floating grassy islands became a regular occurrence from now on.

One night there was no dry land and I had to paddle all night, wearing my mosquito-net. The full moon made the lakes mysteriously exciting, and far away I could hear the music of bamboo flutes. The flutes like everything else in Chambri, belong either to the Sun or the Moon, and there is a balance between the two (rather like the Chinese concept of Yin and Yang). The lakes belong to the Moon and a hierarchy of gods and demi-gods with names like Iambuke and Mali. There are also spirits of the lake. The most powerful lake-spirit is Munbonk (usually a crocodile, though he comes in several other forms), and people call on his aid for good fishing and good weather. The people of Chambri also belong to either the Sun or Moon.

They are a small population of about 1,500 people, living in three villages: Aibom, Indigai and Wambunai. I went to Aibom village which is situated on a cone-shaped island where I discovered the source of the top-quality clay which is used for making the firebowls. Aibom has to rely on its trade of firebowls and cooking pots, because they have no sago palms for *saksak*. The firebowls are reputed to last several years, and even the frying dishes last a year. Alongside the pottery market the people also traded *buai*, so I bought some to give out along the way.

Back on the main Sepik I stopped at Kaminabit, where I found a luxury tourist lodge. It was closed up, but by chance the owner and his daughter arrived shortly after me and invited me to stay the night. His name was Sapa (Czech), and in addition to running the lodge he bought and sold local wood carvings which he exported to America. It was good to hear English being spoken, and to drink a glass of wine with supper. Sapa's purpose in coming to the lodge that day was to make it ready for a party of tourists, and to take a trip up a side-river to hold a market. He said that I would be welcome to accompany him.

A guest-room was assigned to me, and I slept in a proper bed with sheets. In the morning I studied my map to see where Sapa's market-trip was going. It would go south, up the tributary Korosameri and then onto the Blackwater river. At the top of the latter I noticed a lake which lay in remote mountains. The mountains whose streams drained into the lake would be the head-waters, and on impulse I decided that after visiting the markets I would continue up Blackwater river to its headwaters in those mountains.

Accordingly, we set off to market, with my small canoe tied to Sapa's big motor-canoe. The Korosameri was muddy and we sped upriver for hours, stopping nowhere until we turned off up Blackwater river and went in to a village called Sangriman. It looked like a disaster area, since about thirty per cent of the huts had fallen down in a recent earthquake, but once the people heard that Sapa was there to buy carvings they hurried to their huts to collect them together and set up an instant market. Bustle and activity surrounded us as each man added his carvings to the long line that was growing up beside the main path through the village. The line grew continuously. There were cult hooks, spears, and shields carved and ochred with protective motifs; old canoe prows of crocodile's heads, and canoe shields (formerly used in times of war). The shields adorned the canoe prows, and were more for magical protection than physical. They were made of sago bark painted with ancestral faces, and decorated with long white feathers. Also for market were three-legged stools, spears, and spear-throwing weapons. The spear-thrower was a three-foot (1-m) length of bamboo, with a slot at the side for the spear end. It worked like a catapult, hurling the spear *longwei tru*. A man demonstrated it for me.

Sapa browsed along the line and when he had seen everything he went back stopping by each man and offering prices for items that he wanted. If the price was not accepted he moved on; if it was, the carving was carried off to his canoe. I was busy keeping inventory for Sapa and coping with the chaos of people trying to charge us for merchandise we hadn't bought, or naming prices higher than he had offered. But it was good-natured trickery.

When order was restored we cruised on upriver. At Kabriman village the river became blocked with salvinia. Sapa's big canoe could go no further and he would have to return to the lodge, but before his return he stopped to call up another market for carvings. After the market we picnicked on the river bank eating fresh-bread sandwiches and drinking beer from an ice-chest.

Sapa left and I stayed overnight in Kabriman, knowing that my canoe was small enough to take a short-cut through the grass-swamp and meet the river above the block. This would enable me to continue up to the headwaters. The villagers lent me a nicely-built hut, and the following morning, after breakfast of wild duck and *saksak,* I untied my canoe and set out across the grass-swamp.

The vast flat expanse of floating grasslands was quite different to anything I had seen before. It was a blazing hot day so I stopped to swim. The water was black-coloured but clear and warm, with patches of water-lilies and white flowers. Ahead lay blue hills and beyond them were the mountains of Blackwater's headwater area, where I was heading.

It took me five days to reach them. The lush green grasses which grew from a floating network of roots and salvinia opened into a mass of small lakes joined by a labyrinth of channels. I got lost, and a dark stormy cloud blew up in the east. Soon the wind grew stronger and colder, and it roughened the water into waves. Obviously I would need shelter from the storm, but none was visible. There was one solitary tree, standing root-deep in water. I tied the canoe to a low branch and climbed up into its branches to scan the near-distance for any sign of shelter. There was nothing. Meanwhile the storm was approaching fast, so I climbed down the tree into my canoe, arranged the plastic sheet round myself and the backpack, and waited for the rain. It wasn't long in coming and as I huddled in the canoe I felt some trickles of water on my neck. Then a lot of rain came in and I got soaked, and I thought 'Why am I sitting here getting wet and miserable, when it would be nicer sitting in the top of the tree?'

So I climbed back up to the top branches, and perched there while the storm raged, and the branches swayed wildly in the wind; it was exhilarating.

19
The Blackwater Villages

Later that day on the eastern side of the grass-swamp, I arrived at Kraimbit village and made an exciting discovery: some boys were awaiting their initiation and skin-cutting ceremony. This was the ceremony dedicated to crocodiles that I longed to see. No date had been set, but the *kansol* (councillor, or headman) said that it would be held fairly soon when the time was right, and when everyone was ready. For these people there is no need, and little use, for a structured time-clock; time is hooked around events.

The boys had been awaiting initiation for about five months already. They had been confined to the *haus tamboran*, where they lived and slept, and food was brought in for them. It was taboo for the boys to be seen by women during their waiting-time, but because I was treated as an honorary man, the boys were brought to meet me inside the palm-frond enclosure which hid the *haus* from the village. The boys were young teenagers; they wore woven grass waistbands with a bunch of grass at the front, and told me they were looking forward to their initiation with pride. Skin-cutting isn't compulsory at initiation, and to have it done or not is the decision of the boy's father and uncle. Many men in Kraimbit bore the scars of skin-cutting: raised welts in a series of dashes from their chest over their shoulders and down their back to the thighs. The lines symbolise the scaliness of a crocodile. Circles of cuts on the men's chests represent the eyes of a crocodile, and the star mark on men's stomachs is simply called the mark of the crocodile.

During the pre-initiation period the boys were undergoing tests and learning about the role of men and about the secrets of the *haus tamboran*. Where we stood outside the *haus* there were five upright stone obelisks and some very old wooden carved faces half-buried in the ground, among a group of *buai* palms and colourful shrubs. The *haus* itself was old and undecorated but the village was in the process of building a new one which would take a year to finish and it was going to be a beauty. Already in place were the stilts, floor, and thick support posts carved into grotesquely phallic human figures; their bodies crocodile scarred, their eyes staring, mouths open and tongues hanging far out.

As well as building a new *haus tamboran* the villagers were also having to build thirteen new huts to replace those that fell down in the last major earthquake. Village life can be hard work, especially when luck (or *masalai*) isn't on your side.

The unexpected arrival of salvinia seven years ago was one of the heaviest blows that nature could deal. Whereas in the past fish had been very plentiful, now they were difficult to catch because they hid beneath the carpets of the weed which grew until the giant lakes were nearly obliterated. Many people couldn't find enough food to support their families. Sometimes villagers would try to keep open canoe-paths through it, but salvinia grows quickly and soon covers any still water.

Occasionally it caused a tragedy, as when a canoe was found enmeshed in salvinia with its occupants dead from hunger and exhaustion. No-one had any idea how to kill salvinia. Chemicals would be no good, since they would be expensive and would kill the fish too. Perhaps there was a fish or animal that would eat salvinia and could be introduced to the rivers. I wished I knew the answer.

Brigita, the robust and friendly girl with whom I stayed in Kraimbit, asked me if I would come back for the skin-cutting ceremony and was pleased when I said yes. I decided to return in a few weeks to see if things were in preparation. Meanwhile I would continue on into the headwaters by retracing my route through the grass-swamps until I met the Blackwater river, and could go upriver. Brigita said that there were two villages upriver, Kanengara and Kuvemas, and beyond them in the mountains was Blackwater Lake.

Accordingly I left Kraimbit and after an hour's paddling I came out onto the river and went up it to Kanengara, but I didn't stop there for long because I wanted to reach the next village, Kuvemas, before nightfall. The river got narrower and flowed more strongly, and I could tell that I was paddling uphill. Flocks of wild ducks sat on floating islands, and a storm began to gather behind us, so I hurried. When my canoe slid out of control and hit the grass, it disturbed a multitude of insects and frogs which croaked continually. The river flowed along beside a ridge of hills, winding occasionally. I met no-one. At the end of the ridge the river turned sharply back on itself and went south into hilly land, now getting close to the mountains. The storm began to rumble and the sky to darken.

Before the storm broke I had reached Kuvemas and was sheltered in a large family hut. It was occupied by a man and his two wives, his married children and their children. Juli and Martin Mera, a young couple, took care of me during my stay, and introduced me to each member of the family. Martin explained their inter-family relationship and told me that the village had six main family lines, and some sub-groups. Each person has three names, his own name, his father's name and his father's father. They said their ancestry went back to three basic ancestors, whose names were pig, *guria*, and cassowary.

As night drew on I could hear occasional dogfights below us under the stilts. Certain privileged animals were brought inside, and these included some wild piglets, striped black and tan lengthwise, which the women and girls hugged and cuddled like puppies. Supper was cooked in the clay fire-bowls and 'frying pans' that I recognised from Chambri. It is easy for these people to get to Chambri in the rainy season because a stream forms to take them there. The sago-flour *parems* were much drier and crumblier than before and were eaten with fish and greens soup or smoked fish, or just by themselves. They were good fuel for the body since if I had one or two for breakfast I found I didn't get hungry again until the evening.

At sleeping-time the *haus* was transformed by two long lines of calico mosquito-nets and we all bedded down for the night. I didn't use my hammock when sleeping in family houses because it would have been an insult, implying that their floor and way of sleeping wasn't good enough, so I slept on a floormat like everyone else.

The following morning I lazed and watched two men 'cooking' a freshly-hewn canoe as they fanned the flames across the wood in order to shrink and seal it.

Later the men took me to the *haus tamboran,* which was one of the biggest and most ornate that I had seen. Its upswept gable-ends tapered into long spikes that were carved to represent birds taking flight. The upstairs area was only for sleeping; the living and working area being at ground level beneath the stilts. The floor was of earth, and the sides and centreposts were stacked with carvings; *wan-legs* (one-legged carvings), hooks, six-foot tall masks and long-nosed *tumbuan* masks (masks symbolising *masalai* worn for *sing-sings),* flutes, drums, and weapons. It lacked only the skull-racks of former days that I was assured it once had. An old man was *fighting* (a pidgin expression) a big log *garamut* drum, which had a full-size crocodile head carved at one end. The thudding beat pulsed in the air; it wasn't making music, it was talking. I wondered how it was used for sending messages, and it was explained that each family line has a different call sign. The message he was beating was to two men in the next village to tell them that their pigs had strayed and one of them had been killed.

Groups of three-legged stools and log seats were scattered around several small fires. The fires made the atmosphere smoky, but the shade was welcome. Men sat resting, chatting idly, and using the fire's heat to dry out some tobacco leaves which I had given them. Tobacco is a social habit and was particularly appreciated because little grew there and the people relied on local trade to buy it. I dried a piece of leaf for myself, stroking it through the flames until it was brittle and ready to crumble. There were various ways of smoking tobacco — in a pipe, rolled slightly moist as a cheroot, dried crisp and crumbled into a banana-leaf roll-up, or rolled up in newspaper. I had tried using writing paper, but found it burst into flame when I drew on the cigarette, whereas newspaper (a traded item for this purpose) burned correctly and didn't taste too hot.

The other gift I had brought for people was *buai* since everyone from kids to adults and old folk loved to chew it, and loved the person who brought it. A stem of ten *buai* cost only a few cents but it was hard to obtain. At one time the government of Papua New Guinea attempted to make *buai* illegal, but there was such an outcry that the idea was dropped. I had now tried it a few times, but it still didn't produce any effect — perhaps it needed years of accumulation to work. But I was only idly curious, I didn't need the extra energy, having plenty of my own, nor did I feel the need for an artificial high.

In the jungle and hills behind the village was a stream with cascading rock pools where some girls took me to swim. The younger and more daring girls played at sliding down the smooth rock and falling into the deep clear-water pool below. I couldn't resist the temptation, and joined them. Some of the girls displayed the scar-marks of the crocodile skin-cutting ritual on their backs though unlike the men their stomachs and breasts were not scarred. When I asked them why they had had it done, they said 'laik bilong mi' (I wanted to).

During my stay I began to learn to carve wood in the traditional way. The men were rather surprised that a woman should even think of carving wood, but they accepted it with good humour and also allowed me to work carvings inside the *haus tamboran*. It turned into a hobby which would last until the end of my voyage. My teachers were usually old men, who spoke of bringing out the spirit of their ancestors in their carvings.

That was rather advanced for me and I concentrated on more basic things such as learning to use an axe or a tomahawk as it was called. It had a metal blade (unlike the stone ones I had seen earlier) and was used to chop out the rough shape of the carving. The rest of the shaping was done with either a tomahawk or knife. My first attempt was worked from a piece of broken canoe and turned out to be half-man, half-bird. Actually it looked quite good, and the men took me more seriously from then on.

When the knife-work was finished the carving had to be 'cooked' in a fire, to singe away any rough splinters and to seal the wood. The next step was to get some bark, and shred and twist it to make string for its ear-rings and nose-ring.

To paint their carvings men used ochre from clay and powdered stone in red or yellow colours. White paint came from adding water to the lime used with *buai*-chewing. It was necessary for me to abandon my former concepts about use and arrangement of colour, and adopt their simplistic approach. Paint brushes were no problem: for big paint brushes there were slices of coconut husk; and for fine brushes we would break a stem off a hibiscus bush and chew one end until it was shredded into a fine brush.

When I left, two men gave me carvings they had done as a present; both carvings were big beautiful primitive works of art.

On leaving Kuvemas I continued up Blackwater river until finally I reached the mountains. The stream was now just a narrow way, and it was often hard work paddling upstream against the current. Also it was disconcerting to feel the stream's current flowing underneath the floating grass-banks. After several hours of canoeing I came to an area of shrubby water-bushes where the stream began to zig-zag, and the glassy-smooth water showed such a jumble of reflections that, in the midday haze, it was hard to tell what was real and what was just a reflection. It was difficult to see the way. At one of the pools which was covered with water-lilies and red dragonflies, I stopped to fish. Overhead two hornbills whirred, and some wild ducks flew in a V-formation. I rolled a smoke of tobacco leaf, and held the fishing line between my toes as I rested in the hot noon-day sun.

Later, I began looking for a way onto the great lake which I knew lay nearby. Soon I felt a stronger current and noticed a gap in the bushes. The canoe fitted through and I paddled out on to the lake. A cool breeze blew across the water causing sparkling, rippling waves that splashed against the canoe side, and kept the lake clear of salvinia. It was as the map had implied, a big blue lake enclosed by green mountains which provided the headwaters. Paddling out I flexed my muscles, they felt strong and supple.

I kept paddling for three hours, across the middle of the lake and up to the far end, where there was a small island. A stream coming in the south-east led to another smaller lake and to Mesca village. In the rainy season it is possible to paddle on from Mesca to the Korosameri river.

The area around Blackwater lake looked uninhabited: open grassy banks went up into the jungle-covered mountains that held the lake. I followed the shore around until at the top of a bald lakeside mountain I spotted a high-gabled *haus tamboran* and huts on its summit.

The village was Anganamai, and it was made up not of the big family houses like Kuvemas, but of a number of smaller huts. An old woman and young couple invited me to share theirs. They spoke a different language from the Blackwater river people and had different ways; they were more like mountain folk.

At dusk I went to wash in the lake, accompanied by ten children who sang continually. Sunset was dull and cloudy, and I went back to the hut. For supper we ate *cuscus* (possom) stewed with *tu-lif* (richly-flavoured tree leaves). This was my first taste of possom and it was slightly like mutton. The fire for cooking was set in an earth hearth but they didn't use a firebowl, presumably because they weren't traded this far. That night there was an electric storm with forks of lightning ripping through the night sky. At times the flashes were so frequent that the sky stayed bright like daylight.

In the morning I browsed through the *haus tamboran* on the mountain summit. The carvings were remarkably different from those I had seen before; the majority were bark carvings chiselled into strange phallic men and women. They bore the markings of the crocodile and some had an almost martian appearance. Many had names: one with three antennae on his head represented the ancestor Dejar, whilst two other similar-looking ones were called Mangoto and Uratalish. The men offered the carvings for sale and begged me to buy because none of the carving-traders could reach their village. Prices were very low, so I bought one work from each man. As I went round, the number of men seemed to double. They pulled every trick to make me buy extra, but I didn't mind because I liked their work, and they would make good family presents. When I had made my final choice we piled the carvings into heaps of six and tied them in bundles with bark string. I was impressed with the bark string — it was long and so supple that it could be knotted, and withstand considerable strain. Also I bought some *buai*, which grew in the mountains behind Anganamai.

In another hut the men showed me their most sacred of carvings, a very ancient figure called a *wan-leg*, which was believed to have been in Anganamai before the village. We all sat down as they told me its legend — of how a female ancestor had told her son that when she died a tree would grow on her grave and that he was to fell it and carve a drum from the trunk. When she died the son did as he was told but from the left over wood he made some carvings of faces, enclosed by a series of semi-circles upheld by one leg. They became known as *wan-legs*, and to his surprise, he found that they were endowed with the powers of

209

speech and movement. In war expeditions, I was told, the figures, bounding along on their single leg, were used to precede the warriors, to kill and sow confusion in the enemy village. The *wan-legs* lived in the *haus tamboran* until the day that an inquisitive woman looked at a *wan-leg* while pretending to pick leaves and was killed for her sacrilegious curiosity. From that day on the *wan-legs* lost their ability to move and speak.

This story led on to other *masalai* and ancestor stories. The *masalai* here were depicted in their carvings as long-nosed caricatures of humans, their bodies usually hidden beneath overlapping grass skirts. *Masalai* could be spiteful, kind, or indifferent and could be found in the lake at every point and inlet. Their ancestor caves were deep in the mountains and were said to house piles of skulls and still to have the remains of ochre paintings on the cave walls. I made a mental note to visit them if ever I passed nearby.

In the afternoon I thought it would be nice to go fishing. I got a few of my things together and went down to the lake, to the spot where I thought I had left my canoe. But it wasn't there. Thinking I must have made a mistake I searched the whole area but still couldn't find it and gradually it dawned on me that it had been stolen again. I was angry and disappointed and felt let down. I went back to the village and by asking around I discovered that someone from the other village had taken it (there were only two villages on Blackwater Lake). To help me, one of the men stood up on the bald hilltop and yelled over the lake that I wanted my canoe back. He told me that it would be a while before it was brought back and that meanwhile I could borrow another canoe for fishing.

It was a long canoe, heavier to handle than mine but easier to steer in straight lines. I parked in a patch of waterlilies, and pulled up a couple of their juicy edible stems to munch, then baiting my fishing line with a sago grub, I cast it into the water and sat back to wait. (In pidgin to fish is *thro-im-awei-huk.*) An hour passed by and the lake became glassy in the evening stillness. Just as I was about to give up I felt a tug on the line and pulled in a *big-mauf* (barbel). Now, in better humour, I paddled back to the shore where to my surprise and pleasure, I saw my canoe. I checked over it to make sure everything was there and noticed that my canoe-rag was gone, which was inconvenient but not disastrous. I poled the canoe deep into the reeds so it was completely hidden from view and made my way back to the village.

In the evening there was a *sing-sing*. It started rather dully with just two men playing drums, one girl chanting, and others ambling round in a circle. A few more people joined in, singing a monotonous chant of 'oh-ey-ah-oh', but I went away and had supper of wild pig and *saksak*. My host had somehow managed to get thoroughly stoned, but he was very amiable.

Later I went back to the *sing-sing*, it was still low-key, so I circled with them and learnt the chant and rhythm. Slowly the wheel turned. Often it halted and everyone relaxed for a minute then started again, spinning steadily through the hours and gradually gaining momentum. Now ten times the original size and still growing, people were stomping around vigorously, the women's grass skirts flicking with each step, and their long flat breasts keeping time. As the circle turned, waves of harmonising bass, tenor and soprano voices washed over me. I used the sound as a mantra and it relaxed me into a different consciousness. At midnight I retired to sleep, but the chanting and dancing went on until dawn.

In Anganamai (as everywhere) all types of local people came to visit me during my stay. The old folk came to look and marvel; some thought I wasn't real, and others were worried because I was twenty-nine and had no babies. When I explained that I didn't want to stay at home and have babies, many of the women agreed heartily, but I wondered if they actually understood. Most of the village babies screamed in terror at the sight of me, but the older children were full of curiosity and followed me wherever I went; and when I stopped they sat down to watch me. Sometimes I enjoyed their company, but at other times I felt crowded, or as though I was a freak in a zoo, and then I would tell them all to go away. But I didn't like to send people away too often, because I had chosen to place myself in their lives in a way that attracted their attention, and a compromise was reached when I discovered that they understood the phrase 'Give me space'.

Some of them were in poor health with septic tropical ulcers, malaria, filaria, dengue fever or snotty noses and hacking coughs. TB wasn't uncommon and when they coughed straight into my face (they had no idea of germs or how they are spread), I worried that I might catch something. Their curiosity was only natural, and it did give rise to some funny moments as well as frustrating ones. Perhaps the funniest was when they saw me brush my teeth with toothpaste for the first time. Some people gasped with alarm as my mouth began frothing, others just stood and stared with amazement. They have their own indigenous methods of cleaning teeth and they had never seen anything like this before. They use *skin-dwai*, the bark of the cinnamon tree, which they chew; it is excellent for killing germs and strengthening the gums, and I often used it myself as well.

It was not yet time for me to go and find out whether Kraimbit's skin-cutting ceremony was in preparation, so I decided to move to its neighbouring village, Kanengara, and continue to get acquainted with the area in general.

When I left Anganamai, some of the villagers stood on the hilltop and as I paddled away they sang out their traditional farewell. The song floated over the water, growing fainter as I paddled away from them and continuing long after they had disappeared from sight.

Kanengera village was situated on a central high ridge of solid land in the midst of marsh-forest and a maze of lakes with salvinia and floating grass islands. Looking out from the end of the ridge I had a wonderful view over this waterworld. Usually there was a canoe or two with men fishing or going about their daily business. It was the season for gathering reeds for matting, cutting sago palms for *saksak*, and felling trees for new canoes. People stood to paddle their canoes, enabling them to see clearly over the tall floating grass. I had begun practising my standing technique, but wasn't at all steady — standing in a lightweight wood-hewn canoe is little easier than standing on a log.

While sitting overlooking the emerald flatness, I watched two separate storms circling far off and letting loose their rain on the landscape. Someone brought me a fresh coconut full of milk. Hornbills flew upriver and a solitary white heron stretched out its long neck for take-off then crooked it into a double-bend to fly. Luckily for them the herons have little meat on them and consequently are not hunted.

Kanengara was made up of two villages; on the ridge-end was the community school, trade store, first-aid post, and a closed-up mission house, while a mile further along the ridge was the original indigenous village with its *haus tamboran*. A small hut in the old village was offered to me, and a group of *skul-munkies* (school children) were delegated to carry my luggage there. I took the entire contents of the canoe with me, dividing the baggage and carvings into child-sized loads which made enough packages for twenty small porters. The village was set on the ridge, only one hut wide, and it formed a line along the ridge top. As soon as we got to my hut a storm broke and the boys, after helping me stow away my luggage, stripped off and went outside to play football. I watched them splashing through the clay puddles, playing to no rules, with no referee, just every player for himself in the torrential rain; they were having a marvellous time.

The following day the boys offered to take me for a walk, and we all set off down the ridge into the swamp. The going under foot was firm at first but the path that led through the dense sago-palm forest was underwater, with narrow plank-like strips of bark lying in the murk. For the first person in line the water was clear enough to see where the strips lay, but once the bark-strips were stepped on they stirred up clouds of mud and were more difficult to find. I followed the leader taking care to put my feet exactly where he had put his, and angling them outwards to prevent them slipping down between slats and getting pinched.

We were all barefoot. I had forgotten my jungle boots and early on had taken off my thong sandals which were worse than useless. There was no alternative to the path since to either side of us the swamp was deeper and more treacherous for the lack of bark strips. Squat, thorny sago palms closed in on us from both sides and stretched back into an evil-looking gloom. The branches of the palm were heavily studded with needle-sharp spikes, some of which poked up through the slats in the path. They were excruciatingly painful to walk on and we occasionally had to pause to pull them out of our feet. Twice I overbalanced and nearly fell; it would have been safer to fall in the swamp than to grab the trees for support.

I was thinking how close it all was to a living nightmare when the leader called out *'Run huri-up, poison snek'*. Ahead of us I could see the long dark body of a snake slithering and swimming along the path toward us. I froze, uncertain where to run, and the boys hopped around in excitement but as soon as the snake sensed us it recoiled and sprang like a whiplash away into the forest.

After about an hour's walking we came to a mountain and climbed its steep side to the top, to Yamandenai village, where we stopped to *kisim wind*. I felt exhausted but the boys didn't seem to be affected by either the walk or the steepness of the climb to the village. Outside some huts we met three old men who welcomed us and said that they had a question to ask me: they wanted to know what the word 'Independence' meant, because several years ago they had been told that their country became Independent, but nothing seemed to have changed. I tried my best to explain what it meant, and the boys laughed gleefully because they had brought someone who knew the answer. The men also asked me if I wanted to stay the night and after a moment's hesitation I thanked them and refused. If I had known about that appalling path I would have brought some things for the night, but as it was, my clothes were damp and I didn't want to sleep on a hard floor-mat without any dry covering. From the huts the boys led me over that ridge and down to a lake, a smaller one than Blackwater lake, lying in a vast landscape of marsh and mountains. I lingered there watching the sun set and dreading the return journey through the swamps, and knowing that every extra moment that I delayed would make it worse because twilight doesn't last long in equatorial places.

I called to the boys and we returned to the huts, waved goodbye and headed back to Kanengara. The deep gloom of the sago palm forest, the dank swamp and the whine of mosquitoes were a hellish combination. After miles of having to walk knee-deep in the swamp I could only set myself on automatic reflex and think about better things.

It was a relief to arrive at the base of Kanengara's ridge where there were some fresh springs that we used for washing and cleaning up. When I arrived back at my hut I was so weary that I fell asleep, but was quickly woken by a friend who had brought some supper for me to eat — wild pig and *parem* which tasted delicious to me. After supper I fell asleep again until the middle of the night when something startled me awake, and turning on my flashlight I saw a large rat inside my mosquito net by my feet. I grabbed hold of the net's hem and pulled it up to allow the rat to escape, but it panicked and ran the wrong way inside the net behind me. I lifted up more netting and fortunately the rat escaped, although some mosquitoes had taken the opportunity of getting in; but I was too tired to care and went back to sleep.

One morning the children took me to their school, a government community school where the teachers were nationals of Papua New Guinea and they asked me to teach some morning classes to the older pupils. At 8 o'clock we grouped for morning assembly on a hillside promontory overlooking the endless maze of lakes and greenery. The children formed lines and began a marching exercise which was part of every school assembly (*skul asembli*), then they gathered in front of a tall flagpole. During the raising of the national flag everyone sang the national anthem. It was set to a melodious tune with each line ending on a short sonorous note which rang out over the vast water-garden.

After the morning's teaching I went for coffee with Tino, the catechist at the mission. He had a young but serene and kindly black face, and he turned out to be one of the most genuine Christians that I met. We had just finished coffee when we heard the motor of a small single-engined aeroplane. It circled the hill, alerting everyone of its arrival, and landed on the rough grassy airstrip down at water level. *'Balus'* (plane) *'bye fal-daun'* (*fal-daun* means to land!), they shouted as they hurried towards it. It brought a Catholic brother from Timbunke (which is a Catholic mission downstream on the main Sepik), who had come to visit the mission and bring supplies for the clinic and trade store. He helped the pilot to unload the supplies which villagers hastily began carrying to the mission-house. Then he invited several people, including myself and the pilot, to come up to the house for refreshments. During this I realised that the plane gave me a chance to mail some letters, and when I asked the pilot, he agreed to post them for me at Wewak. He would be leaving in half an hour, so I hurried back to my hut to collect the letters. It was fortunate that they were already written although in fact I often wrote letters which I collected and kept until finding a way to post them. My parents had said that if ever they lost touch with me and three months were to go by without any message, then they would try to trace me in case I needed help. In the five years that I had already been travelling I had twice been over the deadline, and on both occasions my parents had traced me successfully without using government or police help. Even in the Sepik it would not have been difficult to find me since my whereabouts were part of the local news.

It was time for me to check out the nearness of the skin-cutting ceremony in Kraimbit. Some school children who lived in Kraimbit said they would take me there on Saturday, when they went home for the weekend. It sounded odd to hear the word weekend since I had long ceased knowing what day of the week it was, but of course for a school the weekend was relevant, especially when some children only went home at weekends. Villages like Kraimbit, Kabriman and Kuvemas were too far away for children to paddle to school daily so they lived in *haus bilong skul-munki* during the week; one *haus* for each village.

The boys recommended an early start so I spent Friday night at their rickety old house that was precariously balanced on tall stilts on a steep hillside. The people of Kraimbit needed to replace it with a new hut but because they were busy rebuilding those lost in the earthquake and the new *haus tamboran*, they didn't yet have the time. The old house wasn't so bad when I knew where the dangerous flooring lay and was able to avoid falling through it. During the night we were woken by a storm and had to go out through the rain to the *haus kuk* (kitchen), where we sat until the storm and winds had abated and it was safe to go back. The mosquitoes were dreadful and the rain blew in through the broken wall. When finally the wind dropped and we were allowed to return to bed, I slept with three children under a huge mosquito net.

For the first hour of the way to Kraimbit we had to walk in the sago-swamps again — how I hated those sago thorns and splinters — until we came out at a lake where their long canoe was moored. I sat in the middle of a line of twelve young paddlers; we looked like part of an armada. The lake was badly overgrown with different types of waterlily, fuzzy surface weeds, maroon ferny weeds and of course the salvinia. Getting through the matted stretches of salvinia was a test of the children's skill and I was impressed by the fact that no steering commands were ever given, and that they acted instinctively as a team. The floating islands and invisible paths in the grass were the worst hazards, and sometimes we had to get out onto the floating grass to push the canoe through. It took two hours to reach Kraimbit.

The news of the skin-cutting ceremony was that it was drawing closer but not yet the right time. The boys waiting in the *haus tamboran* looked a bit fatter and more sleepy-headed than when I had seen them last. These people have no concept of or word for boredom; the closest is *mi laze* which means to rest, be tired or fed up.

From the lack of any visible preparations it seemed likely that the ceremony was a matter of weeks away, and I decided that I should definitely stay in the Blackwater area so that I could return to Kraimbit nearer the right time. I returned to Kanengara with the boys on Sunday and arrived in time for a church service at the mission. It was held in the open-sided hilltop church, with hymn music provided by drums. Going to church is something of a social event, bringing together people from different villages who do not often meet. Many had brought things to trade, so after the service there was a small, noisy and colourful market.

The market trade was mostly in *buai*, *daka* and *skin-dwai* which were brought down from the mountains nearby and usually exchanged for *saksak* (from the sago swamps) and tobacco (from the Sepik direction). I bought some *limbum* leaves to use as a covering for baggage in my canoe and a few meagre tobacco leaves. I didn't need to buy the banana leaf wrappings because the mission store sold sheets of newspaper which was cheaper and better. Every time I bought some pieces of newspaper I read them avidly before smoking. The articles didn't often make sense because they were continued on missing pages and anyway were several years out of date. Once I managed to buy a page with a crossword on it which was a real treat, and I had to stop myself filling it in too quickly so that I could enjoy it longer!

While still at the mission, I managed to get treatment for a small tropical ulcer on my leg. The ulcer had started as a mosquito bite which would not heal; I must have scratched it and it became infected. In this hot and humid climate you only had to scratch a bite or cut and it would go septic, soon turning into a tropical ulcer. The clinic's nurse gave me a spare bandage and a little jar of antibiotic powder so that I could continue the treatment. Tropical ulcers are particularly unpleasant because the infection eats back into the flesh and looks hideous. The local people were in a worse state than me, but they didn't seem to bother about theirs and although the health clinic was free, they often just left their tropical ulcers to get dirty and rotten.

To fill my time I decided to get back into my canoe and go down the Blackwater river to Kabriman. Having lost my canoe-rag I now used a handful of absorbent salvinia for mopping and drying the canoe's floor. It was a nice change to be back in my canoe, on my own, and since I was travelling downstream I didn't have to fight the current, and just rested my paddle and floated.

A crocodile swam lazily upriver and as if by mutual agreement we ignored each other and he passed by. Now I had to begin looking out for a line in the tall grass that would show me the short cut to avoid a block in the river that I had been advised was further down. I kept a careful watch, but when I came up against a dead end I realised that I had over-shot it and I was lost. I stood up in the canoe in order to see over the grass and to see if I could find any signs of a way out, but there was nothing, nothing but masses of small, still lakes. It was very quiet; there wasn't another soul in sight. Since I couldn't go forward I turned back and began following a more promising narrow creek.

Suddenly, from out of the stillness I heard a frantic rustling and six pigs emerged from the grass swimming toward my canoe. It was an alarming and totally unexpected sight which I could have found amusing if they hadn't looked so menacing. I quickly sat down. As they got closer I made threatening noises and gestures, to make them swerve away, but they kept coming straight at me. I back-paddled until I got clear then stopped and thought how silly it was to be afraid of some pigs swimming in water.

The pigs had gone to the bank on the other side of the creek, so thinking it was safe I paddled forward again. Immediately, they turned, plunged back into the water, and swam at my canoe again. I couldn't believe it. I paddled forward more strongly, but two pigs swam to cut me off, and one went to the back and began pushing the canoe with his snout, rocking it crazily. I tried to lever him away with my paddle but other pigs began to jostle alongside. It was a frightening experience and only when I was well clear of them did I stop to wonder that it had all been about. To give it a rational explanation, I decided that probably they were semi-tame pigs that were trying to get the sago feed they thought I was bringing to them.

On reaching Kabriman I found the village almost deserted. Most of the menfolk were away in the forest, looking for good trees to make new canoes. The women were down at the end of the village, thrashing some bundles of reeds, flattening them, and laying them to dry in the sun. They would be used for thatching roofs and basket-making. No traffic came or went from anywhere; the river was now blocked in two places downriver, cutting the village off from the outside world. Mosquitoes were plentiful.

Late afternoon I went fishing and caught a small *makau* (the tastiest Sepik fish) for my supper. I was preparing it in my hut when a chicken flew in through the window, squawking loudly, and promptly laid an egg. I hadn't had a fresh egg (apart from crocodile eggs) for ages and I boiled it for supper. I ate it slowly, and thought about the stacks of them in western supermarkets; but I didn't really miss such things.

The occupants of the huts on each side of mine were fighting and shouting angrily at each other. Women shouted louder and more angrily than men; there was no withholding of feelings, and every drop of rage was expressed. To get away from the noise I went for a stroll, and met a group of young people singing in *tokples* (their own language) and in pidgin about fishing in the lake below Mt Sanmari. Some children stopped to dance, in realistic imitation of their elders. At dusk a fierce storm blew up and we all dashed back to our huts. It raged all night and in the morning I discovered that lightning had struck one hut and burned it to the ground.

At dawn the chicken came back and conveniently laid another egg in the basket for my breakfast. It was calm again and cloudy, a good day for paddling, so I set off upriver.

At Kanengara I received news that my friend Tino (the catechist) had been struck by lightning. Only his hand was hurt and since he was sleeping I didn't disturb him. Instead I continued on upriver, making a total of eight hours that day paddling upstream until at sunset I reached Kuvemas where Martin, Juli and their family gave me a lovely welcome. After supper of wild pig, *tu-lif* and *parems*, I went around with Juli to visit some of the friends I had made on my last stop there. One of the girls, Evita, was confined to her family house and hidden behind improvised curtains so she couldn't be seen by men, which Juli told me was customary during an adolescent girl's first menstruation. A week later Evita would be taken secretly to wash, and the other womenfolk would dress her in a new grass skirt, and decorate her with ear-rings and strings of beads after which they would have a special *sing-sing* for her coming out, which was called *Abouoin-jam*.

While I was learning all this I heard the mournful wailing of a bamboo flute, coming from the *haus tamboran*, so I wandered over to find out what it was about. The man with the flute was shuffling around among the carvings under the *haus* stilts, lost in a trance, blowing his feelings through the flute. Someone explained to me that a man had died and that after death the spirit needed to be freed from the body; the wailing and keening of the flute was to encourage the spirit to come out.

I spent several weeks in the Blackwater area, re-visiting villages and getting to know people and their customs. Men took me hunting, and tried to teach me the local language; women showed me how to cook in the local way, and to weave baskets; and young girls took me fishing and taught me their songs. Slowly I seemed to become part of their lives, sharing with them, and belonging in their families.

20
The Ancestral Cave
of Anganamai

Just as on my last trip from Kuvemas, I paddled again to the big lake in the mountains, but this time I went to Anganamai to ask for directions so that I could go and look for their ancestral cave with the paintings and skulls that they had mentioned before. A village elder said that the cave was in the headwaters of the Karawari river, and it would take at least a week to walk there and back. He elected his son to be my guide, and said that we should start out the next morning at dawn after the night-long *sing-sing*.

The *sing-sing* was to celebrate the giving of a baby to a childless couple by one of their relatives. It was an unusual *sing-sing* in that it seemed to consist of many short scenes like a play. The people behaved like actors: the young couple were painted in red ochre and sat on stools, with the donated baby on their lap, on the open swept hillside; other people lined up and presented the couple with gifts, but it was aggressively performed with one man ordering them to give and commenting on their meanness. Someone gave a chicken, then picked up a stick and beat the chicken to death in front of the couple. The stick missed the chicken several times and everyone burst out laughing. This scene that would have upset me in England, didn't upset me here. I had come to share their lack of sentimentality over animals and to recognise their importance as a much needed source of meat. A child in rich *bilas* of yellow bird of paradise feathers and *kina* shells gave them a basket of pig meat, and another gave *parems*. All of this was done seriously with solemn faces, although the scene changed slightly every time a man hammered on a drum. Two boys arrived, sat by the couple, and began to kindle a fire. The play went on for nearly two hours, getting progressively more incomprehensible until it developed into a feast and a typical *sing-sing*.

221

The party was still going on when my guide and I left Anganamai at dawn. My guide, Francis, also brought his wife and baby along for the trip. I wasn't sure why, until I realised her *bilum* was full of bedding and *saksak;* she was his pack-horse.

The headwaters of the Karawari river lay in the mountains to our south-east. The first day was a hard day's walking, up a rough mountain behind Anganamai then down and across muddy marsh-forest. The sago thorns were a painful three inches long but although my companions were barefoot, mercifully I had remembered to wear my jungle boots. The boots were a mixed blessing when it came to tramping through the pools of stagnant rainwater and many streams because the water often came over the top. It wasn't worth taking them off, and full of water, they squelched for the rest of the day's walk.

Leeches, black slug-like things, with front and back suckers, hung invisibly in the vegetation beside paths, waiting to latch onto anyone who passed by. They left a stinging sensation when I pulled them off my skin, and those which had already sucked blood left a spot that bled profusely due to the anti-coagulent that they injected when they took the blood.

Then we climbed a bigger mountain. Forest roots tangled underfoot, red-shelled fruits with orange conker-like nuts and red bell-flowers grew on shrubs beside us, while overhead I glimpsed orchids and a bird of paradise with long yellow-white tail feathers. Some of the trees were leaning over but had been stopped from falling by other trees. At a shallow pool we paused for a drink of water, Francis and his wife flicking the water into their mouths with their hands and me using a curled leaf as a cup. I still couldn't flick it.

Later Francis stopped to show me some tracks where two men had passed and returned. Their return prints were much deeper, indicating that the men had probably been hunting and come back heavily laden with a wild pig.

We went on through the dark, dense forest until at midday we stopped by a cool stream for a picnic of dry *parems.* After one more mountain we reached Brumoh. Brumoh comprised two huts, belonging to an old forest man who raised tame pigs, and increased his herd by capturing wild pigs. We had a delicious supper of pork.

The second day took us from Brumoh to Banditua. In the

afternoon a storm broke directly overhead quickly turning the streams into raging torrents. We had to swim one of them; most of the others were spanned by single fallen trees, and were more slippery with boots than if I had been barefoot. The forest dripped and was misty; the rain brought out a multitude of leeches. Francis was becoming a nuisance, he complained *'Legs bilong me laze; hed bilong me pain; bell-i pain; gimme smok'*. My tobacco was almost finished. Whenever I smoked, Francis nagged at me to give him a smoke too and I felt I couldn't say no. So now I had finished all the leaves and was down to the last dregs. Maybe that accounted for my bad-temper.

Banditua was a cluster of huts on top of a mountain, which overlooked the Karawari river and the many mountains surrounding it. Spiky *pandanus* trees, *buai* palms, coconut palms and fern trees were all around. I wandered among them and didn't feel happy. Francis was complaining about being hungry, so I cooked up some rice and tinned steak as a treat, but he only ate a little and said it wasn't tasty. Then he lay down and said he was sick because he had no tobacco. It made me want to slap him; he had not brought any of his own tobacco to start with.

I slept in a half-built hut and coughed all night. In the morning I saw a woman beating a boy's back with a broom of twigs, then pinching his skin between her fingers and taking a sharp sliver of bamboo, slicing a series of cuts across it. This was done to produce decorative scars. When the blood stopped running we had breakfast of pig and *parems*.

For the next stage of our journey we used a canoe and three paddles to take us down a small stream. It led among tall, aged and mottled trees which often arched over the stream and formed a roof above our heads. Tendril roots trailed down from high branches to brush the water. At times we had to get out of the canoe and climb over fallen trees, pushing the canoe underneath. We went to a village where we had heard that people grew tobacco plants, but when we got there the village was deserted except for one old lady hiding in the back of her hut. I asked her if I could buy some tobacco leaves, but her face was immobilised with fear. With her eyes fixed on me, she began to gibber and, seizing her *bilum* and a firebrand, she ran away. So that was that, no tobacco.

Gradually the stream became deeper and faster, with many

sharp corners and brown mud banks. Piercing bird calls could be heard above a chorus of crickets that sounded like jet-planes getting ready for take-off, their noise stopping as we drew level and beginning again as we passed. The stream ran into a river; it wasn't yet the Karawari, we were just in the headwaters. That evening Francis pointed to a faraway mountain, which he called Mt Kaprimari. A faint white mark showed the location of cliffs near the cave. It was a long way distant.

As we drew closer, over the next couple of days, we had several glimpses of those white cliffs, always from different angles. One day near an abandoned hut I saw a wooden gun for poisoning fish. It looked like a firework-rocket, with a head of two hollowed halves of wood. White milky poison (a type of tree sap) was used to fill the hollow space. To fire the gun you pushed the handle which acted as a plunger, shooting the poison out of the cracks with great force to spread rapidly through streams dammed up by local folk for this purpose. It blinds and paralyses the fish, which all rise to the surface and die, and are collected. It is a shame that even the tiddlers die, but conservation isn't a concept which existed here.

We stopped at three garden-hamlets, where we parted company with Francis' wife and baby. She said they would wait for us there. We also parted company with our canoe, leaving it tied to a tree in a hidden side-creek. Francis located a footpath going south and found his way without mistakes, even though admitted that he had never been this far from home before. He was now out of his territory, and somewhat frightened by that, but his instinct for pathfinding was faultless. Again I glimpsed the distant white cliffs on Mt Kaprimari. The next village we found was called Yermat. Nearly everyone was out, but once we explained our errand to an old man he walked over to a big *garamut* drum and began hitting it with a pole as tall as himself, in slow wooden thumps, which got faster as his message grew longer; I wondered what he was saying.

While we waited for some kind of response we ate a delicious meal of roasted turtle and *pandanus*. The meat was pale and tender, not at all fibrous and more like shellfish. The *pandanus* stained my fingers bright red and as I looked at myself with my mud-splattered legs and red-stained hands I smiled at the thought of how horrified my family would be if they could see me. Just as we were finishing our meal an elderly man emerged from the trees and came over to speak to us. He had arrived in response to the drum message to offer to guide us to the cave. He hadn't been there since childhood but he was confident that he would remember the way.

He insisted that we use his canoe which was rather small for three, but although it sat very low in the water, surprisingly little water spilled in. We were going upriver against the current so the paddling was mostly hard work but it eased up when we cut across river corners and caught small up-spinning currents.

Then we branched off up a small tributary and followed it until it was just a brook. It was often too shallow for a canoe and so we frequently ran aground and had to push it free. We also had to push it up each set of stony rapids. The stream forked several times until I lost track of our whereabouts though I could see that we had come to Mt Kaprimari. Finally we beached the canoe and started walking up the stream bed. We walked for two hours before we stopped and made camp beside a deep rock pool. In the pool Francis managed to spear a fish, and one prawn for our supper, while for bedding we collected mounds of broad-leaves. I wished they were tobacco leaves; not smoking was proving difficult and making both Francis and me edgy. I had already tried smoking other types of leaves from a variety of trees and bushes but the majority tasted sickly and made me cough.

But I forgot my problems when the old man began to talk, and describe his visit to the caves as a child. His eyes went out of focus as he recalled the past and said that the paintings were done by an ancient person who lived in the cave at the time the world was created. I fell asleep to the legends of the sun and moon, and slept deeply until dawn. The old man had woken long before us and had already re-kindled the fire, and when we woke he was cooking some plantain-bananas for our breakfast. He urged us into a very early start.

A steep but straightforward scramble took us up through steamy forest which was so humid that sweat ran down my face and dripped from my chin. Leeches were numerous, and orange-spotted butterflies flew out of our way. At a clay outcrop the old man told Francis and me to put clay marks on our legs and bellies, since we were seeing these sacred paintings for the first time. When we had climbed about 1,000 ft (300 m) we reached the cliff base and struggled along underneath, holding onto rubbery rope-like creepers, to prevent ourselves from falling down the steep crumbly pale-grey shale which slid away under our feet. Luckily the creepers held firm. We stopped to rest perched on a tiny ledge, and as I looked at the evidence of years of erosion and landslides beneath us I hoped there would still be some of the paintings left. Scanning the cliffs above us I could see how the lighter-coloured rock was freshly eroded, flaking away in layers, while the darker rock was weathered and old.

According to the old man the cave should have been wide and shallow, formed between an overhang of cliff and a flat ledge of rock, but that was not what we could see. Much of the cave had clearly gone, though as we progressed along we found more remains of the rock ledge and arrived under an eroded overhang which the man said had once formed the cave. We looked up at the long overhang directly above our heads and saw ochre paintings in red and yellow primitive shapes and symbols. Much of the artwork had been lost through erosion and I felt sad to think that it would all soon be gone forever. We could still see the fading shapes of crescent-moons, circles, combs, something like birds, and that most elemental of cave-paintings — hands outlined in red ochre, some life-size and others enlarged. Francis was awed by the place; his face showed fear, respect and reverence.

We crossed between the remnants of ledges by clinging on to the creepers making sure that two of us were never holding the same plant since there was a staggering fall below us. At the back of one of the precariously balanced ledges we discovered the fragments of skulls, long bones, joints, and ribs, many of them in the later stages of disintegration. In another spot I found a piece of an old *wan-leg* carving.

I rested idly up there. The old man brought me a yellow furry-tasting fruit, which was sweet, and had big round shiny seeds. As I sat there I made another find; a small tobacco plant growing from a crevice. A seed must have been dropped by a bird. I picked it and we made a small fire to dry out one of the leaves for smoking straight away. The old man brought a bamboo *susaf* (jew's harp) out of his *bilum*, which he began to blow and hit to produce a melodious zingy tune.

Looking from the cliff's ledge out over the mountainous

jungle, I remembered how we had seen the cliffs as a distant white splash from various points in that immense view. On our journey back to Anganamai I often glanced back at the cliffs, and as they gradually receded into the distance I was aware that they were disappearing into my past, soon to disappear out of existence.

The way back was hindered by paths overgrown with vegetation and containing deep pockets of bog and swamp. There was no concept of path maintenance or anything like that even though the Australians had tried to encourage villagers to improve their trails during their days of colonisation. At Yermat we parted company with the old man, and at the next hamlet re-gained Francis' wife and baby.

It was a long hard trek back to Anganamai that was not made any easier by two near-disasters. One occurred when I tripped over a root, and as I jabbed my walking stick down for support, it went straight through a mesh of roots and into a hole — and I followed it head first. I landed in soft earth in a dark hole, surprised but not injured. Just above my head was the forest floor of roots and I realised that the hole had been washed out by rain. After climbing out and shaking the earth off my clothes we continued safely until the second near-disaster which happened as we were crossing a ravine.

The bridge was a fallen tree and its smooth trunk was very slippery as I edged along it very carefully with my feet pointing sideways for a better grip, and tried not to look down at the steep rocky gulley and the trickling stream which lay about 20 ft (7 m) below us. There were no convenient handholds since the tree's branches were almost out of reach, and the trunk angled downhill. I knew that I was in trouble when the foot carrying my weight slid forward. Instinctively I jumped sideways, pushing off with my other foot and leapt into some bushy branches close by. Luckily, the twigs cushioned my landing, and I was just pulling myself towards the bank and safety, when I heeard a yell and saw Francis slip off the bridge as well. He landed nearby and as we both scrambled up the bank we agreed we had been lucky; it felt good to be unharmed and alive.

At the hamlet of Banditua our arrival coincided with about twelve other travellers; a heavy load for a three-house hamlet but there was more a feeling of festivity than resentment. The people were all of the same tribe and had much news to exchange as they passed through on route looking for trees to make into canoes, for ironwood for hut stilts, for *buai*, and to go hunting. The land was tribal territory and everyone in the tribe had rights to some things, yet certain trees were owned by particular family lines — Francis' family, for example, owned the rights to some *buai* trees which had once been planted by a deceased relative.

There was no fish or meat in the village, and one elderly man proudly presented me with a bowl of sago-grubs that he had collected for me. How could I refuse? My body needed nourishment but I certainly couldn't eat the whole bowl of maggots even though they had been cooked. I solved the problem by inviting the man's direct family and Francis and his wife to share the bowl with me. After supper the man dried out a pawpaw leaf and rolled it up as a cigarette inside a strip of banana leaf and gave it to me, and for lack of anything better to smoke, it was alright.

I was feeling below par, which probably was due to my recent poor diet and excessive exercise combined with an unpleasant cough that I had caught from some children in Anganamai. It all made me tired and discontent but I strived to present a smiling appearance.

Later everyone gathered for stories and got wet when rain swept into the half-built hut. The storm gained force during the night, sending cold furious gusts of wind through the hut walls. Thunder rolled and lightning cracked and flashed overhead. The arrival of a sow and twelve piglets seeking shelter in our hut just added to the noise and confusion; we chased them outside, but it wasn't the most peaceful night I had ever had.

Inevitably, in the morning all low-lying land was heavily flooded and the creeks were impassable. While we waited for them to subside a little I learnt a new song in *tok-ples*.

On the final lap of our walk we filled the *bilums* and my backpack with *buai* that we bought from the man at Brumoh. It was high quality from a source-point of *buai*-trade. My share was for my friends in the Blackwater villages.

We detoured for a cassowary hunt but didn't catch one; and caught a *mumut* (forest rodent) instead, which we cut into small pieces and roasted on twig-skewers. It tasted much like rabbit. Despite the good times, Francis continued to winge and complain about things and generally to make life unpleasant. I was happy to get back to Anganamai.

Anganamai, Kuvemas, Kanengara. As I neared Kraimbit I heard *garamut* drums sound out at my approach and people came running to say hello. I felt that I had arrived home.

21
The Skin-cutting Ceremony

The situation in Kraimbit was unchanged: everyone was still waiting for the time of skin-cutting to be nominated. I went to pay my respects to *kansol* Gallus (and give him some *buai*), and as we talked about the business of waiting, it transpired that the skin-cutting was now overdue because the villagers were waiting for one initiate's uncle, who was away downriver. He had been away for months, but they could not proceed without him because he was responsible for holding his nephew during the cutting ceremony. Messages had been sent but he had ignored them, so I offered to go and look for him and ask him to return. My offer was accepted.

Taking my canoe I left Kraimbit and journeyed down to the Sepik. It took several days to reach the village but once I was there it was easy to find Uncle Marcus. But it was less easy to persuade him to come up to Kraimbit; he said that he was flat broke and had to sell a big carving before he would leave. The carving was uninspired and he was asking 100 *kina* (£75) for it. It was a ridiculous sum but I agreed to wait until some tourists came by, and I used the time to get supplies of goodies for the *sing-sing*. As gifts, I bought beads and *buai*, twenty ropes of tobacco leaves, three old newspapers, salt, rice other provisions and four shotgun cartridges.

When I had done all I wanted to, Uncle Marcus still hadn't sold his carving but he had received money from somewhere, because when I found him, he was blind drunk.

During his hangover, the next day, he agreed to leave for Kraimbit and asked if I would also take his friend Otto who was ill with a fever. Otto had family in Kraimbit and he was going there to be nursed. It took over three days to get back, partly because the river had become choked with salvinia, and partly because there were so many rainstorms.

Kraimbit welcomed us all. Uncle Marcus invited me to sleep in his family hut and told his two daughters Matilda and Marirose to look after me. We had supper of *binatang* (grubs) and *parems*. I still could not get used to the squishy grubs and just took a few which I tucked into the *parem* hoping it would disguise their flavour and texture. In the hut was a big wooden bed which Matilda and I shared, but the wood was rigid and hard and I would have been more comfortable on the palm-strip floor.

The next morning my bones were aching badly enough to make me go back to sleep for most of the day. Marcus didn't help matters by saying that he had thought of some urgent business downriver and wanted to leave immediately. What he meant was that he could not face his home responsibilities but it wasn't my place to say that to him and I felt too upset to say anything. I felt sure that if he left, the skin-cutting would be delayed indefinitely.

I got up in the late afternoon and took presents of *buai* to *kansol* Gallus and tobacco to his wife, a fat and jolly lady, who smoked her tobacco leaves as big rolled-up cheroots. During our conversation I mentioned Marcus' plans to leave and on hearing this Gallus said that he would speak to him. Later as we sat idly talking I heard the sound of bamboo flutes begin to issue from the *haus tamboran,* and asked Gallus for permission to go inside. He spoke with some men sitting near us and turning back to me said that although no female had ever been allowed inside their *haus tamboran* before, the elders had decided that because of the way that I had come to visit them, alone by canoe, I would be allowed to go in whenever I liked — though I must never tell the womenfolk what I saw and learned.

Inside the *haus tamboran* four men were playing bamboo flutes of varying lengths whose ends were *bilassed* with woven bamboo-cane and cassowary feathers. The two shortest flutes (females) were played by men facing each other, and circling counter clockwise; they held transverse flutes with both hands and changed the tone by partly-covering the hole with their index fingers. Around that pair of men circled the two other men, also keeping the same complex slow-foot rhythm. They played peaceful gentle notes, some strong, some quavering; the tune was called the song of women. The difference between male and female flutes is their length and the side to which they are

231

played, so that when played as a male/female pair, they lie together.

As I listened my eyes rested on the hut's centrepost, a large black phallic carving of a man whose white-painted face was ringed by insets of tortoiseshell. It had hair of bark, a feather-bag, and the horny casque of a cassowary hanging round its neck. Its body, with hugely exaggerated proportions, was covered in dust and cobwebs. In the past when centreposts were put in, it was traditional to soak them in enemy blood first. Another out-dated custom was that before initiation a youth should have killed one enemy.

These young initiates were asleep on palm benches, they looked even chubbier than a few weeks before; *skin i redi nau* (skin is ready now), having been fattened for the 'crocodile's bite'.

The flautists were still circling when I bade them all goodnight and went to say goodnight to Gallus. Gallus had some news for me: Marcus had been persuaded to nominate a date, within a week or so, for the ceremony.

Early in the morning, Brigita collected me and we went to gather the fish from her nets. She was a little upset that I was staying at Marcus' hut and not with her as before. I reassured her that we were still friends, and was pleased to be living next door to her parents, Mama and Papa Lucas. She smiled and relaxed more, and as we pulled in the fishing nets she told me the story behind a weirdly-carved wooden head that I had noticed outside the *haus tamboran*. Many years ago some women had been pulling in their fish baskets, and inside one basket, among the fish was this wooden head. Its weight broke the basket but they put it in their canoe and took it back to the men of the village. The men assumed that it was a *masalai*, and placed it among the old stone obelisks outside the *haus tamboran*, where it had stayed ever since.

Brigita netted four fish, no *masalai*, and on the way back we picked some *tu-lif* to cook with fish for a late breakfast. *Tu-lif* is so deliciously-flavoured that I wondered why it wasn't traded or used as a dried herb in European or Asian cookery, though the fresh leaves took several hours of cooking before they released their full flavour. Their savoury richness was one of the best flavours that I have tasted. While eating, I suddenly remembered

232

my tradition of eating with a knife and fork, and seated at a table, but it was only a memory.

In the afternoon there was a meeting to discuss potential candidates for the position of *kansol* because Gallus wanted to retire. The *Big-men* talked vociferously, but there was no 'getting down to business' nor any sense of urgency — things would be decided in the Melanesian way. We were all sitting on the grass beside the wreckage of a family *haus* which had fallen down in the earthquake. Its stilts had collapsed and the back wall had buckled, so that it lay tilted with its front gable staring skywards. The spiked gable-end was a carved man topped with white birds' wings outspread, now pointing straight to heaven.

While the men talked, a group of women sat picking the lice out of each others' hair, and a white-painted widow, with ropes of blue-dyed bark, around her neck and arms, sat puffing on a pipeful of tobacco. Another woman found a grasshopper and broke off its hind legs and gave it to her child to play with.

Babies were crying and noisy children were playing among the crowd until some boys brandishing stout sticks chased them away. Many of the boys had recently had their nasal-septums pierced and were wearing loops of bark-string through their noses, rather as we wear gold sleepers after we have had our ears pierced.

The men were debating whether or not to nominate some younger men, but most agreed *im i tumus big-hed*. They also agreed that Otto, who had now recovered would make a wise *kansol* because he was sensible and well-respected, but they didn't seem to be trying to take a decision and went on to discuss others. When a thunderstorm broke and the first spots of rain fell, I said *kokorian wajerm* (good-day I go now) and retired.

I felt feverish, but no sooner had I lain down to sleep that night than someone screamed and all hell was let loose. I sat up to see that a long brown snake had come inside our hut. The screams brought some men rushing over and we all ran outside while they killed it. I stumbled back to bed as soon as I could. The night seemed interminably long as I tossed and turned in a lather of sweat one minute and shivered with cold the next. Long before dawn I woke feeling too uncomfortable for further sleep, so I dressed and went out. A light was flickering in Papa Lucas'

233

hut, so I went in and sat with Mama, and cried because I felt so ill.

I didn't go to practise carving with the old men that day. I had a piercing headache, my bones ached, and I was in a hot and cold sweat. I guessed that I had malaria. Marcus' hut was full of screaming brats, so since I couldn't lie peacefully in bed I stayed on my feet; my feet were the only part of me that didn't hurt. Fortunately I had enough chloroquine left to treat the malaria.

In the evening there was a small *sing-sing*. I went to it but didn't stay late. Inside the *haus tamboran* a man was beating a long-waisted drum with crocodile-skin top; the man shambled in a slow circle followed by three men chanting in waves of sound. According to a bystander the sound could be translated as a black cockatoo turning into a white one, with a chorus about a strong woman climbing a mountain.

The men went round in tight circles, their chanting now all in different timings. Other men had joined them. Someone asked me if I would like to join the circle. Round and round we went, yeh-ee-ah-hoo, yee-oh. My thoughts spun idly, until I was jolted by the idea that I didn't belong here, and I felt suddenly self-conscious. What was I doing among these people?

On the next day I felt totally grotty: high fever, skin burning, sweat pouring out. I slept and lazed until late afternoon when I tottered down to a small pond in the sago grove, and using a coconut shell to scoop up the cool water, I poured it gratefully over my burning body.

In the evening there was another meeting to discuss the *kansol* election. Candidates were being selected. I listened to their names and asked Brigita why they didn't use tribal names, and she replied that they used 'christian' names to show that they were Christians (in addition to their own beliefs). It surprised me to realise that we use the same expression, our first name being our christian-name. The choice of candidates was still being debated; *Big-men* like Simon and Willi were not eligible because they couldn't read or write. Marcus told me that they wanted to elect him, but I thought that was untrue, since he would have been a rotten councillor. Papa Lucas would have been an excellent one, but he said that he had too much other work (cutting sago palms, building a new house, etc).

My fever increased and the days became blurred. I lay sweating between delirium and semi-wakefulness. The floor-mat was hard, and I longed for a feather bed, and for sympathy. And for my mother, who would have comforted me and asked what I fancied to eat or drink. I wanted some toasted cheese and a milk-shake. In the depths of delirium, I thought I was underwater, deep-sea diving without air tanks. I made seven dives, all of 1,000 feet, but the worst part was that when I was halfway up I couldn't tell which way was upwards any more. I fought the water, not knowing which way to go or if I would ever find the surface again.

Somewhere in the blur I heard Marcus shouting at me, shouting that I must get up and go to work on my carving. But I was too ill and when I did get up a day later, I was so weak that the knife kept falling out of my hand. Marcus later admitted he was afraid that if I had been left to sleep I would have died and that he would have been accused of killing me.

I recovered in time to watch the election. It was won by Otto who had 57 votes to the other candidates' 26, 22 and 18 (total adults in Kraimbit 123). There was an all-night *sing-sing* to cele-brate.

Life drifted into a gentle routine. I studied carving in the *haus tamboran*, where every morning some old men grouped to play their bamboo flutes, and *lapun* (very old) men sat around with the firelight flickering on their dark faces and illuminating the aged bumpy crocodile markings on their weathered backs. There were ten men playing flutes; their notes blending with barking dogs, roosters crowing, and the wind rustling in the palm trees.

My carving was a large hook carving of tough *garamut* wood. The image of a man with eyes like flames was emerging; he was holding a giant-sized tadpole, which was also part of his body and it had crocodile scales. Its tadpole head hung down as the hook, and its face was identical to the man's face. Florian was teaching me about grains of wood and how to 'sharpen' the carving with a *tomahauk*. When I questioned how to drill a hole in my carving, someone showed me how to use a string-powered drill. The drill was composed of two sticks: one stick was upright and had a headless nail as a drill bit; the other stick was horizontal with a hole through which the upright stick was slotted; and a long piece of string was tied to both ends of the horizontal stick, then wound spiralling around the upright and attached at the top. By

235

pulling the cross-bar downward fast the string was forced to untwist and spin the upright stick.

I put down my carving when Gallus came along to tell me that a date three days away had been nominated for the big *sing-sing*. The message about the *sing-sing* date was pounded out on a big *garamut*, audible to villages miles away. Kraimbit became a hive of activity. Everyone busied themselves preparing fresh sago flour *(skrub saksak)*, gathering baskets of sago grubs, smoked fish, cutting grass for the floor of the *haus tamboran*, and making the village neat. Others went off into the mountains to hunt wild pigs, *cuscus* and bandicoot (a large rat), or to collect stacks of firewood and *buai*.

The repairing or making of *bilas* was equally time consuming; threading beads, braiding armbands or renovating head-dresses. Papa Lucas was making my decorations, so I used the time to wrap presents of tobacco leaves in newspaper. Marcus' daughters helped me divide it into enough pieces for every adult in Kraimbit. It felt like Christmas.

As part of the preparations I washed my hair; the girls helped me, pouring water, out of coconut shells, over my head. While my hair was drying in the sun I let Brigita brush it and she offered the dubious compliment that my hair resembled the silky-trailing roots of salvinia.

One day as I worked my carving in Gallus' *haus wind*, I saw that Gallus was cutting an old canoe in half, and making a lid to fit. It was a coffin for his mother, a very old lady who had announced that she was ready to die, but that she would try her best to wait until after the *sing-sing*, so as not to cause another delay.

A setback occurred in the timing when one initiate's parents announced that they hadn't had time to prepare sago or collect firewood, so the *sing-sing* was delayed for two days. The message was sent out by *garamut* to warn the neighbouring villages, but the people at Tungibit didn't hear about the change of plan and they arrived decorated in full *bilas*, ready to *sing-sing*. At first they were puzzled by the lack of celebrations but when the delay was explained to them they got upset and refused to go home. With a show of mock-anger they went marching toward the *haus tamboran*, trampling shrubs underfoot as they went and chanting that they were going to *sing-sing*. They pushed their way aggressively into the *haus tamboran* but no-one offered resistance and soon a throbbing drumbeat began to issue from behind the palm frond screen.

The Kraimbit villagers stood back, uncertain about how to react, then one by one the old people began to join in the festivities. The younger ones hung back, ashamed of their lack of *bilas*. Then all in a rush they began frantically adorning themselves with nearby bush-leaves and soft ferns; they smeared coloured muds on their skin and stuck a few feathers in their hair, then joined in.

Men stayed inside the *haus tamboran* whilst the women were allowed to dance around the outside. They circled it with mincing steps, their hips swaying provocatively and their arms outstretched. I hesitated by the obelisks, before joining in. We circled faster, with long bounding strides, grass skirts swishing sideways and heads tilted back in a full-throated chorus. After a few rounds with them I went inside the *haus tamboran* and joined the men.

The previous nights of *sing-sing* were lethargic compared to the high-stepping dance-trot and the volume of song from the increasing numbers of dancers. Drums and lime gourds were used as musical instruments, the gourds were played by scratching them with ridged cassowary-bones to make a whirring noise. Occasionally everyone stopped to chew *buai*.

While the drummers rested a group of nine men played flutes creating a lively melody as they attacked the notes to make them shorter and sharper. Then the man with the female flute arrived, and the tune deepened and hesitated, making the men pause and hover above the ground as they stepped; their legbands of shells clinking in time. The last flautist seemed to be out of time; and unsurprisingly it was Marcus who was so stoned on *buai* that he was holding his undecorated flute backwards.

Suddenly it was noticed that an uninitiated youth from Tungibit was inside the *haus tamboran*. This was forbidden by clan law. There was an uproar. As his penalty for this wrong-doing, it was decided that he should undergo the skin-cutting initiation.

Dusk became night; thunder and lightning heralded rain. But inside, the dusty and smoky atmosphere was lit with kerosene lamps, and filled with music. Intertwining bass, tenor and soprano voices sang 'oh-ee-ay' in waves that surged, receded and swelled again. I got up and merged with the wheeling dance circle; I wasn't sure how the Tungibit men would react to my participation, but when I stopped for a breather their *Big-man* came over and spoke of their pleasure at seeing me with them.

A man came in with his dogs, back from a long day's hunting with a wild pig slung round his shoulders. He shook the rain from his hair and someone went to call the women to cook the pig for a feast. (I was already full from a huge supper of *makau, tu-lif* and palm hearts.)

Torrential rain had forced the womenfolk to shelter, they were all in a spacious house nearby. Later when I ran through the rain and scrambled up the ladder, the scene was in total contrast to the male celebration. Groups of women suckling their babies, sat cross legged on the floor around lanterns; small children were asleep on folded mats, while in the centre of the hut five grandmothers stood, singing a baleful-sounding song about their happiness for the crocodile to scar their boys. They stood swaying slightly and stamping their feet regularly with force. Most of their songs had words, and were stories about their children or *masalai* (every child also has a *masalai* name). Sometimes they chanted sounds, blending harmonies, swinging their arms and flicking their hips with a stamp-jump that landed them facing the opposite direction. The floor shook with their stamping and the air vibrated with their chant which plummeted to a surprising depth and rocketed up into a contralto.

The Tungibit clan decided to stay in Kraimbit. There were only two days before skin-cutting time, so it was better to be where the action was taking place.

Breakfast was of pig and *parem,* and I spent the morning helping Brigita to make her *bilas* by weaving armbands of bark string and sewing cowrie shells onto them. After that I went to visit Gallus' mother, who was preparing to die. Ndanowe, was shrivelled to skin and bone; she had frail fingers, sunken hollow cheeks and wisps of poppled grey hair. Her voice was as thin as her body, I couldn't understand what she said, but someone translated into pidgin for me. She talked about her life and her children, and her approaching death, which she welcomed. She was no longer able to move about; it was time to die. She was a great great grandmother. Gallus, her first son, had only one child; the second son had children but they had died; while her daughter who had produced eight children, now had grandchildren and so on.

In dying she believed that although her body would rot in the ground, part of her would remain forever. They would never see her, but she would always be there, with the other ancestors, watching over her line.

My afternoon was spent hunting wild game (without any success), and in the evening there was another *sing-sing*. It was more like going to a party. I felt completely at home, wandering around greeting friends, listening to the music, and when I felt like it dancing and joining the others on the dance-floor. After dancing a number or two, I chatted with friends, rolled up some tobacco and drank some water.

When it was time for me to go home, I thought of my flashlight (whose batteries had died days ago), and instead picked up a bunch of shredded *pangal* (palm stems) which when lit, burned with a good light.

The final day before the skin-cutting ceremony was spent duck-hunting. We used the four cartridges that I had bought and the one shotgun in the village. It was difficult to know who to choose for shooting the gun: the gun-owner deserved a cartridge, and myself, so that left two others; but every man in the village claimed to be the best shot. With a cartridge you don't just kill one duck, the shot sprays out and can kill as many as a dozen birds. I didn't offer one to Marcus, as I feared he would miss altogether, but I gave one to his eldest son, who was said to be a good shot. Gallus didn't want one and he advised me to give it to a lame man called Philip.

We set off paddling our canoes through the maze of lake-pools. We passed scores of wild ducks which scattered out of our way, but Philip guided us past them to take us to his favourite hunting spot, herding more ducks towards it as he went. He took us to a small pond covered in red water-weed, and there on a floating grass bank was a large flock of ducks. We glided silently through the reeds, and Philip fired just as the ducks saw us and began to take flight. By waiting for that moment he got more ducks in his range of shot. He was unlucky to score only twelve, and two of them sank before we had time to dash over and retrieve them.

The total bag from four cartridges was twenty three ducks. We kept plenty and gave away plenty. Matilda cleaned some for the fire immediately. Marirose began stoking the firebowl to make *parems*. I prepared the *saksak* for the *parems* and cooked the first few. Marirose stoked the fire, breaking the firewood over her own head.

When the fire's heat got too intense I went off to take a bath in a cold clear spring among the sago palms. After bathing and eating, most people began to put on their *bilas*. White ochre was put on first; but it didn't show up well on my skin, so we used black and red. On my forehead they painted the mark of the crocodile, my cheeks were outlined and dotted, and my arms were decorated with bands and snake-patterns. Papa Lucas put feathers in my hair and gave me legbands with soft ferns. Brigita gave me a grass skirt to wear over my own skirt. I was ready to join the *sing-sing*.

People from the villages gathered at the lakeside, all in full *bilas*, their plumed head-dresses rippling in the breeze. Most feathers were set in grass sockets that acted like springs, making the feathers dance with every movement; some had thick clusters of cassowary feathers and one man had the blue-shimmering plumes of the *guria* bird. The crowd formed a procession through the village. Drummers kept pace. We marched to the *haus tamboran*, and waited beside the *tumbuna* carvings and stone obelisks, while the men brought the young initiates outside.

They emerged through the palm-fringed doorway, their hands clasped on the crowns of their heads, with leaves sticking out of their mouths. Suddenly all the women of their families surged forward and grabbed the boys from the men, encircling the boys, and tearing at the leaves in their mouths; it was quite a scrummage. The womenfolk were forced away by the men, and they ran off, flicking their grass skirts and kicking up their heels. Each boy was held by his uncle standing behind him and holding his hands up for people to see his young unscarred chest. The boys were naked except for yellow bark-string bracelets and a bunch of grass with a penis-cover which came up into a pointed prow above the hip-band. The men walked the boys in circles round the stone obelisks. Then there was a lull while everyone was given food and *buai*. Dusk became darkness, kerosene lamps were lit, and there were stern warnings to the men about no fighting as the male and female groups separated into the two *hauses*.

Somehow the atmosphere in the *haus tamboran* had turned sour, men looked surly, and tempers started to flare. There was a desultory attempt at forming a *sing-sing* wheel but no one joined it. They just sat stony-faced on the palm benches, muttering angrily.

The cause of the trouble was that the *kansol* from Kabriman was drunk. It was probably mainly jealousy that made them cross; they wondered where he had got the liquor, and why he hadn't shared it. But the Kabriman *kansol* was oblivious to criticism, drumming superbly, singing with gusto, and behaving perfectly well.

Tempers and tension brought the *sing-sing* to a halt and for half an hour it teetered on the brink of a fight while everyone still refused to *sing-sing*. Some men tore off their head-dresses and threw them dramatically on the floor. I kept quiet and out of obvious sight. Actually I sympathised with the *kansol*, he wasn't misbehaving in any way and I couldn't see the harm. So when another attempt was made to re-start, I joined the circle and then others joined too. Slowly the situation eased, and when I could hear singing coming from the women's house, I went there to relax.

Few women were seated, most were dancing and chanting a song about cutting skin: shell anklets jangling, grass skirts swinging, breasts bouncing, and faces painted white, rapt in song. During an interval I distributed my gifts of tobacco to the women, then returned to the *haus tamboran* to give the men their share.

Their dance had changed, a drummer stood in the centre of a single ring of men, shifting from foot to foot and chanting a rippling yodel that merged with the dust and smokiness. In the deep of night the *Big-men* asked me to leave the *haus tamboran* for a short while since a *tumbuna* secret was ready for performance. The *kansol* explained that all the men would go to the end of the village, taking the boys with them, then come back and find some *masalai* waiting inside the *haus*. While the men were gone they posted a guard on the women's *haus*, and any woman going outside was questioned and watched with suspicion.

241

When they returned we heard the bangs and crashes of fighting, and finally there was silence. Throughout the long night the *sing-sing* lapsed often to near silence as the men fell asleep on the *limbum* tables that lined the walls; the tables were wide enough to hold rows of bodies like canned fish. Then after a minute of silence a lone voice would pipe up, and another until there was a strong chorus. The song was regenerated as men urged each other on with staccato 'ow-ow-ow' sounds. When I rejoined them I could see the results of the fighting, as the men were still rubbing the bruises and grazes on their bodies — and someone had punched Marcus.

In the women's *haus* during the quiet intervals one or two would stand up and do a strange sort of dance-act, with a story behind it which was chanted by a solo female and chorus. Everyone thought that the stories were funny and they roused them to laughter and more song.

As the first light of dawn streaked the sky, the cocks began crowing and the men filed out of the *haus tamboran* with the three initiates, then circled some huts and returned. No-one said that I couldn't be there so I watched as two figures wearing *masalai* masks with long noses and big round eyes, their bodies hidden beneath grass overlaps, whirled around brandishing sticks of palm with which they beat the boys. I backed into a safe corner, realising that this was the part of the ceremony which I had missed last night, now being repeated. Its purpose is to allow the boys to prove their bravery and it is important that no-one tries to run away. The *masalai* spun, cavorted and whacked at everyone; they didn't spare the youngsters, they thrashed them. Then all the men started raining blows on each other, and after the confusion the two *masalai* were not there any more probably they had slipped away to Gallus' hut to change back into *Big-men*.

Dawn was heralded by a chorus of cockerels; steam rose from the warm thatch, and the grass was heavy with dew. As the sun rose the men took the boys to be washed in the lake. They walked in single file, symbolising the crocodile walking through their village, moving silently between the huts. On their return to the *haus*, the skin-cutting began.

The three initiates sat on smoked banana leaves laid on the floor, leaning back onto the chests of their uncles. The atmosphere was charged. The first cuts of the razor drew the mark of the crocodile on the boys' stomachs, and continued up their chests to their shoulders and arms in a wide series of short dashes, representing crocodile scales. Circles were sliced around their nipples, like eyes. Blood poured down their bodies, one boy was screaming with pain. I felt weak and stunned. Time seemed to stand still. The boy who screamed was the one they had caught in the *haus tamboran;* he felt more pain because his mind was alert and his skin was hard, whereas the boys who had stayed seven months living in the *haus tamboran* were soft and flaccid, and their minds were tranquil. When the boys chests were finished everyone went outside. The boys lay on fresh leaves while their backs were cut, the men deftly pinching and slicing the skin in lines from shoulders to thighs, with embellishments mid-back.

It was a weird ritual that I watched through a mist of blood. One boy was still screaming, and bamboo flutes poured their melody into the sunny morning. When the cutting was finished the initiates' wounds were packed with red mud, to ensure that the cuts remained open and that they formed the right scars. (This particular red mud was reputedly high in sulphur which seemed to prevent septicaemia.). Then their skin was annointed with thick honey-coloured and sweet-smelling plant oil, which was brushed gently onto their skin using white feathers. The boys were exhausted of emotion and lay quiet with their eyes closed.

Two girls came forward for skin-cutting. The cutting was done by two old women, pinching and cutting open the girls skin on both sides of their backs.

Voices asked me if I was ready to be marked by the crocodile, and when I finally answered yes, they started cutting the crocodile's star-mark on my shoulder. I felt apprehensive but not afraid. The crocodile cutting was extensive on the boys but I trusted them to treat me gently. I turned my head away and held on to my proxy sister Matilda. The first cuts didn't hurt, but he went on ripping. I was trying to count the lines but there were too many; many more than I had expected. Blood trickled down my arm, but I refused to look, I didn't want to disgrace myself by fainting. Sweat poured down my face; the crocodile was biting; the women were chanting; the flutes were rejoicing. At the end I felt dizzy but knew it would be a scar I would bear with pride for the rest of my life.

By the time all the skin-cutting was finished the sun was nearly overhead, and everyone retired to their huts to sleep for a few hours. The initiates were woken up mid-afternoon and they stood while their hair was cut, their skin was re-oiled and re-ochred, and their faces were painted in thin wavy lines of alternating colours (the effect was the same as I had seen on carved masks). The human artwork was completed by hanging pearly *kina*-shells round their necks, and tucking ferns and foliage into their armbands.

The whole village assembled at the new incomplete *haus tamboran*, some people climbing up its frame and sitting among its grotesquely-sculpted pillars. The boys were made to sit on log-seats in a row facing everyone. One by one the *Big-men* of their family picked up a heavy *limbum* stick and went over to the boys, to teach them the rules of manhood. Using the stick they thrashed the ground in front of each boy to emphasize every rule and point made. This final stage of initiation was called *sarba tanogas*, to school the initiates in clan law, instructing them in time-old taboos and rules of conduct. One elder spoke of whom they should look for in marriage (here it seemed customary for first cousins to marry each other, thereby keeping the family property intact). I was surprised when Otto, the new *kansol*, came up to me and thrashed the ground in front of me. He spoke about my sharing myself with Kraimbit, and the secrets that Kraimbit had shared with me.

Some *Big-men* took several turns at talking to the boys, as they thought of things they had forgotten earlier. Various *Big-men* spoke to me, giving me the orders of the *haus tamboran*. Dust and grass went flying as the stick hit the ground. Close to the end someone put the stick in my hand, so I thrashed the ground and spoke of my happiness to be among them, and thanked my proxy family and all my friends for the kindness they had shown me.

One man told us the history of his clan, naming their forefathers and naming all the *haus tamborans* they had built. Yambung was the ancestor who had started this one, and he had been the keeper of the sacred shell which Yowi now held up aloft for all to see as he declared their history.

Pouring rain brought everything to a stop and we all ran for shelter. There was a small *sing-sing* that evening, with a mellow atmosphere followed by an early night because we were all tired.

244

At dawn I got up and went to drink coffee in the *haus wind* (because the babies in our hut were yelling), and saw the crocodile line of fifty-five men with the initiates in their midst again wending their way through the village. Soon I heard flute music drifting out from the *haus tamboran*, mixing with the noise of axes splitting wood, chickens clucking and babies crying.

Later the initiates went off into the forest and cut some sago hearts, which they brought back for all their relatives, who had fed them for those seven months of confinement. Their biggest debt was to their uncles; it would take years to pay that debt off, and it would be done in *buai* and tobacco.

The boys prepared the sago hearts for cooking, chopping them up with *tu-lif* and coconut, and cooking them in pans of boiling water. They 'turned' it all in sago flour, and stirred it until the whole thing was one gelatinous mass. All the relatives ate the food, they couldn't send their bowls back until they were empty, and there was a complex interchange of specific foods. For this event the initiates' bodies were painted with white circles; they still wore the grassy loin-cloths and woven pointed prongs, plus the facepaints of the previous day.

At midnight when all the women were asleep the men collected their spears and formed a crocodile line. The crocodile would walk the boys into the forest, and there would be a spear-throwing ritual.

Again I woke at dawn, but it was to the sound of a single drumbeat and voices raised in a mournful wailing. Its meaning was obvious: Ndanowe had died. She had held onto life by a thread until the *sing-sing* was over, and now she had let go.

Everyone gathered in Gallus' family house. His mother's body was wrapped in cloth and laid in the little coffin-canoe. The villagers filed past her, weeping as they put the lid over her and hammered it shut. I sat on the floor with Marcus' family. Men straddled the coffin, roaring their grief, and some women clasped it sobbing and wailing. All the old lady's family came to hold her coffin, lying on it, kneeling by it, touching it, and singing their lament. Their bodies were racked with sorrow, and I felt tears stinging my eyes. A group of women stood and chanted a mournful dirge and others joined in with outbursts of grief.

The *sing-sing* went on all day and all night. I retired to doze in a little hut beside the big one, their dirges mixing with my dreams.

At sunrise they buried Ndanowe's coffin on a dry island in the marshes. A chapter in all of our lives had come to an end.

22
The Last Lap

My canoe was ready, loaded up with my backpack and piles of
carvings, all securely covered with leaves of *limbum*. I went
around the village saying goodbye, and people brought me gifts
of carvings from the dim recesses of their huts. It was sad to say
goodbye. My friends came to see me off, and we waved to each
other until I was out of sight and had vanished back into the
grass-swamps.

The water level had dropped considerably; the tree I had
climbed when I was lost before was now standing on dry land;
the short-cut where I had been terrorised by pigs had also dried
up, and most other routes I had used had become blocked with
salvinia. I stood in my canoe and scanned the water for interlinking channels. Late afternoon I reached Kabriman. I stayed in my
usual hut, and the villagers brawled and fought, amongst themselves, just like last time. Two women beat each other with
sticks, screaming insults, another woman ran past me pursued by
a furious man and I heard a series of punches and more shouting.
Then some young men and women began quarrelling and most
of the children seemed to be throwing tantrums too. The weather
also turned stormy, but at least the strong wind kept the mosquitoes at bay.

Next morning the river was sprinkled with small red flowers.
My canoe with its cargo of art which had increased again overnight, felt super-heavy, which made it less unstable and easier to
steer, although it was slightly leaky from a hole at the front.
Mountains receded into a blue haze. Down among some water-
lilies a white heron, was fishing. Flocks of ducks scattered out of
my way. I met a friend from Kuvemas, paddling to Yesabit, so
we kept company for a while.

Suddenly he broke off mid-sentence and motioned silence.

There was a man with a shotgun in a canoe gliding through the reeds, aiming towards a flock of ducks. He fired once, just as the ducks took flight, and he scored twenty-six hits. We helped to retrieve the fallen ones, and in return we were given two birds.

We passed a large lake and went down a channel to Yesabit. I had intended to go on downriver in the afternoon but I changed my mind when some men offered to take me crocodile hunting that night.

The following day I reached the joining of the Blackwater and Korosameri rivers. The grass-swamps were left behind as the river began to have solid banks, with low bushy forest above them. At the junction with Korosameri river there was a big whirlpool, and a definite line where the black water joined the muddy brown water. On the bank opposite the junction was the village of Mumeri. People called me by name and showed me where to park. Many willing hands helped me to unload my cargo and take everything into a *haus-wind*. Someone brought me a basket of freshly-cooked prawns. I ate so many I felt too full to move, so I relaxed, chatted, swopped songs, and finished the carving I had been working on. It should have been the day for scrubbing my crocodile scars to re-open the cuts in order to produce the correct scar, but I chickened out, though I still anointed it with oil and ochre, which had to be done daily.

Prawns for supper and prawns for breakfast, and in between there was heavy rain. The river had been low, but by morning it was in flood — rushing along in spinning whirlpools and sometimes heaving in glassy sheets with foaming troughs, racing suddenly sideways across the river and taking the canoe with it, forcing me to fight for control. There were many floating patches of salvinia, which moved faster than me; the gaps in them altered and closed, and weed massed around the canoe. Currents jostled me and water boiled up from below; it took all my strength to steer a sane course.

Suddenly and without warning my canoe hit something hard, the stern swung round, I paddled frantically but couldn't prevent the canoe from swinging broadside to the river. Another jolt, and the canoe stopped moving while the river kept racing on. Water rushed around and came spilling in, the canoe had wedged against something, but my paddle found only deep water; nothing was there. It flashed through my mind that it could be a

waterlogged tree, floating beneath the surface. Salvinia was building up. The wind was tugging at the *limbum* which protected
my luggage, it flapped crazily and I tried to hold it down with my
feet. I felt near to panic; then simultaneously I was jolted again
and was free. Free, and hurtling downriver broadside.

Later in the morning I came to the joining of the Korosameri
and Karawari rivers, the *masalai* was sleeping quietly and the
eddies were gentle fun. At midday I arrived at where the river
split into two halves around a long island at its junction with the
Sepik river; I was back in Middle Sepik and stopped to look at
the different types of carvings at a village called Mindibit. From
there, I didn't take the shorter route to the Sepik because the
current was coming upriver, so I went the long way but it was
annoyingly calm and sluggish.

It grew broader, and a strong wind gusted upriver making
waves that slapped against the prow. I knew that I must be
getting close to the main Sepik. The wind increased, some waves
poured into the canoe, and although I paddled on the leeward
side of the *pitpit* it gave no shelter. Storm clouds were rising and
spreading into an angry anvil-shape and waves were frequently
spilling over the canoe prow. The river seemed to be about a mile
wide and I wondered where on earth the Sepik had gone. I saw
two huts and decided to stop for the night.

Three charming old couples and their fourteen children lived
there. Unfortunately the mosquitoes were ferocious and at dusk
they became horrific. A woman put some smouldering coconut
husks around our feet to discourage them with smoke, and gave
me a raffia-fringed flyswat, which I flicked around myself continually to lessen their biting. We sat in a group talking; the old
man recalled the Japanese invasion of the area; I had already seen
a couple of wrecked war planes rusting in the damp jungle of the
Middle Sepik, and several half-sunken rusty boats.

We ate supper (fish and *parem)* soon after dusk. Two of the
women gave me necklaces of beads and seeds, and I gave everyone
some *buai* and tobacco. Immediately after supper we retreated
from the mosquitoes and continued the conversation from inside
our separate nets.

Early the next morning the mosquitoes were still there and
worse than I had ever known. I brewed coffee and set off downriver taking my breakfast of fish and *parem* with me. One by one

I killed the mosquitoes in the canoe, and since they don't fly over large stretches of water I didn't attract any more. Peace was restored.

In the light of morning I found that I was approaching the muddy Sepik. It wasn't a difficult junction, the two rivers just slid together and became one huge river. I took my place among the flotsam and jetsam of salvinia and dead wood in the current.

Ignoring the current's unpredictability, I floated, eating fish and drinking coconut milk. From around the bend ahead came a big tourist ship with rows of deckchairs and white people, taking a luxury cruise up to the large village of Ambunti. Now I knew that I was back in the Middle Sepik.

As I neared Timbunke Catholic mission a speedboat passed me; it contained a nun in a white habit. At midday I reached the mission, and met the Catholic sisters who invited me to lunch. We ate things like bread and butter, and cheese and jam. The Catholics run a health centre here, and have some small clinics, such as at Kanengara and elsewhere on the river. The nuns whom I lunched with had spent twenty years working here, doing patrols, teaching child care and hygiene.

The village at Timbunke is extremely old; its *haus tamboran* is the oldest on the Sepik. In the *haus tamboran* were seven boys who had been through the skin-cutting ceremony and were due to emerge that evening. The initiation customs here were different from those of Blackwater; there was no waiting period before skin-cutting and the boys were simply rounded up on the night and cut at dawn. After skin-cutting the boys had to stay for three weeks in the *haus tamboran* while their crocodile scars healed.

Apparently there hadn't been a skin-cutting ceremony here for many years, and the men had been overly enthusiastic about rounding-up the boys: one was only eight years old. Their marks weren't as extensive as those of the Kraimbits; their chests hadn't been cut, and they were scarred with lines only along one arm, shoulder, and on one side of the back, and there were embellishments in the shapes of lizards and arrowheads.

For their coming-out the *haus tamboran* had been surrounded by a palm-frond fence whose gateway opened like the upper jaw of a crocodile. The 'jaw' was made of woven palm leaves with a hanging dry grass fringe, and on the end of its nose was a carved man's face.

Early in the evening I joined the crowd of villagers who sat outside the enclosure. Drumming and whoomping sounds came from behind the fence, and above it I glimpsed the waving white plumes of head-dresses. The gates' 'jaws' opened and out danced a double line of finely-*bilassed* men. Their bodies were painted red and white, and they were wearing head-dresses of white shells and feathers, and *arse-grass* of red leaves. Pairs of men were holding poles between them and while striking the pole with batons they sang a chant of 'hoo-hoo'. These were all the *Big-men* of the *haus tamboran*. The front three men held ten-foot (3-m) wands decorated with black and white feathers. As they 'hoo-hooed' and retreated backwards into the enclosure, they stamped their feet making their anklets jangle, and when they danced forward they shook their chests and jangled their back-strings of shells.

The 'jaws' opened again and they re-emerged and went back again, doing this many times, and 'hoo-hooing' faster each time.

The seven initiates were sitting outside on flattened *limbum,* they were ochred white with red mud over their scars. Around the boys danced another group of men, waving sticks and singing a happy-sounding chant; these were the boys' fathers and uncles. More of the skin-cutting ceremony was explained to me: the initiates' emergence from the *haus tamboran* symbolised crocodiles hatching from eggs; the boys sitting on the *limbum* represented the baby crocodiles swimming on the mother's back. Later the dance would change to a thrashing movement similar to the action of the baby crocodiles falling off her back into the water to play. The boys, like the crocodiles, are now old enough to fend for themselves.

Some men threw white lime dust over the procession of *bilassed* dancers, and hung ropes of *buai* on their shoulders. The last in line also had a role: he swept the path as they retreated to clear away any lurking evil. A jester appeared and tempted the line forward with *buai*. The crowd sat among the palm trees on both sides of the open *sing-sing* area; I was warned not to sit directly below any palm tree since the coconuts were ripe and heavy and likely to fall at any time. The sun began to set and dark storm clouds rose up in the east. It didn't rain but the ground gradually turned into a sea of mud beneath the dancers' trampling feet. The double line reached the far end of the palm-lined avenue. Suddenly from the 'crocodile-mouth' gate came a rabble of men brandishing *limbum* whip-twigs threatening the boys with the beating they would have to withstand the following morning, to prove their fearlessness.

As twilight darkened people lit small kerosene lanterns. Some women in grass skirts called me to have supper at a big *haus* where we ate boiled frogs legs and sago jellied in water (which kept sliding through my fingers).

Back at the *sing-sing* the initiates were still grouped centrally, and their fathers were ambling up and down, legs bent with knobbly knees, and painted tails of grass and feathers swinging behind them. Their song sounded dismal. The crocodile line emerged from the *haus*, the men were waving wands and fire-brands, 'hoo-hooing' and shouting snatches of garbled song. The fathers' song was entirely different, dismal yet tuneful with cackles of laughter each time the line turned and vanished down the gate's dark throat. Women in grass skirts danced vigorously.

It was a starry night without rain. Some *bilassed* jesters rushed out of the gate madly waving flaming firebrands and sending showers of sparks like golden rain. They brandished them in the faces of the oncoming procession, trying to drive the men back. They *sing-singed* all night. I left them in the early hours.

After only a few hours' sleep I was woken by the tolling of the mission bell and I got up to go to the morning service which was a communion. As the priest intoned 'Drink ye all of this for this is my blood' I heard the distant drumming from the skin-cutting ceremony, and my thoughts drifted as all sorts of words and images came into my mind: wine, blood, God, spirits, *masalai*, devils, *sanguma*, crocodiles, church services and *sing-sings*. I couldn't make any sense of them.

After Timbunke, I became aware that I was approaching the end of my journey, and that the crocodile ceremony had been the climax of it. Each day the river was getting rougher, and although I enjoyed it, I couldn't see any point in continually getting soaked, and many people told me that my small canoe would not be able to cope with the big waves down towards the estuary. Unfortunately my map didn't have a mileage scale to tell me how far it was, because I only had one half of the map and this made it difficult to judge distance. When I asked people about distance they replied in days not in miles. Taking into consideration my slow speed I estimated that the estuary was about four days away, and looking on my map I saw a riverside town called Angoram which would be about two or three days away, and which had a dirt road linking it to Wewak, so I decided to end my river-journey at Angoram.

I floated downriver very lazily with a warm gentle breeze helping me on my way. It was tempting to try setting up a sail, but instead I sat back and listened to the songs and screeches of birds along the shore. Occasionally there were riverside clearings in the *pitpit* where people had planted gardens of tobacco, yams, sugar-cane, and rubber trees. Prawn baskets were set along the water side. A family from Karawari river came travelling downriver on a big raft of tree-trunks, with a shelter built on it and four new canoes tied alongside. They were on their way to sell the tree-trunks, canoes and *saksak*, though one canoe would be kept for their journey home.

Late in the afternoon I stopped at Tamburnam village, a long narrow village with huts of an interesting design. The huts were big; their front faces had two eyeholes cut in them up high and a protruding thatched lip, which made the door shelter, and reminded me of *tumbuan* masks.

A friendly group of people came over to talk with me and told me that each family line in the village bore the name of a bird, animal or reptile. I stayed with the crocodile clan, in a big house with a man and his three wives. We ate prawns and swopped stories until it was time to sleep.

The following day the river widened out with islands and continual loops in its course. The sun was blazing hot but the sky was tinged pink by smoke spiralling up from a wide line of bushfires. The paleness of the smoke meant that it was probably only burning *pitpit* and dry grass, and since the forest seemed too wet to burn I didn't think that fires generally caused problems for villagers near the river. The fire could have been started by people clearing land for new huts or gardens. As the smoke spread it filtered the sun and the whole sky turned pink. I watched the columns of smoke rising as I picnicked on smoked prawns and water melon and drifted downriver.

Further on, some young men at the shore saw me and paddled out to ask if I would have sex with them. This was the first time that anyone on the Sepik had propositioned me and I was angry. It deterred me from staying at the nearby village, Moim, so I carried on until I passed a garden-hamlet where a man was 'cooking' his new canoe.

While Antn cooked his canoe, fanning the flames against its wood, I sat in the shady *haus-wind* beside the canoe, and drank coconut milk. I felt frazzled by the sun. After the cooking Antn collected some tools and a partly-finished carving, and came to work in the shade. His tools were two *tomahauks;* one was called Karen and it had a crocodile-head handle, and the other was called Warame, and was carved as a man's snarling face with bared teeth. He was working on a small figure, which he later gave to me. Its name was Tumbet Kandiman; the first name denoted the type of wood, and the second was its ancestral name.

The mosquitoes were bad. Next day I paddled down to the first mouth of the Yuat river, which has its source somewhere up near Mt Hagen.

I went upstream for a few miles and passed various villages then took another route back to the Sepik. In the water there were clusters of the fluffy yellow flies that I had seen in metamorphosis nearly four months ago. I wondered how I had changed.

I stopped at Kambaramba, a village built on grass islands in some lakes, that had no solid land for crops, no sago palms, no trees for firewood no house materials and no palms for roofing or floors. Everything had to be traded in from outside, and since their only marketable commodity was their women, prostitution had become an established trade. There was no moral stigma, it was simply their way of existing. The money was given to the girl's parents and the whole family lived on it. Nowadays there is the extra problem of salvinia which means that fish are hard to find and people often go hungry. I hoped that when my voyage ended I would be able to find out if anything could be done to help.

On this whole stretch of the Lower Sepik there was little dry land for cultivation and when a large floating island came downstream people would paddle out in canoes to tie ropes to it, then tow it back to their village where it would be tethered and planted with yams.

After a misty start the morning became scorching hot. The air rang with the chirring of cicadas; colours intensified as the sun rose higher; I splashed water on my face, it felt good. Soon the breeze strengthened, blowing against the current and creating rough waves; I had to mop and bail out the water which spilled in as I went along. When I needed a rest I turned up a side-stream which led to a pond with a small village on its bank, set among palm trees. A crowd of excited people came out to meet me and took me to rest in a lovely old *haus tamboran* which was lined with paintings on bark-strips sewn together. Its beams and posts were well-carved, and the centrepiece was a sacred statue. Newly-picked coconuts, some fish and *parem* were given to refresh me.

Now I was beginning to feel more than just daily tiredness, I was weary from having come a long way over the past four months, but the voyage had been more than worth the effort, and my joy was tinged with sadness that it was almost over.

All along the Lower Sepik the village-people called out, '*Sepik meri*', and paddled over to me as I went downriver, bringing fruit, pawpaws, water melons, sugar-cane, fish, a new mosquito-swat; everyone wanted to give some small token and to help me reach the end of my journey.

A motor canoe came chugging upriver. In it was Sapa, the Czech trader and lodge-owner. He stopped to hand me a cold beer and give me the keys to his house in Angoram, and told me to make myself at home. He was going to Kaminabit and would be back in three days.

The wind was beginning to build into a storm and I felt glad that Angoram was not much further. As I rounded a large bend in the river, the village came into sight and people spotted me. By the time I was alongside the village riverbank, it was packed with people waving and cheering, calling greetings and congratulations. Above the cheering I heard one man shout '*Sepik Meri* (Sepik woman), *Sepik meri, yu pul-kanu long wei tru, yu win-im Sepik wara, yu win-im tru.*'

And so my journey ended.

Glossary

arse-grass — bunches of long-bladed cordyline leaves worn by men
arse-ples — home
bailer shell — domed sea-shell
barat — ditch or gulley
Big-men — important men
bilas — self-decoration
bilum — string bag
binatang — grubs, maggots and insects
bride-price — cost of buying a wife
buai — betel-nut
bugarap — broken, out-of-order
cargo — goods
cuscus — possum
daka — pepper-vine
dokta-boi — man trained in first aid and basic medicine
dream-haus — special hut for dreaming
garamut — large drum hollowed from tree-trunk
gengong — jews harp
grass — hair
grilli — ringworm infestation
guria — earthquake bird
guvmen — government
haus — house or hut
haus-buk — library
haus-kuk — kitchen
haus-sik — hospital
haus-tamboran — spirit house
haus-wind — hut with open sides
kansol — councillor
kaukau — sweet potato
kiap — government officer
kina — shell, formerly money
kuru — 'laughing death'
lapun — old

limbum — palm leaf-pad
long-haus — a hut which is 50-150 metres long
luluwai — headman
makau — fish
mami — type of yam
masalai — nature spirit
moka — exchange ceremony
mumu — ground oven/fire pit
omak — bamboo tally-stick representing pigs given away
pandanus — pulpy red fruit
pangal — stick of palm-leaf
parem — thick pancake of sago flour
pig-kill — type of celebration
pitpit — tall grass
ples masalai — place of spirits
pulpul — grass skirt
race — competition
rascal — robber, thief
saksak — sago flour
sanguma — evil ghost spirits
skru-bilong-leg — knee
sing-sing — celebration
sing-sing race — musical competition
skin-dwai — bark of cinnamon tree
skul-munki — school child
suan — white heron
sumting-nuting — not important
susaf — jew's harp
toea — money (kina & toea)
tok-ples — language
tu-lif — type of edible tree leaf
tumbuna — of the old days
wan-leg — one legged carving with mythical powers